ADELAIDE LITERARY AWARD 2020

ADELAIDE LITERARY AWARD ANTHOLOGY 2020

SHORT STORIES

Volume One

Selected by
Stevan V. Nikolic
Editor-in-chief

Adelaide Books
New York / Lisbon
2021

ADELAIDE LITERARY AWARD 2020
SHORT STORIES ANTHOLOGY, Volume One
Special Issue of the Adelaide Literary Magazine

February 2020
ISBN: 978-1-954351-67-7

Adelaide Literary Magazine is an independent international monthly publication, based in New York and Lisbon. Founded by Stevan V. Nikolic and Adelaide Franco Nikolic in 2015, the magazine's aim is to publish quality poetry, fiction, nonfiction, artwork, and photography, as well as interviews, articles, and book reviews, written in English and Portuguese. We seek to publish outstanding literary fiction, nonfiction, and poetry, and to promote the writers we publish, helping both new, emerging, and established authors reach a wider literary audience. We publish print and digital editions of our magazine twelve times a year. Online edition is updated continuously. There are no charges for reading the magazine online. (http://adelaidemagazine.org)

EDITOR IN CHIEF
Stevan V. Nikolic
editor@adelaidemagazine.org

MANAGING DIRECTOR
Adelaide Franco Nikolic

FORMATTING & TYPESETTING
Vesna Trpkovska

WEB DATA & CONTENT ENTRY
Dilip Challani

Published by: Adelaide Books LLC, New York
244 Fifth Avenue, Suite D27, New York, NY 10001
e-mail: info@adelaidebooks.org
phone: 917 477 8984

Printed in the United States of America

Best short stories by the Winner,
eleven Shortlist Winner Nominees
and eighteen Finalists of the
Fourth Annual Adelaide
Literary Award Competition 2020,

selected by
Stevan V. Nikolic
editor-in-chief

With deep gratitude

this Anthology is dedicated to Adelaide Literary Magazine

contributing Authors.

Our Heartfelt Thanks.

Contents

FINALISTS

THE WINNER

The Optimist

by Joram Piatigorsky

Mr. Mellows squirms his 6-foot 5-inch hulk onto a flimsy wooden chair. The low tabletop presses down on his knees. A bare 40-watt fluorescent light in the center of the ceiling flickers from the ceiling in the barren room; brown stains mar the blond, dusty hardwood floor. The gray paint on the walls is peeling. A cockroach lies belly-up near the warped door with an empty hole where the doorknob used to be. A dark cloud eclipses the sun, sharpening the relief of the crack in the glass pane of the curtainless window.

In a plastic-framed print on the wall, a young woman wearing a straw hat with a pink ribbon milks a Jersey cow in a barn surrounded by aspens bearing golden autumn leaves. Rocks with red and copper-green veins protrude from a creek.

A young reporter from the Front Royal Magazine sits across from Mr. Mellows. He centers his horn-rimmed glasses against the ridge of his nose and reviews his notes. It has taken him almost a year to arrange this interview with *the* Mr. Mellows of United Steel Corporation. He hopes a successful interview will improve his chances of being selected for a community events reporter by the Potomac Gazette – a more illustrious publication.

Mr. Mellows scans the room, scratches his neck and runs his fingers through his thinning hair. His eyes lock on the farm girl gripping the udders of the cow.

"Makes me envious," he says, sweating in the July humidity of Washington.

"What's that?"

"The print. Is that the life, or what? A sweet girl, countryside, nature."

"Yes, sir. Know what you mean. Let's get to work."

The reporter reads his first prepared first question.

"Mr. Mellows isn't your real name, is it? What's your birth name?"

"That's irrelevant, isn't it?" answers Mr. Mellows. "I answer to Mr. Mellows. I made Mr. Mellows who he is."

The reporter searches for a response.

"But, sir, people want to know more about you. Nobody even knows your first name."

"First name, last name, middle initial. Big deal."

Appearing slightly flustered, the reporter presses on. "My name is Bob," he says.

"Just Bob?" asks Mr. Mellows.

"Ringling. Bob Ringling."

"Related to the circus family?"

"Not really. Everybody asks me that. Gets annoying."

"See what I mean? Why don't you call yourself Bob Circling, eliminate the annoyance, Pick your own name."

The reporter scratches his chin. "I thought I was interviewing you."

"Yes, correct. But I'm not sure why. What have I done worth an interview?" Mr. Mellows asks with false modesty.

The reporter shakes his head. "You're on TV, on billboards; there's even talk of you being selected by Time magazine as the Man of the Year."

"Ridiculous. I'll never beat out Mayor Gargano. Do you know that his wife's a Rockefeller?"

The reporter ignores the question and looks at the second question on his list. "The rumor is that your parents emigrated from Europe just before World War II.

Is that true?"

"Excuse me for switching the subject, but why is everything so run down here? The place looks like a war zone."

The reporter clenches his jaw.

"You asked for a neutral site without publicity. You didn't want me to come to your house or office or restaurant. A commercial real estate agent let me use this place. It's a dump, but it's the best I could do."

"I like it," responds Mr. Mellows, who finally reveals that he's capable of smiling. He looks lingeringly at the farm girl.

"About your parents," the reporter says, trying to refocus the interview. "Were they also in business?"

"Heavens no! My father was a molecular biologist, may he rest in peace, and my mother worked for a tree company."

"A tree company?"

Mr. Mellows thinks a moment. "Yeah. She was tiny, only 4-foot 7, and loved to climb trees, heaven knows why. She didn't weigh enough to break the small branches, so she was able to get to places that are hard to trim. Most of her work was on the estates of rich guys."

"Pretty dangerous. Did it teach you to take risks like you've done in your work?"

"You bet, except that she fell off a tulip poplar by a tennis court on her fortieth birthday and bye-bye. I was 12. That made me the only child of a single parent. My dad told me to get used to it; nothing lasts forever. You might write that down. He was tough."

"Wow! Quite an experience for a 12-year-old."

The reporter scribbles *'nothing lasts forever, tough father'* on his pad.

Mr. Mellows puts his left hand in the pocket of his gray cotton pants; coins jingle. He loosens his maroon tie and undoes the top button of his shirt, crisp white except for the symmetrical grey discolorations under his armpits.

The reporter wipes his brow. "Your father must have been a big man to have a tiny wife and a huge son like you."

"Not really. He was about 5-foot 10 at a stretch. Don't *ever* try to psyche out nature. It'll fool you every time. Nothing's predictable. That's been a guiding principle of mine. You can write that down too."

"Yes, sir."

The reporter writes on his notepad *'nothing's predictable, guiding…'* He stops writing before finishing and looks lost in thought.

"Hello?" says Mr. Mellows.

"Sorry."

The reporter asks another question.

"Was your father a well-known scientist? That is, were you exposed to fame as a youngster?"

"Hardly, although it depends on what you call fame. Most of the people in his building at work knew him, as did a dozen or so scientists around the world. He got an award once, from a pharmaceutical company. No, it was from an entomology society. He studied sticky stuff on the bottoms of the feet of certain kinds of bugs. I forget their scientific name. Busted his ass and sweated every detail of his work, and nobody cared, except a few peers. They argued like crazy as to who discovered what first. Man, it would make a boring movie! Watching him taught me a lot about life, even though it sort of broke my heart."

Mr. Mellows hesitates. "Science is fascinating though. Something about it that's...well...that rings true..." He looks sad and then adds, "Science doesn't depend on perception to be right."

"Is that what you learned from your father?"

Mr. Mellows checks his gold Rolex and then stares at the print on the wall.

"Mr. Mellows, what did you learn from your father?"

"Yes, yes. Excuse me. She's so pretty. I mean, *really* charming. Like the girl with a pearl earring by Vermeer. Know that painting?"

"Yes, sir." The reporter looks at the print and then returns to his question.

"About what you learned from your father. What was it?"

"Give awards, don't get them. The percentage is much higher, and everybody else waits on the edge of their chair rather than you. Makes you far more important, and you don't have to say thank you or grovel explaining how you don't deserve it, that it's all due to others, and...well."

The reporter scribbles some notes, underlines a phrase.

"Mr. Mellows, how did you make USC so financially successful and innovative? The use of large sheets of pliable, green steel that's comfortable to walk on, like grass, and generates energy from soil heat. That was brilliant! How did that come about?"

Mr. Mellows stands up and paces the room. He sneaks a look at the farm girl again, whispers inaudibly to himself and turns to the reporter.

"The first thing I did when I took over the company is strip titles from everyone. Hierarchy stifles creativity. It helped morale and ideas flowed like water. A green, soft, energy-producing woven steel grass substitute was just one of the ideas, and it came from a new recruit. Young people are too foolish to be cautious. You're young. Know what I mean? Do you take chances?"

The reporter doesn't answer. He asks, "Didn't that create insecurity for the senior people?"

"Are you kidding? Equality is a great thing. It gives everyone the same opportunity."

When the reporter hears "equality" and "opportunity" his eyes shine.

Mr. Mellows continues. "Everybody wins. I coordinated the show, like a…a….manager of a baseball team. Yes, that's it. All the baseball players in the major leagues are great athletes. So why does one team do better than another? The manager, of course. He decides who does what, when, why. He's the person who deserves the credit. That's why managers are always getting fired if their team doesn't win. The owners know that a different manager may make them winners. What an inspiration, a great manager! You can write *that* down in your notes. 'Management is art'. Yes sir," beams Mr. Mellows.

The reporter writes on his pad *'management is art'*. He also adds some comments to himself in messy handwriting with a disapproving expression on his face.

Mr. Mellows walks to the print and closes the fingers of his left hand around an imaginary udder. The reporter watches.

"It would be an inspiration to…*younger people*…to hear how you began such a successful career," says the reporter.

Mr. Mellows gazes at the floor.

"My path to success? I never did or said anything that the majority didn't agree with. Then I implemented it. No need to be a 'lab hermit' doing stuff that no one cares about. I never believed in originality by obscurity. It's reverse snobbism. Listen to the voices out there. It's like my garbage company."

"Garbage company, Mr. Mellows?"

"Yes! It was a hoot."

"A hoot? Garbage?"

Mr. Mellows ambles back to the print, rubs his index finger along the top of the frame and winks at the farm girl.

The reporter looks annoyed.

"Oh, it's kind of silly, really. I was just out of college. That was just over forty years ago. The local government wanted to put a county dump – a landfill – in a large field in a posh neighborhood. They said everyone needed to pay their dues. Land filled with crap and germs and ugliness is what they meant. I hate euphemisms, don't you?"

"I guess so."

"Well, when I read about the landfill in the news, when newspapers were still in hardcopies, I convinced several families in the neighborhood to start a garbage business, to take advantage of the situation rather than whine about it. I told them they could make money living next to a landfill by picking up trash and dumping it across the street. It would be a local convenience. One fellow had a wooded lot that was just… *there*…doing nothing but looking pretty…so I convinced him to make it a parking lot for our garbage trucks, which would be camouflaged by trees. I got some investors to go along with the idea and arranged the zoning by calling my business 'Estate Purification Assistance'."

Mr. Mellows winks at the reporter, then says in a low voice implying complicity, "The local government interpreted 'purified estates' as more valuable than 'unpurified estates', know what I mean? 'Purified estates' translated to higher taxes, so they had no problem giving us the proper zoning. I guess I don't hate euphemisms after all." He pauses. "I disbanded the business after a couple of years although it made money."

He rubs his right thumb and index finger together indicating it made a lot of money.

"Some people may knock the green stuff, aspire to higher ideals, like poetry or how bugs walk on the ceiling, whatever. Without money…well, nothing's done and people starve. You might want to write that down too. Money counts."

"I guess," says the reporter. He writes *'money counts'* and follows it with two question marks. He looks at the flickering fluorescent light as if it bothers him.

"Well, young man, it isn't easy, is it? The idea of interviewing me was more appealing than actually doing it. Right? Am I correct?"

The reporter focuses on the tabletop like a little boy being reprimanded. "No, sir, it's not so easy. You're not helping. I mean. Your life is…*interesting.*"

"Sure is."

"*Amazing* is more like it. You make things work, you twist and turn, and there you are at the finish line, smiling and alone. But…who are you, really?"

A siren screams in the street. Mr. Mellows walks to the window and looks below. He sees mid-day traffic, a few pedestrians, some trash on the sidewalk, a leashed dog pissing against the lamppost, while its owner, a middle-aged Chinese woman, looks the other way. Mr. Mellow turns to the reporter, straightens with resolve, ignores the radiating nerve pain down his right leg due to spinal stenosis, returns briskly to the table and sits down.

"Let's go on. I promised you an interview and an interview is what you will get. Who am I? I told you. I am Mr. Mellows, a self-made man with a self-made name. I carved my way through life, like a sculptor. Do you understand? Each time a chess piece moves, the game has a new structure, the opportunities are not the same. I am the chessboard. The pieces are my life. I am the substrate for the game. The game cannot be played without me. Without the chessboard, without me, the pieces would have no place to move. Without land, architects couldn't build houses, without air, pilots couldn't fly planes, without nature, scientists couldn't discover anything. The medium is everything. Do you understand that?"

"No, sir, not really."

Mr. Mellow looks at the fluffy clouds above the aspens in the print.

The reporter writes '*chessboard, medium is everything*'.

"After the garbage, I mean 'Estate Purification Assistance' business, I was asked to be an advisor for the state government on urban planning. I thought it strange since I had no credentials in that area, but they told me the concept of merging sanitary engineering, as they called my garbage business, with the suburbs was brilliant. Before I knew it, I was on the zoning commission, planning changes in traffic patterns, designing recreational facilities at the junctions between urban and suburban areas, joining different lifestyles as it were, and so on and so forth. I was given a green medal when I decided to leave after a couple of years."

"Why green? Do you mean for energy conservation?"

"Maybe. The bronze part dangled from green cloth."

"What did you do then?"

"Good question. I always had a weak spot for science, I guess because of my father, but mainly I saw it as another way to make a buck. I figured I could get support for anything scientific if people thought they would benefit from the results. They forget about the gap between the science and the reality of having it be useful."

He glances at the farm girl. "If only she were real."

Mr. Mellows continues.

"Anyway, I thought I would challenge myself and start a biotech company. I didn't know any medicine or molecular biology or fancy stuff like that, but I knew people dreamed of cures to nasty diseases, everlasting life and eternal happiness. And that's what biotech was for me, at that time, anyway: promises. I didn't pick a stereotypical problem like cancer or blindness or diabetes. No sir. Those obvious areas were over-crowded. Competition's a nuisance. I wanted to solve everyday issues that people didn't realize were problems. I settled on a rather silly idea when I think of it now, but it worked, however not as I expected it to. Life is full of curve balls. I wanted to make sweat smell good, appealing, *sexy*. I know one can simply put on cologne or perfume, but I figured people would like to find a way to make their own sweat appealing rather than cover it up. Vanity, you know. I got $50,000,000 of venture capital from the Miss Universe Foundation, and I established a company in Florida, where they sweat a lot. That was good for another $10 million. At first, I called my company 'Sniffme'."

"What happened?"

"Never touched the market I targeted. Had to change the name. Too bad. I liked it. My group of researchers busted their collective ass to find a chemical that could be ingested to make sweat produce a sweet aroma, but nothing really caught on."

"So, you lost money?"

"Of course not! We came up with a cream made from crushed cranberries, or was it strawberries? Whatever. Anyway, it attracted lobsters. Lobsters are a big industry in Florida. Do you know that lobsters have noses? Well, I didn't either, but they do, and they are attracted to good smells, good for them that is. We caught them by the thousands and made a ton of money since everyone loves to eat them. I changed the name of the company to 'Taste'em'. I met a scientist who spent his whole life studying lobster noses and he never made a cent. Actually, he begged for money to continue his research by writing grants all the time. Scientists are weird that way. I always went where the money is rather than try to have the money come to me. You can write that down too."

"Yes, sir," said the reporter as he jotted down *'went where the money is'*.

A musical sound distracts Mr. Mellows. He reaches into the inside pocket of his suit jacket that is hanging on the back of his chair.

"Hello," he says into the cell phone. "Senator Birch's office? I'll wait."

He excuses himself and walks to the far end of the room.

"Yes, Senator, this is Mr. Mellows. Good to hear from you. It was such a pleasure having lunch with you last month. No, no, I have all the time in the world. You're not disturbing me in the least. What's on your mind?"

Silence, except for the low rat-a-tat-tat of syllables flowing from the receiver, and the "uh-ha, yes, umm, interesting, ahh, yes, of course…. hmmmmm, absolutely," uttered by Mr. Mellows.

The reporter waits, looks around and fixates on the print on the wall. His pupils dilate. He puts down his pen, leans back in his chair and smiles. He looks relaxed for the first time.

"It's a wonderful idea, Senator. Increasing the visibility of steel will certainly harden the resolve of the American people. You can rely on USC. We must not let terrorism frighten us. Steel is impenetrable, resilient, shiny, strong. It says don't mess with me. A model suburban showcase of steel houses with built in steel furniture powered by the steel-grass lawn says, 'Bring industry back to America'. What an idea! The houses will be bomb proof, tough as…as…won't need repairs. Yes sir, with your support and taxpayers' money, we can do it. What's that? You need cost estimates and a slogan before the President writes his campaign speech next week? No problem. Consider it done. And thank you sir, for your confidence, support, for your great idea. It's an inspiration. America owes you a debt. How about lunch next week, sir? Oh, of course, of course, I understand. We'll lay low. Until later. Bye."

Click.

"Excuse me for another minute, Bob. That's correct, isn't it? Bob? I need to call my deputy."

Mr. Mellows is alert, as before battle. He calls his office.

"Hello. Stacey, get Karl. Quick. Karl? Cancel all meetings for the next two weeks. I don't give a royal damn what we agreed on, just listen. Remember the steel family houses? It's no joke now. Quiet! I told you to listen to me. I'll tell you more later. Damn it, Karl, you're working for me. That's better. Talked to our Senator just now; he swallowed. Who would have guessed? There's big money here. Get Sam and his crew to come up with blueprints for steel houses in which everything is steel: toilets, tables, chairs, everything. Yes. I know, it's crazy. Don't argue. Tell the econ guys to gear up for cost estimates. And we need a catchy slogan. See you within the hour. Don't breathe a word of this to anyone. I told you things always work out for the best. It's all about having a positive attitude. You pessimists slay me."

Mr. Mellows replaces the phone in his jacket pocket. He re-buttons his collar and tightens his tie.

The reporter writes *positive attitude, don't be pessimistic* in bold letters and underlines it three times.

"Let's finish up, young man. I've got to leave in a few minutes."

The reporter is quiet, distant. His gaze turns to the print of the girl milking the cow. "She *is* lovely, isn't she? I mean the scene and everything," he says.

"Yes, indeed. Wouldn't it be nice to live among the aspens, milking cows and chasing butterflies?" answers Mr. Mellows. He looks past the framed print to the dead cockroach on the floor.

"You're divorced, Mr. Mellows?" asks the reporter.

"Yeah, a long time ago. You married?"

"No, no…not… yet," says the reporter. "Do you have any children?" he asks.

"A daughter, Cynthia. She has two kids…oops, three. I forgot the little one, almost a year old now. Cute little guy, at least when I saw him six months ago. It's hard to get time to go to Chicago. Anyway, we must close now. Got your story? Business is waiting."

Mr. Mellows puts on his jacket and brushes the dust off the lapel.

"What a spot you picked for the interview! Filthy. I hope it's sold before it deteriorates any more. So, what are you going to say about me?" He looks at his Rolex.

The reporter clips his pen in his shirt pocket. He picks up his notes, pauses and places them back on the table.

"I wrote down what you said, Mr. Mellows."

The reporter gets up and tucks in his shirt. He walks to the print and stares at the pretty girl. "Beautiful, isn't she?"

"That's a bit much, son, but I know what you mean."

"Thanks for the interview, Mr. Mellows. I can't begin to tell you how grateful I am for your time, and your insight. It's been…*useful.*"

He moves towards the door without his notes.

"Certainly. Not so fast. Will I see the story before it's published? I don't want any wrong statements to appear."

"The story is on the table, sir. I've got to go before it's too late."

"Wait. Where are you going? Too late for what? Don't you need your notes?"

"Not where I'm going. I've got my eye on this small farm in the country about 100 miles from here, close to where Becky lives. I'm on my way to buy it before someone else has the same idea. It's a great…*opportunity*. Becky loves it. Do you know a cheap place around here where I can buy an engagement ring?" the reporter asks.

He goes out the door and begins to walk down the stairs.

Mr. Mellows stands alone in the doorway.

"Charles Melinski," he shouts to the reporter. "My friends call me Chuck. My parents came from Poland. My mother never climbed trees. She died three years ago."

The reporter stops and looks back over his shoulder. He smiles. Mr. Mellows is standing still at the head of the stairs, his tall frame bearing down on his right leg riddled with nerve pain.

"Thank you, Mr. Mellows," answers the reporter as he steps out the front door of the building onto the sidewalk.

Mr. Mellows yells at the top of his lungs, "You're an optimist, young man! An *Optimist*, with a capital O!"

A car horn drowns out his voice, and the reporter disappears from sight.

The Miracle of Estelle

For the third time in a row Benjamin didn't have a single matching pair in the cards he held in his hands. His frustration doubled when Estelle flashed her triumphant smile announcing. "Gin!"

"It's not all luck, you know," she said in a self-satisfied way that rubbed Benjamin the wrong way.

Every Wednesday night, Benjamin accompanied Melinda, his wife of forty-two years, when she visited "poor crippled Estelle." Melinda was more charitable than he was, always willing to help those in need, which is one of traits he loved about her. But, no matter how needy Estelle was, he was irritated watching precious time escape as he played gin rummy with ungrateful and annoying Estelle rather than attend to his unfinished work. The scientific manuscript of his postdoctoral student needed revision, he hadn't prepared his upcoming lecture at Harvard, and his never-ending list of administrative duties for Georgetown University weighed heavily on him.

"Larry didn't come to see me again this week, as if he's too busy to have lunch with his sick mother," Estelle whined, "and my TV flickers so much I can't even see Oprah without getting seasick. The repairman won't come for another week. I'm always last on the list."

"Come on, Estelle," said Benjamin. "Give it a rest." Melinda shot him a disapproving glance. Shit, thought Benjamin. I can't win.

"My legs are cold today," Estelle continued, ignoring Benjamin's comment and straightening her back in the wheel chair. She was paralyzed from the waist down and extremely sensitive to temperature changes ever since the onset of a baffling nerve degenerative disease three years ago. She had moved from

Chicago to Bethesda to receive medical treatment by a well-known neurologist at the National Institutes of Health. None of her doctors knew if and when this mysterious ailment would stop progressing.

Benjamin asked Estelle about her illness as she dealt another round of cards. "It's God's will," she said, with an astonishing lack of anger that she expressed for other subjects.

"Have courage, Estelle. Maybe Dr. Jensen can help you," said Melinda.

It's not God's will, thought Benjamin. It's got nothing to do with God. It's genetic or viral or maybe something else here on solid earth.

Although Melinda spoke kindly to Estelle, Benjamin wondered what she was really thinking. Two hours ago before coming to play cards that evening, Melinda had said, "Here we go again, dear. It does get tiring, doesn't it?"

Once again, he had suppressed asking why they had to keep going to Estelle's every Wednesday night, like robots. Instead he asked, "How do you think God will reward us for our 'Estelle mitzvahs'?"

"Perhaps by a surprise or two, who knows?"

Melinda had learned to side step his sarcasm. Also, the Jewish New Year was in two days, which pacified her. Rosh Hashanah and Yom Kippur were the only religious observances that Benjamin shared with her. He claimed he was a High Holy Day specialist.

Estelle looked more in her late sixties than her fifty-two years. She had aged overnight when her husband abandoned her a few months after she lost the use of her legs. He had claimed it had nothing to do with her disease, but Melinda didn't believe that. Gray roots bridged Estelle's white scalp to thinning, dyed brown hair, her one effort to appear presentable.

Since her sickness, she'd neglected caring for home or body. Her clothes were often stained and her shoes dirty; scattered objects, old newspapers and unwashed dishes lay around her small apartment. She had gained at least twenty pounds on her short thick body since she had joined the temple six months ago. Her pudgy face lacked expression, even when complaining, and her tiresome monotone triggered a defensive reaction in Benjamin. However, he fought his instinct to strike back, not always successfully, since he knew she had not attacked him personally. He was doing this principally for Melinda.

Benjamin did have a forgiving nature. He saw Estelle's fingernails coated with dull red, peeling polish as worn weapons that had lost their threat, unlike claws of a predator, calming his desire to snipe at her. It was not what she said or her appearance that irked him most, but rather it was her certainty about everything. Always the academic scientist, he rebelled against opinions stated as facts or beliefs not supported by evidence.

Benjamin walked into temple the following Friday morning clutching his prayer book but thinking about the lecture he was missing at the university on stem cells. "Nice day," he said to Melinda, then gazed at the cloudless blue sky.

"Yes," she answered as she passed the entrance of the temple.

As the Rosh Hashanah service started and the empty seats disappeared, he noticed a thin diagonal scratch in the back of the polished pew before him. He leaned forward to see a tiny heart at its base etched into the wood from the same sharp point. LN + PDU were printed in pencil underneath the heart. He speculated these as initials of imaginary people Lynn Nussbaum + Peter Denon Ukevitch? Why not, thought. Everything we hear in Temple is imaginary. Then he wondered whether 'Lynn' or 'Peter' made the scratches, and whether they really loved each other, or maybe someone just imagined phantom people like he did to entertain the old guys, like him, doing their duty on Rosh Hashanah.

"Look, young lovers," he whispered to Melinda as he pointed to the heart. "Shhh. Not so loud." She abruptly turned the page of her prayer book and he got the message.

"Rise as the Arc is opened," commanded the new rabbi, who had just replaced Rabbi Magnum on his retirement. Young Rabbi Fraenkel was the future: the changing of the guards to continue the never-ending cycle that kept treading back on itself.

"Please be seated," the rabbi said after the Arc was closed.

"All rise and turn to page 93 in your prayer book. Let us read responsively," said the rabbi a little later.

> *O Lord, You have been our refuge*
> *From generation to generation.*

The rabbi motioned for the congregants to be seated again.

Up and down, up and down, won't need to go to the gym today, thought Benjamin. A trickle of sweat slid down his cheek. He wiped off the perspiration with his fingers and rubbed his eye with his knuckle. The September heat was oppressive in Bethesda.

Practicing his speed-reading skills Benjamin skimmed forward in his prayer book, blocking out the background voice of the rabbi.

> *The Lord is King, The Lord was King,*
> *The Lord shall be King throughout all time.*

He was baffled why so many smart people repeated such nonsense over and over. If they meant the King is Nature, why didn't they say so? If they meant there is a supernatural force out there protecting people or directing events…well… how could anyone really believe that? He questioned for the umpteenth time what he was doing here, and then reminded himself of Melinda's devotion and his vows so many years ago "…in sickness and in health, until death do us part."

His leg touched hers and she smiled. "Please rise." Up again. Benjamin noticed strangers of all ages studying their books, standing as instructed, like soldiers, except for the girl in the stroller next to her young parents. Benjamin looked down at his feet and wiggled his toes. Obedient little fellows, he told himself, feeling disconnected from his body. I guess we all do what we're told, he thought, becoming strangely angry at his toes.

His mood mellowed as the congregants' joined the Cantor's deep voice in song and he saw Melinda swaying with the tune. The age-old melodies had become familiar over the years that he had attended Rosh Hashanah services with Melinda and were separate in his mind from the mechanical religious observances. It was as if the music and prayers, although under the same roof, had little to do with one another.

Benjamin tried to sing along with Melinda and the rest of the congregation but couldn't maintain the melody for more than a few moments, adding to his frustration at the service. He had difficulty pronouncing and didn't know the meaning of the Hebrew words, which often made him feel as an outsider, instead of imagining, as he usually did, that the others were chained within. It was as if he had not earned entrance into the privileged inner sanctum of Jews, or that birthright was insufficient to join this holy setting. Yet, he didn't feel rejected either. Rather, he felt that he had an illicit membership to an exclusive club.

A sense of estrangement was not new to Benjamin. He was the first American citizen of his family, having been born in New York a few months after his French mother and Russian father emigrated from France just in time to escape Hitler. His parents neither sent him to Hebrew school nor attended services themselves as he grew up assimilating new customs in a foreign land that they now called home. He was an American/ European/non-observant Jewish refugee raised in a peaceful country. He felt no more a ritualistic Jew clinging to past traditions than he a felt a target of Jewish persecution and Nazi extermination. Singing itself was difficult for him personally as well. His father was a musician, but Benjamin was tone-deaf and self-conscious when he sang. He imagined himself a deficient mutant when singing among others. His lips attempted to form words without sound for the rest of the song.

Benjamin, bored, started thinking about Estelle. He assumed that she was at the service and wondered who brought her to the temple or where she was sitting. He hoped Melinda wouldn't ask her to join them for lunch after the sermon, a tradition he had with her every year. Also, he didn't want to be stuck with Estelle that afternoon. He was looking forward to catching up on his work. He scanned the crowd looking for her didn't see her anywhere. The wheelchair should have been easy to spot.

"Where's Estelle?" he asked Melinda. She shrugged. "I don't know."

Benjamin's attention was diverted to the Cantor starting his journey up the aisle carrying the Torah. Many congregants shuffled along their rows in his direction. A gray-haired man eager to reach the Torah maneuvered across Benjamin and Melinda's row to reach the aisle. The end of his tallit, tassels dangling, was clutched in his fingertips and his arm extended towards the on-coming Torah. A changing flux of hands holding either prayer books or edges of tallits danced around the ancient Torah as it proceeded down the aisle. Golden rings, jeweled bracelets and cuff links screamed opulence while the act begged humility. No icons allowed, said the Jews. Yet, Benjamin saw them tied to ritual and the Torah. Were those not icons of a kind?

The books and tallits touched the Torah, ever so lightly, so lovingly, so reverently, and quickly receded to the lips of their owners for spiritual nourishment, a taste of honey. Benjamin recoiled from the programmed bonding between Torah and Jew. He found the subservience as unpalatable as the evangelists on television Sunday mornings praising Jesus Christ. Save for the rare scholar, why *kiss* a book or cloth after it touched a scroll that he had neither read nor understood? Why use lips; why *kiss*? It has nothing to do with the passion of lovers with moist lips, open, or with lips nuzzling on an infant's neck, or even with the social masquerade of lips smacking air as cheeks brushed past each other. To Benjamin, this Jewish kiss meant, "I'll obey, I'm yours," less like the fearful kissing of the Godfather's ring than the obsequious kissing of the Pope's. He would have preferred to *touch* the silver case of the Torah with his fingers. But, it was so distant, he thought, to touch but not to feel, so unsatisfying, like the *near* contact of a gentleman's lips meeting a lady's hand. He could not bring himself to extend his arm, to tap the Torah and touch his lips. Apart from the hypocrisy for him, it was an ostentatious performance, like yelling "Bravo!" at a concert, to stand out as a connoisseur, a true music lover, one who belongs, yet plays no instrument and cannot sing in tune. He looked at the other congregants touching and kissing, avoiding each other's eyes to make it all more sincere. The bowing, the swaying, the yarmulke and tallit, the reaching to touch the Torah in a mass frenzy – all distasteful public displays and badges of belonging – thought Benjamin. Was all that necessary?

What about the others, like himself, who were born members of the so-called Chosen People (chosen by whom?), but chose to look forward, not backward, and settled with being a member of the human race, despite their flaws, the product of eons of evolution, rather than being confined to an encapsulated group, special, claiming a singular privilege to misery? Every year it was the same: he watched, a peeping Tom, a Jewish peeping Tom, watching Jews.

But then other nagging questions rattled around in Benjamin's mind and confused him. A*m* I participating in earnest? I'm here, aren't I? I'm always here on Rosh Hashanah. I'm a Jew with a Jewish wife celebrating the New Year with other Jews. Don't people need family? Don't I? I am a product of history as everyone else here. He responded to the songs, rose to the call, read, on cue, that God is one, all-powerful, benevolent, never to be doubted, always to be honored. Did it really matter that he did not believe the voice of certainty in the prayer book, or that his hand was not among those seeking the Torah, or that his lips were not brushing against the object made holy by contact with the Torah, or that he was an Atheist, with a capital A? He was there, willingly, wearing his talllit and yarmulke. Doesn't the uniform define the person? Wouldn't a person camouflaged in a white sheet and sporting a pointed hat listening to the Grand Wizard be branded a member of the Ku Klux Klan whatever his private beliefs? Do thoughts trump actions? No. The messy informal appearance of a research scientist, like himself, was part of that person. He was *there* all right. With Melinda. If a modern day Gestapo invaded the temple at that very moment he would be incarcerated with her and the others.

He re-centered his light brown yarmulke (left over from the Bar-Mitzvah of Danny Shapiro, a friend of his daughter) and re-arranged his white and blue tallit to cover the full expanse of his shoulders, which sagged a bit with advancing years. He gazed at the Cantor walking along the aisle at the far left of the chapel heading back to the bima. Few remained around the Torah, a touch here, a tap there, kiss, kiss, the bees quieting as the hive prepared for the next phase.

Various members of the congregation went to the bima to read their assigned words of Hebrew, a plea was made to buy Israel bonds, more chants, up, down, yawns, the chapel door opened, closed with congregants taking breaks to sip water from the fountain or relieve themselves or maybe just chat with a friend and express condolences for a sick family member, or congratulations for a promotion, whatever, and then back to the sanctuary, the rituals, the service that put all lives on hold for the day, playing guiltless hooky from work, with pride and comfort and sense of community. It was their tribe, after all, for centuries, and it was Rosh Hashanah.

Happy New Year! Last year was wonderful, a blessing. Touch wood; *touch* again. Next year in Jerusalem! Maybe next year all our dreams will come true. Maybe. *Maybe.*

Benjamin pondered what thoughts filled the minds of the other congregants at this very instant. His six-foot, four-inch frame allowed him to see over the heads in front of him (except for one very ugly purple hat that blocked his view) and it all looked ordinary, a group of people observing the Jewish New Year, as expected of them. His thoughts turned more scientific and he wondered how many of the strangers in this holy chamber would be dead next year, how many malignant tumors were in the room, how much anxiety, how many would hear devastating news within the week about their health, or their jobs, or their children (God forbid). Then he gave himself a break and wondered how many orgasms would they generate today, and how many conceptions, wanted and unwanted, occurred last night?

This scene may have appeared commonplace, but so do tragedy and ecstasy from afar. A room full of people is high drama, he thought, the stuff of literature and life, just notice, think, *imagine*. His thoughts returned to the contradictions of authenticity: was it mind or body, beliefs or actions? Could he be religious and not religious at the same time? Who wins the battle of competing truths?

And then Benjamin heard a human voice that put aside his tiresome conflicts. It had a wondrous quality, like the first chirp of a bird at dawn. The tapestry of suits, dresses, jewelry, hair shades, scarves, the background of people that had distracted him, surrendered to the feminine melody so fine that it sounded like a single violin string caressed by a bow containing a hair plucked from the head of a child-angel. The voice was not powerful or tutored like that of a soprano's trained for opera, but free like air filling the sanctuary, entering his body with every breath.

Benjamin's invisible shield melted. He glanced at Melinda beside him and took her hand in his. She squeezed his fingers. He closed his eyes and imagined the ebb and flow of tides in a calm sea where life originated. His face relaxed and the creases lining his forehead disappeared. The warmth of that single voice made him shiver in the September heat. It didn't matter anymore whether there was a God that was good or powerful or existed at all. With Benjamin's hand in Melinda's in his private dark space of closed eyes, there was no inner or outer group; that one human voice kidnapped his conflicts.

Benjamin leaned close to Melinda and asked, "Who is singing?"

"I don't know," she said.

"Where is it coming from?"

"The choir, I think."

Benjamin scrutinized each person within the choir standing at the front of the chapel. No lips were moving, yet the spellbinding voice. He searched the congregants for the woman who sang, but found none. Again he examined the choir carefully, and then he noticed a space between two women standing in the second row. A metallic flash caught his attention. He squinted and thought he may have identified the source of the voice. He shifted in his seat trying to see her more clearly.

Estelle! Yes, he was sure now. She was trapped in her wheelchair as usual. Her eyes were shut and except for her lips, she was perfectly still. Oh my, Estelle! Benjamin wondered whether she plucked the notes out of the heavens and blew them gently to the audience. This was not Estelle's gin-rummy voice Benjamin heard on Wednesday nights.

The older couple in front of him stopped whispering to each other. The rabbi stopped fiddling with his tallit. Even the baby stopped fidgeting in the stroller. The occasional coughs, the muffled chatter, the turning of pages, the restlessness all ceased. This voice was for listening, not joining or interrupting. It demanded no action and claimed no certainty; it was from another world where understanding came simply from being a part of it. Estelle was singing purely and beautifully. That was all. The preaching of the rabbi, the chanting of the cantor and the rituals of the congregants seemed insignificant. Benjamin's desire to prove his identity to himself or to anyone else dissolved. He imagined symphonies playing in the heads of the deaf. And then as Estelle's voice had permeated the sanctuary, it eased to its conclusion without fanfare.

A solemn hush lingered. There was no applause, no bow. There would be no headline in tomorrow's newspaper: "Estelle Changes Lives: Jews Honor the New Year". A lady in a wheelchair had sung her song to a congregation at Rosh Hashanah. But Benjamin knew that he would carry this sound with him when the sun set that evening.

Rabbi Fraenkel broke the magic of the moment with a mundane sermon about the importance of retaining Jewish roots through observance.

After the service he saw Estelle being wheeled to the lobby by her son Larry. She was criticizing him for pushing the wheelchair recklessly. Benjamin saw that her purple-red lipstick, too heavily applied, spread unevenly beyond the boundaries of her parched lips.

"Estelle," said Melinda. "That was wonderful. I had no idea…what a voice you have."

"Yes, yes, absolutely, amazing. I didn't know. You never said anything," added Benjamin.

"Thanks," she said. "God, it's hot in here. Do they think we're made of plastic or something?"

She laughed coarsely, as usual, starring straight ahead with her deadpan bug-eyes. Her blue sweater was rumpled and her canvas shoes stained. Her earrings were too small for her big ears, and she was wearing a gauche necklace with large blue, glass beads.

Such a mess, thought Benjamin. She was as obnoxious as ever. Just seeing her in her wheelchair made him shy away. That her divine voice had returned to some mysterious place within her haunted him.

"Good singing," said a passing congregant as he raced out the front door. "Happy New Year!"

"Yes," said Larry to no one in particular. "Good singing."

Benjamin moved close to Melinda as they left the Temple. He removed his yarmulke and tallit; the service was over; the New Year had officially begun. Larry wheeled his mother out behind them. Benjamin turned as bright sunrays filtered through the leaves of a nearby tree and brightened Estelle's face. A slight breeze made shadows dance on her cheeks. He took a step in her direction and touched her arm.

"Thanks, Estelle. We'll see you next Wednesday?" he said.

He could not be sure but hoped that the small movement of Estelle's lips was a smile.

"I guess," she said. "Wednesday."

Melinda took Benjamin's arm and they headed together towards their favorite small Greek restaurant where they always ate lunch after Rosh Hashanah services to usher in the Jewish New Year.

About the Author

Joram Piatigorsky lives with his wife in Bethesda and devotes his time to writing after a lengthy career in science research. He has published short stories and essays in literary magazines, a novel, Jellyfish Have Eyes (IPBooks; Adelaide Books), a memoir, The Speed of Dark (Adelaide Books), and two short story collections, The Open Door and other tales of love and yearning and Notes Going Underground (Adelaide Books), and an essay collection scheduled for April, 2021 (Adelaide Books). He is an avid Inuit art collector and blogs at his website (www.joramp.com).

SHORTLIST WINNER NOMINEES

Appalachian Curses

by Brooke Reynolds

The weighted rubber soles of Cassandra's Columbia hiking boots crunch through the melting leftover patches of snow. Where there isn't snow, wet orange and brown decaying leaves intertwine like a crotchet blanket to spread across the forest floor. Her arms stretch out so her hands graze across an emerald sea of ferns. She pauses to rest, leaning against a nearby oak tree. Her fingers pick at the spongey moss that invades its trunk. Whenever she needs a good therapy session to work out a situation, Cassandra seeks sanctuary here in the Appalachian Mountains.

Saplings bend and twist at odd angles, their new spring growth forever stunted by the dense canopy above that refracts the late morning sun. Cassandra sucks at the rubber stopper of her Camelback, allowing cool water to flow into her mouth. Her stomach pinches, forcing a gag. She searches through her bag and pulls out a granola bar, eager to keep the nausea away that always seems to intensify on an empty stomach. If she's lucky, she'll only have to deal with this queasiness for another three phases of the moon. Though she's heard some must endure it up until evacuation.

She still hasn't figured out how to break the news to Chad. The conversation's been easy to avoid. Thankfully Chad's been in Mississippi for the past week setting up a new plant. When she finally gets around to telling him, he'll be ecstatic, once the initial shock wears off. She's just not sure how to feel about it yet. It's not like they were preventing anything, but she's the one that has to go through bodily disfigurement. Having a tiny piece of each of them is inspiring and terrifying all at the same time. Imagine a tiny copycat being with her long nose, doe eyes, and introvertness combined with husband's insane level of stubbornness; the idea terrifies her.

With nausea subsided, she continues her trek. She comes upon an overturned birds' nest at the base of a tree. A predator or the wind from a storm must have dislodged it from one of the branches above. Its previous inhabitant, a single white and brown marbled egg, lies abandoned underneath, cracked and spilling its liquid contents onto the ground. She picks up the nest and runs her finger around the inside. She marvels at its softness, a layer of padding formed from the undercoat of a grey fox woven between a mesh of twigs and mud. She packs the nest away in her bag and continues on.

Blocking her path is a fallen tree, the base wide enough that she must swing her legs up in the air one at a time in order climb over it. Its trunk is covered in small shelf like groupings of tan and white mushrooms. Being a member of the foraging community, Cassandra recognizes the characteristic gills running the full length of the underside of each one, making these delicious oyster mushrooms. She collects a small cluster and takes a small bite to test if they are too mature or leathery in texture. Her teeth glide through a tender cap. Satisfied, she adds them to her collection.

She ventures deeper into the forest, along a winding path that pulls her further away from society, so deep that the only sounds she hears are chirping birds and the rush of water from a nearby stream. Sweat acts as a glue, sticking her clothes to the small of her back. Its unusually warm for late March. She abandons the path to seek water to cool off. As she gets closer, larger and larger rocks climb out of the ground beneath her until she reaches a knee-high cliff dropping down to a rushing stream. The water is chaotic, jumping from rock to rock, forming a white froth of bubbles. She stands at the waters' edge and breaths deep.

A cool breeze ripples through the trees. She unzips her favorite black hooded sweatshirt and fans it out, thankful for the relief. Her fingers pick at the holes in the cuffs from extensive wear. She bought the hoodie at a Trapt concert in her freshman year of undergrad, back when she used rock concerts as her religion. It's all black with the band's logo splattered across the front in red and white dripping letters that split apart from the zipper. She removes it completely and drapes it over a nearby rock. She crouches down to the waters edges and plunges her arms into the cold mountain stream. She grabs the smooth stones at the bottom as the current beats against her skin.

A baby's wail breaks the silence. Her eyes search up and down both sides of the stream but she sees no sign of human life anywhere. The crying is consistent, loud, and urgent. It brings her to her feet. She follows the sound south. Her stomach twists. What if someone abandoned their baby out here along the trail?

She jogs after the sound, following it several hundred yards. It doesn't get any louder. She changes direction and heads north, backtracking to the water and continuing on. The crying doesn't get any louder. Maybe a mother is carrying the baby and they're walking along the trail. She tries east. Then west. No matter how far she travels in any direction, the crying never gets louder or softer.

Then, it stops. An abrupt quiet with no soothing, wind down. Just stifled silence. She reasons that the mother must have finally soothed it by shoving a pacifier in its mouth. The hair on her arms raises. What if something else found it?

"Hello?", she shouts. Her lungs suck in a deep breath and she holds it for fear that the sound of her own breathing will smother a response.

No reply. A forced exhale spews from her mouth. She's unsure how long she was holding in that breath. Cassandra rubs her head. Did she imagine the whole thing? Eager to get on with her hike, she wanders back to the trail. A strange sense of relief overcomes her. She's proud of how she responded. Perhaps there is a mothering instinct deep down under her hardened exterior.

"Please, my baby."

A voice jolts her out of her thoughts. Limping towards her is a woman in clear distress. She's dressed in black, loose draping clothes. Cassandra thinks she sees writing on the woman's shirt, but there's so much mud caked to her, it's hard to tell. The woman bears a mangled right leg, her toes pointed off to the side. Dried pine needles stick in amongst a tangled mass of brown hair. Before Cassandra has time to react, the woman's in front of her, crying. Mascara melts down her face like wax dripping from a lit candle. She grabs hold of Cassandra's shoulders. Her hands are grimy, with dirt caked up under each of her nails, like she's been clawing at the earth. She shakes Cassandra.

"Help me, please. My baby, I've lost my baby!" The woman has a hard Eastern European accent, making her words sound muffled. She lets out a guttural yowl.

As the woman shouts, spit sprays, hitting Cassandra in the face. Cassandra's conscious screams at her to run from this crazed woman in the woods. Clearly, she must be on something to lose an infant in the woods or she's lying. Cassandra's heard stories of meth heads attacking hikers on the Appalachian trail. This could be just a ploy to catch her off guard. Deep in the bottom of her Camelback is her Swiss Army knife. If Cassandra shoves the woman back with both arms, she may have enough time to grab the knife.

The woman collapses to her knees, groveling at Cassandra's feet. She buries her face down in the dirt and claws at the earth as she cries.

"My baby boy. Please. I fall asleep and wake and he's gone. Why they take my baby?"

Something pulls at Cassandra heartstrings. The act appears genuine. This woman doesn't possess any real threat. She carries no pack or supplies, no place to conceal any weapons. Cassandra kneels down next to her. "It's okay. I'll help you. Where were you at when you fell asleep?"

The woman looks up and points behind to the direction she came from in the woods.

Cassandra slips her pack off and unzips it. She reaches her hand into the bottom and grabs the knife. It's concealed from the woman by hiding in Cassandra's palm. She feels for a front pocket and realizes she left her hoodie back at the stream. The knife slips into the front of her jeans instead, just in case.

She helps the woman to her feet. The woman stumbles and grabs at the front of Cassandra's shirt. A hand brushes Cassandra's stomach. "Ahh, you with child."

Cassandra looks down at her stomach. How did the woman know? There's no baby bump yet.

The woman responds like she can read Cassandra's thoughts. "A mother always knows."

Cassandra avoids any further discussion. "Take me to where you last saw your baby."

They walk in silence, with the woman out in front dragging her mangled leg. The ground changes to a bed of dried pine needles as they come upon a section with mostly evergreens.

The trees are spread further apart, allowing them to see quite a long distance in any direction. They approach an area where the needles have been disrupted, fanned out from the center creating a large nest like a deer would use to bed down at night.

Cassandra kneels in the center of the bed and runs her hands over the needles. Off to the right she finds large tread boot prints. She points to the tracks. "Those tracks are too large for you or I. If we follow them, we'll find whoever took your baby."

Cassandra leads the way, keeping her eyes peeled to the ground to follow the tracks. The woman trails close behind. Cassandra sneaks a look back every few yards to make sure she's still being followed. The woman wrings her hands and with her eyes narrowed, stares straight at Cassandra. Mumbled words in her native language are spat at Cassandra. At first, Cassandra reasons that the woman must be muttering prayers to herself. It's the stern look in the woman's eyes with just the slightest hint of a smirk on her lips that makes Cassandra keep patting her pocket to check and see if the knife is still there.

The pine needles disperse and the ground becomes littered with a light coating of leaves again. After a few more steps, the tracks stop. Cassandra walks in a circle, trying to see if maybe whoever they're following made a sudden turn that she missed. She pauses. The birds have all gone silent. It's too quiet. She whips around and the woman is gone. When was the last time she looked over her shoulder? She calls out but no response. It had to be only a minute before she lost the tracks. She calls again, but there's only silence.

Her feet drag her to the main part of the trail and she follows it back to the gas station rest area where her car is parked. She's feeling exhausted and slightly delusional. Had she imagined both the baby crying and the strange woman? Her spinning head she blames on the pregnancy.

She pops into the gas station and grabs a bag of salt and vinegar chips and a Gatorade flavored green. It could be melon or lime, but to Cassandra they all taste the same. She heads to the check out and the cashier rings her up.

"Nice day out for a hike."

"Uh, huh." She pays for her items and turns to leave. Hanging off the counter is a lost cat sign. It makes her think of the woman. "By any chance, did you see a woman stop by here with brown hair and all dressed in black?"

"Like yourself?"

Cassandra looks down and sees that she is indeed all dressed in black. "A different woman, with a limp."

"Doesn't ring a bell but I generally don't take notice to people. Why?"

"Oh, you would have remembered this woman. She kept saying she lost her baby. I would have thought her mad, but before she appeared, I did hear a baby crying. I was trying to help her find it. It was weird though because all of a sudden, she disappeared. Like one minute she was behind me saying weird words I didn't understand, and then she wasn't."

He nods his head. "Sounds like you had a run in with the Pearisburg witch, a little urban legend we have. Used to be hikers would see her all the time 'round this area of the trail."

Cassandra unscrews the cap on her Gatorade and takes a sip. "I'm not sure I believe in all those ghost and ghoul things."

"She's very much real, or at least she was. The story goes, about forty years ago a young Czech couple decided to hike the Appalachian trail with their baby. They made it all the way up from Georgia when there was a terrible accident. The husband, carrying the baby on his back, fell into a gorge and hit is head on the rocks, killing him instantly. He landed on the baby. The wife tried to go in after them and retrieve the baby, but ended up injuring her leg pretty badly. By the time she got down to it, the baby was dead.

As one would expect, the loss of both her husband and the baby drove the poor woman into a life of seclusion. She refused to leave the woods and lived off of the land. Whenever she'd come across hikers, her frantic naturalistic manor from years of solitude in the mountains brought about accusations of madness. Hikers would challenge each to other to a sort of scavenger hunt, extra points were given if you could snap a picture with the witch or steal something that belonged to her. It was all an innocent game until a child went missing."

Cassandra places her hand on her stomach. "What's so weird about that? Children get lost all the time."

"This was unfortunately the first in a series of disappearances. A family was hiking right up along where you were, going on ten years ago. They had the typical encounter with the witch, but when she disappeared, so did their five-year-old son. Police scoured the area for weeks but never found anything other than a black hooded sweatshirt. Every few years or so, another child goes missing and another story is created. Some believe she's a ghost and that she died in that gorge years ago with her family. Others speculate that she's still alive, abducting children to replace the one she lost."

Cassandra thanks the clerk and heads home to rest. That night, she sits up in bed, feeling cramps in her lower abdomen. Unsure if she's going to be sick or not, she runs to the bathroom. A sharp wave of pain ripples through her. Like her uterus is a wet rag, it squeezes and wrings, emptying its contents in a forced water balloon exploding expulsion. Her hands grab the sides of the toilet and she shakes. She doesn't need to look to know.

Tears of frustration and anger flood her face. There wasn't enough time to processes the pregnancy before her body spit it out like a foul taste. Chad still didn't know and he never would. This secret she would bare.

In the shower, she washes away her mess. Her hands rub just below her belly button, washing away what will never be. What if this was her only chance of having children? Her one hope of raising a better version of herself, to further her legacy, and now it's lost. The memory of the woman touching her stomach fills her thoughts. Did the woman put a curse on her to try and take her unborn baby for herself? She keeps hearing the words the woman uttered behind her in the woods. Words or incantations? Now she's not so sure she knows the difference.

All her usual supplies are thrown back into her Camelback, plus extras of most items. She will stay in the woods as long as it takes to find the witch who snuffed out her lifeline.

Into the wilderness she goes, off the path and through the trees until she finds herself back at the water's edge where she first heard the baby cry. Stomped into the earth she finds her old hoodie and slips it on. It's here she waits.

A night passes and she stays in the woods. A week passes and still in the forest she remains. Then a month passes, followed by a few more, and soon the forest floor fills with a new layer of fallen leaves. She survives on mushrooms and insects, turning rotten logs to feed on things with legs that wiggle and crawl all the way down her throat. Her typical black attire hangs loose on her shrunken frame. Leaves and twigs stick to the matted mess that was once her beautiful brown hair. As she withers away, she encounters other hikers, begging them to help her find the woman who took her baby. They mock her but she never stops looking.

About the Author

Brooke Reynolds is a veterinarian from Charlotte, North Carolina. When she isn't saving animals, she enjoys reading and writing fiction. Her stories have appeared at such online and print markets as Massacre Magazine, Fantasia Divinity, The Literary Hatchet, Ghost Parachute, Riggwelter, Ricky's Back Yard, Coffin Bell, Ink Stains Anthology, Sanitarium Magazine, The Horror Zine, Nightmare Press, and Black Hare Press. Her forthcoming novel Healers is set to be published by Adelaide Books in early 2021. You can follow her on twitter @psubamit or check out her website reynoldswrites.org.

Sweat

by Jonathan Maniscalco

The moisture that dripped down the Thinker's head became not just noticeable but downright attention dominating as exertion was relinquished after the running stopped and rest was allowed to pervade. Sweat itself was a funny phenomenon and it had occupied the Thinker's mind frequently throughout the last few weeks. The Thinker found it funny that the word was permitted to be an adjective when there was plenty of diversity to it outside of the mainstream use. When someone said something *smelled like sweat*, it referred to the hot, full, active sweat from heat or the exercise that had just occurred. There were other forms though with different smells. The most common alternatives being the putrid sweat of sickness, the sour sweat of anxiety, and the stale smell of the sweat you woke up in after a nightmare. All those were drastically different from the common sweat of a gym locker room. And it wasn't like the common usage had set qualities that were totally different from the others. The common use filled a room, but so did the sick sweat, whereas the sick sweat didn't hit you full in the face when you entered the room it inhabited, but instead took a minute to seep into your nose like when in close proximity to the anxiety sweat. And they were all like that. All different sweats inhabited different overlaps of a sweat Venn Diagram, and despite this diversity of strength, aggression, power, and lifespan, the sweat that dominated our vocabulary enough to not need a modifier was the almost boring one our bodies produced from exercise. "Boring is relative though." The Thinker thought, pondering this latest smell. "I suppose I'm using boring to mean common. And it's only common because it's socially acceptable to exercise and smell of it around other people. Whereas we more typically are avoiding people when we're anxious or sick."

"I may be thinking too commonly when it comes to designating exercise sweat as the smell of sweat" The Thinker thought. "Even if that's how it seems to be the way most use it, most isn't everyone." The Thinker pondered while turning around to walk back home.

"Could it be possible," The Thinker wondered, "That like, doctors and nurses associate the base adjective of sweat to the smell of sick sweat?"

"Maybe," The Thinker concluded, "But probably not. Doctors and nurses may be around sickness more than the average person, but it's not like they exercise any less, which would probably nudge them towards the common usage. If anything they sweat more from how much and how long they're on their feet, which would make it even more common for them, especially since not every sick person is always smelling like sick sweat. But what do I know? A lot of this is simply guessing and guessing gets too general too fast. How do I know that they aren't so attune to illness that what I lump into the single smell of *sick*, they can differentiate between the many ways our bodies can be infected. That could even be true with sweat from labor as opposed to exercise. Because what's exercise besides play concentrated to decrease the pleasure benefits for the trade-off of increasing the health benefits for a society too tired and tight-scheduled to commit to open-ended play, so it has to relegate time for the 'health' that should've been covered simply by living. Again though, what do I know?"

That was a question that often came to the Thinker regardless of the thoughts that led up to it. The fascination with the unknown being that discoveries like this had been made insufficient lately due to the status of the Thinker, where the question of, "How does knowing this help?" Couldn't be stopped. And naturally the question was usually fair in the sense that it's rare that any knowledge can directly help us, much less ever does, especially something like the various modes of sweat that are ignored by common vernacular. Not too long ago though the question would not have surfaced because the subconscious answer of "So what if it doesn't." Would have pulled the question down by its insecure coattails, saving the Thinker of being bothered by it. However, now the question was aided by the Thinker's belief that life was progressing too quickly, allowing it to lodge in the Thinker's mind and live there.

"I'm not at all where I thought I'd be at this age," Was something the Thinker had been recently saying out loud to curious and concerned older relatives, prompting offers of dated advice, as well as friends of a comparable age, prompting common commiseration. The Thinker had thus concluded that in order to avoid a future that would continue to wane, change had to be made in order to avoid the insanity of expecting different results without it. To do that, the Thinker had to look to the past for what indiscretions must have occurred. "How does knowing this help me?" had become a way to right the future by learning from the past. The Thinker could not say how this practice of knowledge prioritization could help exactly, but it was change, and something had to change. And the Thinker believed this wholeheartedly due to the motivation in the changes that had been made so far nagged at the Thinker, since these changes subtly made the case that the situation could be dire.

A large part of this fear was rooted in the exercising the Thinker had just done. The Thinker had always been athletic and that must have been a problem. The Thinker had never truly tried to be athletic to the degree that had been spurred on by the first signs of true ageing. The reaction and the success had surprised the Thinker. That the discipline, stoicism, and determination involved in diet, alcohol cutting, and early morning exercise had allowed the maintaining of college level fitness after the tenth-place-decimal that signified youth changed to the first one that lacked it. What could have been accomplished if only the Thinker had applied this level of motivation when age had exuberated young energy? How high or far could the Thinker have gone? No one would ever know and that hole of knowledge manically drove the Thinker to cut anything that could be considered fat, since that's where the error must have been.

"I could be running right now." The Thinker thought and started doing so. Ignoring the aching of shaky legs as weakness that needed expulsion, instead noticing the arms' comparative ease of movement and feeling a need to punish them for their leisure after the run's conclusion.

"But will that help me?" The Thinker thought. "Am I spending too much time on my body? It's too late to be an athlete, if I ever could've been one. Probably not. So what am I doing? Should I be working more? A promotion would help. Promoted to what, though? So do I need a new job? A new degree? A class on being personable? Are those a waste of time, though? Probably. Would another degree be? They take two years minimum. Do I have time for that? I would if it yielded results, but what if it doesn't? Then I'd be even further behind where I am now. I'd have wasted even more time. And if a career is like my body, not utilizing my time could forever keep me from where I need to be."

The need to get to this amorphous place made the Thinker sick with anxiety, and enter the state of running that's similar to a shaky dream, pushing the once humble pace to one that induced new sweat as the Thinker raced faster against no one.

About the Author

Jonathan Maniscalco has taught English to ESL learners in Japan, Spain, Chile, and New York City. A Massachusetts native, he is a graduate of Boston University and is currently completing a Master's Degree at Clark University. Ten Stories to Home is his second published short story collection. His first novel, The Dog Star Burned will be published in 2021.

Grandpa

by Douglas Walrath

Ben wasn't his real name, although everyone called him Ben. His real name was Bernard, but he never liked it. When he left home at sixteen and started life over, he left Bernard behind and became Ben—Benjamin V when he had to sign something official. The "V" didn't stand for a given name either. But other people had middle names so Grandpa decided he should have at least a middle initial.

In the nineteen-twenties and thirties Grandpa Ben and Grandma Lulu lived in a third-floor walk-up apartment on Superior Street in Austin, on Chicago's west side where my father met my mother at the Austin Boulevard Christian Church. Every Sunday we had a family gathering that began at church and ended at their apartment where we ate the roast that had cooked while we worshipped.

When we went to church services Grandpa wore a suit, complete with a vest that featured a watch chain threaded through the vest's middle buttonhole, and connected on one end to a large white-gold watch he kept in the right vest pocket, and on the other end to a small pen knife he kept in the left vest pocket.

Even before I was old enough to go to school, I could sense that going to church was not something Grandpa wanted to do;

he did it to please Grandma. It was one of the accommodations they made to each other that enabled their marriage to endure for sixty years. I thought that's what married people did.

In 1939 when I was six years old, I started to recognize those accommodations. My mother and father had moved out of their bungalow in Oak Park to a larger bungalow with a larger yard in suburban Elmhurst. Occasionally on a weekend they would return to the city to socialize with old friends and I would spend from Friday supper until church time on Sunday at Grandpa and Grandma's apartment.

When I arrived on Friday Grandpa was always at work at the bowling alley he managed. Grandma and I would have supper together and listen to radio programs that she liked. We would sit together on the couch, and she would read a story to me, and then open a pair of curtained glass doors in the living room wall and pull down the Murphy bed.

I loved sleeping in the Murphy bed, though sometimes I was a little afraid that it might fold back up into the wall with me in it. Just in case it did, I slept wrong end to—my feet toward the wall. Then if it folded up with me in it, I would at least be standing up.

I liked waking up during the night after Grandma had gone to bed—especially in summer when the windows were open, and I could hear the noises of the city. The neighborhood around the apartment was so much more interesting than the tame suburb we had moved to. I would sit in the middle of the Murphy bed and look out the windows that faced the alley, past the vacant lot on the other side of the alley, through a wide passageway between the buildings, and watch the streetcars on Chicago Avenue, the next street over.

Streetcars ran all night in those days. Austin Boulevard was the end of the line and they had to switch from one track to another before they started back downtown. Switching was a noisy affair with lots of sparks from the pulleys on the ends of the rods that connected the streetcars to the overhead electric wires. It was worth staying awake to watch the light show.

Sometimes at one or two o'clock in the morning I would see Grandpa slowly making his way through the passageway between the buildings. Shortly after he disappeared from view, I would hear him mount the enclosed wooden back steps that led up to the third-floor landing outside the kitchen of the apartment. When I heard the kitchen door open, I would lie down and pretend to be asleep. I didn't open my eyes as he walked past the door into the dining room and turned to go into the bathroom, but I knew it was Grandpa; I could smell the Smith Brothers cough drops. I was glad he was home.

I always got up early the next morning when Grandma did. Together we would straighten up the covers on the Murphy bed, raise it up into its compartment, and shut the curtained glass doors that hid it from sight during the day. Grandma and I ate breakfast together—always oatmeal and toast.

After breakfast I would sit at the table and wait for Grandpa to appear. He never got up before ten o'clock. He always went directly to the bathroom, filled the tub, and took his bath. When he dried himself and was partly dressed, he opened the door and steam poured forth from the bathroom. Grandpa liked a hot bath in a hot bathroom. Like I did.

I sat in a chair where I could look through the door into the bathroom and watched. He stood in front of the sink in his tank-top undershirt, his suspenders hanging down along the sides of his pants, and smiled at me as he stroked a straight razor back and forth on the leather strap that always hung on the back of the bathroom door. He worked up lather in his shaving mug and spread it over his face.

Grandpa was an artist with the straight razor; he never cut himself shaving. Though one time I watched, entranced, while he pulled a skin tag away from his cheek and zipped it off with the straight razor. He stuck a piece of toilet tissue where the tag had been until the bleeding stopped. He noticed me looking at him. "Got to get rid of those before they get big!" I hoped I could be that brave.

While Grandpa was getting himself ready in the bathroom, Grandma made up their bed and placed a freshly-ironed shirt and tie on the bed. She came out of the bedroom as Grandpa walked into it. They didn't speak or even look at each other as they passed. In a few minutes Grandpa appeared dressed in a shirt and tie, and sat at the dining room table. Grandma set a cup of hot coffee and a glass of orange juice at his place and walked back to the kitchen. Grandpa took a sip of the hot coffee.

Grandma stood in the kitchen doorway. "You were drinking again last night, weren't you, Benny? . . . I knew you'd been drinking when I smelled the cough drops. . . Even when you use the cough drops, I still know. . . You know how I hate drinking, but you still do it. . . Don't you care how I feel about it?"

"Hush up, Lulu, and fix my eggs!"

I waited for something more to happen, but nothing ever did.

Grandma hushed up and fixed his breakfast. Three strips of bacon, two eggs sunny side up, cooked by spooning the hot grease over the top of them, two slices of toast made from her homemade bread, slightly browned just the way he liked it, in the toaster with the doors that let the bread slide down and turn over when you opened them so it could toast the other side.

The toast and the eggs finished exactly together. Grandma placed them on a plate with the bacon and set it in front of Grandpa. He ate his breakfast in silence. It was a liturgy they celebrated every morning. I learned not to be afraid when they did it—like I learned not to be afraid when the preacher shouted at us in the church we attended. After a while I found their homemade liturgy comforting.

When Grandpa finished eating, he would turn to me and say, "Want to go get a paper?"

"Sure!"

We would walk together through the kitchen past Grandma. "Don't you buy him ice cream, Benny, and spoil his lunch!" Grandpa didn't say anything. I knew what that meant.

Grandpa and I went down the enclosed wooden back stairs, across the alley, and through the passageway between the buildings. We walked along Chicago Avenue to the newsstand at the corner of Austin Boulevard. Grandpa always bought three newspapers.

"Want an ice cream cone?"

"Sure!"

Grandpa was the only person who bought me ice cream before lunch. From Walgreen's: two dips of beautiful green pistachio in a special double-sided waffle cone made so the dips sat side-by-side.

We walked slowly back to the apartment so I could finish the ice cream cone before we arrived. Grandpa gave me his handkerchief to wipe my face.

I never mentioned the ice cream cones to Grandma. Grandpa would give me a Smith Brother's cough drop to suck on just in case. "Suck on it slowly," he always said, "don't chew it!" I did, like a grown-up would.

During a visit, right after I turned eight years old, when Grandpa finished reading his newspapers, he said, "Want to play cards?" I was intrigued; no one invited me to play cards at my house.

"Sure."

During the next few visits, he taught me to play casino. It took a while for me to catch on, to learn about the big casino and the little casino and how to take the pot. But I was soon good at the game—though even after I was good at it, Grandpa still won most of the time.

Grandpa loved to win. He would laugh loudly and slap his hands on the table and say, "I won! I beat you!" After a while when I won, I began to do the same.

One cold winter day as we were playing, I saw him cheat. He knew I saw him. We sat for a while and stared at each other. I was scared. Finally, I said quietly, "That wasn't fair."

"I know." He looked at me intently. "You have to keep your eye on people when you play cards with them."

After I caught him Grandpa still won more often than I did, but I never saw him cheat again.

After Friday supper during a visit the next summer, as I sat by the open dining room window to feel the breeze, I heard the sounds of a carnival. When I looked over the tops of the buildings on Chicago Avenue, I could see the lights on a turning Ferris wheel. The next day as Grandpa and I walked away from Walgreens he looked at his pocket watch. "We've got time to go to the carnival. Want to go?"

"Sure!"

We walked together down Chicago Avenue to a large vacant lot located halfway between the apartment and Grandpa's bowling alley. The carnival filled the lot. The rides were just beginning to operate. Grandpa and I went on all of them, twice on the Ferris wheel.

When we walked away from the Ferris wheel Grandpa looked at me like he always did when he was going to say something important. "Come over here with me and I'll show you how to make nickels." He led me to a large table ringed mostly by men. When I stood on my tiptoes, I was just tall enough to see over the edge of the table. People were placing nickels on various squares on the table. The man in charge of the table was throwing dice. When the dice landed, he would call out the number they added up to, and then sweep most of the nickels off the table with something that looked like a rake.

After we watched for a while Grandpa took a few steps away and motioned to me to follow. "Do you know what 'even' means? 2, 4, 6, 8, 10 and 12 are even." I nodded. "I'm going to show you how to make nickels playing double or nothing." He held out a nickel to me. "When we go back to the table you take this nickel, and reach up and put it in the square that says 'E-V-E-N.' Understand?" I nodded.

"Now, here's the important part. When the man throws the dice, don't take your finger off your nickel unless the dice add up to an even number, 2, 4, 6, 8, 10 or 12, *twice in a row!* If they add up to an odd number once or twice, don't take your finger off the nickel. I'll stand across the table from you. If you wonder what to do, just look at me.

"If I nod my head yes, then you can lift your finger off your nickel, but if I shake my head no, don't lift your finger off your nickel. If the man who shakes the cup gives you another nickel, just take it and put it in your pocket and put your finger back on the nickel in the square marked 'EVEN' on the table. Do what I say, and you won't lose my nickel. Okay?"

I was scared, but I said, "Okay."

We went back to the table and I stood on tiptoes and reached up and put my nickel on the square marked "EVEN."

The man shook the dice. "Six," he said. Grandpa nodded. I lifted my finger. The man raked some of the nickels off the table, but not mine. The man with the cup shook the dice again. "Ten," he said. Grandpa nodded. I lifted my finger and the man raked some of the nickels off the table, but not mine. Then he took his rake and pushed another nickel into my square. I lifted it off the table and put it into my pocket.

I put my finger back on my nickel on the table. The man shook the dice. "Five." Grandpa shook his head and mouthed "no." I kept my finger tightly on my nickel. The man reached the rake over toward my hand. He waited, but I didn't take my finger off my nickel. The people who ringed the table began to laugh.

The man with the cup shook the dice again. And so it went for the next ten minutes or so. Whenever the dice added up to an even number twice in a row, Grandpa nodded, and I lifted my finger, and the man with the cup gave me another nickel. When I had five new nickels in my pocket, Grandpa nodded and mouthed, "Let's go." I took the nickel off the table and we walked away. He grinned at me, "You get to go on five more rides, but I want my nickel back. It was a loan." I smiled and gave it to him. I liked winning nickels.

The following winter my father was transferred from Chicago to Baltimore, and then to Scranton and ultimately New York City. He was a rising executive in the Western Electric Company. World War II was raging, and he was married and just old enough to escape the draft. During the War we rarely returned to Chicago from the East Coast for visits. We couldn't buy gasoline for pleasure trips and train tickets were at a premium. By the time the war was over, I was beginning high school. Soon I was a high school graduate and off to college.

After I left home for college, Grandpa and Grandma moved in with my mother and father. He'd had to have a gall bladder operation (too many greasy eggs, the doctor told him). The operation didn't go well, and it took several weeks for him to recover. When he was well enough to return to work, the bowling alley owner told him they had hired another manager. He said Grandpa was getting too old to handle the younger crowd that now patronized the bowling alley.

Grandpa's job was gone, and he and Grandma had no savings. They sold all their furniture except their bedroom set. They sent the bedroom set and a few boxes of heirlooms by moving van to the East Coast. They arrived with their suitcases at the train station in Newark. My parents took them in.

I saw Grandpa whenever I came home during college vacations, but our times together weren't as much fun as they had been when I made those visits to the apartment on Superior Street. By the time I was a second-year theological student we had mostly lost touch; we rarely saw each other. I noticed during a late fall trip home that he had become thin and didn't look well. Most of the time he just sat and listened to the radio. I wasn't surprised when my mother called and said he had suffered a stroke and been taken to the hospital. I should try to get home and visit him; he might not have much longer.

By the time I was able to visit, Grandpa had been moved to a nursing home. When I asked for directions to his room, the woman at the desk said he might not recognize me. He hadn't recognized or spoken to anyone for two days. I walked down the hall and into his room. I pulled a chair up next to his bed and sat down.

I watched Grandpa for a long time. His face was drawn and drooped; he looked worn down. I sat there quietly, wishing

I could bring back what he had been. After a while he stirred and opened his eyes. He squinted like he was struggling to make his eyes focus so he could identify who was looking at him. "It's you," he said finally.

"Yes, it's me." I was pleased and surprised.

He looked at me like he didn't quite believe I was really there.

Then he startled me. "What happens when we die?" He stared at me, waiting for me to tell him.

I couldn't think what to say. The question was too simple for a second-year theological student to answer. I wanted to say something comforting, but I couldn't pretend. Not with him. I could only stare at him. He watched my face. Finally, he said, "You don't know either, do you?" He looked away from me and slipped into oblivion. The next morning he died.

About the Author

Douglas Alan Walrath has worked as an insurance investigator, musician, factory worker, pastor, teacher, farmer, and seminary professor. He is the William Edgar Lowry Professor Emeritus of Practical Theology at Bangor Theological Seminary (BTS Center). He holds degrees in history, theology, and sociology. For many years he travelled the US, Canada, and England as a strategic planning consultant. He is the author or co-author of a dozen books in the fields of American culture, church leadership, literary criticism and, most recently, literary fiction. He lives in Maine where he and Sherry, his wife, garden organically, play traditional jazz, and enjoy challenging conversation.

Struggle Bus

by Rabbi Steven Lebow

Plotkin, a failed science fiction writer, had decided to commit suicide.

He was on the Disney cruise alone because his wife of twenty years, Patricia Plotnick, had run off with a woman from her book club and had taken their two children with her.

He took the tender over to the port terminal and as he exited the terminal he saw there were a variety of shore excursions that he could take.

"Pain Train or Struggle Bus?" asked the tour operator at the kiosk outside.

"What's the difference?" he asked.

"The Pain Train is for people who expect to come back to the ship," he said. "The Struggle Bus comes back empty. Almost every time."

"I'll take the bus," said Plotkin.

When the bus had filled with about twenty passengers it left the terminal and proceeded down what looked like the wrong side of the road, a leftover from the British mandate.

A bus captain stood at the front of the bus.

"Doing poorly today?" he said. "Looking forward to ending it all, or giving it one last chance?"

About fifteen hands went up. The bus pulled up to a small resort and the fifteen got off.

"For those who would like to stay for a while, drink the Rum Slurpy. For the rest of you, try the kool-aide."

The bus left a few minutes later with its last five passengers.

Seeing that the passengers were fidgety the bus captain said to Plotnick. "Making your final plans, or just adjusting to today is the last day of the rest of my life?"

"Does it matter?"

"No," said the bus captain. "Not really."

The bus pulled into the next stop.

"Don't hit your heads," he said. "The restrooms are on the right. The last resort is on your left."

When he returned Plotnick was the only passenger on the ride back to the ship terminal.

"What made you change your mind?"

Plotnick looked down at the tattoos of his children's faces, imprinted on the whorls of his fingertips and said nothing.

"I saw from the questionnaire you filled out that you are a disappointed author?"

"Yes," he said. "In the last year I've written twenty stories and I only had one piece of flash fiction accepted for publication."

"What did it say?"

"This is the end."

"Just four words? Nice," said the captain. "The only thing better would have been The End."

"I considered it, but it seemed a little forced."

"Let me ask you a question," Plotkin said.

"I've heard that all bus captains used to be writers too. Is that true?"

"True enough," he said.

"So what do your do now?"

"Now?" said the bus captain. "We're all editors."

"We still write on the side and in the mean time we run these tours. You know, we bring comfort to the afflicted, and so on."

"Yes, I can see that might be rewarding," he said.

I guess I've decided to give it one more chance. Maybe my next story will be accepted."

"Maybe is good enough," said the captain. "It's always worked for me."

Plotkin and the bus captain spent the last part of the tour in silence.

As Plotkin boarded the cruise he noticed a shelf with brochures. He took one to read as he walked back to his state room.

That night he read the pamphlet "Three reasons to become a Bus captain" and then went to sleep.

Plotkin enjoyed the last days of his trip. For the rest of the cruise the sun was benign and iridescent.

Nonetheless, the seas were still choppy, and exceedingly so.

About the Author

Rabbi Steven Lebow was the first Jewish clergy to perform same sex wedding ceremonies in the deep South. His life and work in civil rights has been featured in the New York Times and the Washington Post, the Wall Street Journal and the Atlanta Journal Constitution, CNN and NPR.

Run, Don't Walk

by Monika R. Martyn

Julia took the lantern in one hand and rested the bundle swaddled in a plain cotton sheet close to her chest. She grumbled something only the walls could hear, but tonight she really resented the nuns for making her do this. The set of keys in her apron pocket jingled as she ascended the short flight of stairs to the dimly lit landing that split into two separate corridors. Julia took a quick left turn and rounded the corner, away from the infirmary. She couldn't tolerate another whiff of the pungent disinfectant and the lingering odor of Augmentin Paediatric. And her feet ached because she was getting too old for this business of transporting parcels. At the heavy steel door that led to the dark basement and toward the tunnel, she inserted the key.

"Julia."

Her name echoed in the stone corridor despite only being a harsh whisper.

"Let me go with you. Please."

The shadow that had been in hiding emerged from behind the wall. It was Mary, the most troublesome of all the new wards under the nuns' care. But Julia liked Mary. The girl worked hard and never treated her like a servant as the nuns and others did.

Despite being against the regulations, Julia handed Mary the lantern. And having company made the journey less daunting, Julia debated her list of excuses within herself. It wasn't like the nuns ever asked if she was scared of the rats, of the ghosts that lingered within every eerie noise and flicker. Mary was genuinely interested.

"Shush. And don't cha ever tell."

The lock sprung open, and the door grumbled on its rusty hinges. A chilling darkness that had been waiting on the other side fell into the small landing.

"Is it Brigit's?" Mary whispered.

Julia nodded. It was the second errand that day, and Sister Emanuel could have spared her at least one walk if they had called Doctor Barnett sooner. But it was all about penance and sins. And these wayward girls had to atone for their mistakes. It was also why she trusted Mary.

Mary wasn't like the other girls. Mary was in the home because she was an orphan like Julia had been, but too pretty to be trusted to roam the streets of Tuam. Which would surely lead her into wickedness.

Julia knew every brick in the snaking pathway. The corridor wound its way like an earthworm away from the H-shaped building and toward the corner beneath the orchard. It was a network of rotten sewage ways not in use since the home was hooked to the town's municipal sewage system. However, Julia believed it had never seen so much waste and misery since she was abandoned at the home when the nuns took over years ago. Julia had been told to deliver these parcels and deposit them next to the others before she could even read.

"This is disgusting." Mary hissed next to her. "Where does this go?"

"To the cemetery," Julia answered. But it wasn't really a cemetery at all. She just called it that to make sense of what she was told to do. What she had obediently done since she was ten years old. One of the sisters walked with her first few times, but even as a child, Julia sensed that the nuns were afraid of the rats and the repercussions if anyone ever discovered the truth beyond the locked metal door.

"What? Where the nuns are buried?" Mary grabbed Julia's elbow and heeled like a well-trained hound.

"No. Be quiet. Or you can wait here. Without the light." Julia asserted herself.

Despite walking slowly and as silently as possible, their footfalls echoed. Mary's hobnail boots thumped loudly on the path, and the lamp projected their elongated shadows. The shape of the sack-like uniforms made them look fatter than they were. Although Julia had walked this path often, she never got used to it. Something just wasn't right about what the nuns asked of her when they handed her yet another deposit and ordered her to deal with it.

When they rounded the slight bend, Mary came face to face with the facts she'd been so curious about and now wished she hadn't been. The enormity of the clothed mummies lining the stairwell leading toward the surface sealed by a cement closure made her gasp; the stench was something unearthly.

"Sweet Mother of Jesus." Mary stopped in her tracks.

Julia took the lantern from Mary, who, despite being deathly afraid, refused to go any further. The beady eyes of a rat crawling over the swaddled corpses caught the light; it squeaked that it wasn't pleased with their intrusion and scurried into the hallway of darkness.

Slowly stooping and depositing her delivery carefully next to the most recent other bundles, Julia crossed herself and said a prayer, "O Lord, let perpetual light shine upon these children. May their souls and the souls of all the faithful…"

Only Mary's heaving retch ended her prayer.

Julia often suffered from nightmares. Seldom did sleep come soundly and prevent the nightmares. Most nights, she awoke drenched in sweat and disturbed by that anxious feeling that a thousand sets of eyes were staring at her and pleading for her help. It was worse when those dreams were orchestrated with sound. Of course, she had tried to talk to Mother Superior on the advice of Sister Emanuel, but the meeting hadn't gone well. The advice still rang in Julia's ears, "we all have a cross to bear, for the sins we're born with."

At ten years old, Julia couldn't think of what that could be since she never knew her parents and what crimes they were guilty of. And then, one Sunday after church, when Julia was only twelve, Father O'Leary asked to see her. That was the uncomfortable last time she ever spent in his presence. Julia developed a cunning defense mechanism just to avoid being alone with him again, although he tried to single her out on several occasions. But he was a man of the cloth and had many sheep to herd to salvation. He quickly found other victims who required his healing hands in places where hands should never come to a rest. Julia still couldn't make sense of that nauseating and overwhelming feeling of being so close to a man and what his gestures and words insinuated. The bigger question of how those girls and women ended up in the dreadful predicament they were in, Julia didn't dare ask. A shudder always went through her when she thought of Father O'Leary panting heavily next to her ear. His hard body pressed against her, and his hand frantically hoisting up her dress and ransacking her coarse cotton knickers and his threatening words that he would have her sent to the Magdalenes.

Thank God Sister Hortense happened to intrude on them. Julia had been so frightened by the unsightly appendage poking from Father O'Leary's trousers, a small whimper escaped into the hand clamped over her mouth. Though Sister Hortense didn't see them behind the pew, she took her time arranging fresh cut flowers on the altar for the Sunday evening service. When Father O'Leary rolled off her, Julia took the opportunity to wiggle away and slid beneath the legs of the altar of the Virgin Mary. She had never been so frightened; her heart thundered so loudly in her ear she thought there was no way Sister Hortense didn't hear it too. Since then, walking the dark passageway was nothing in comparison.

But the memory of that afternoon in the church never faded. It was a constant battle in Julia's head of what happened. The guilt of the dead eyes peering at her in her dreams made more sense to Julia than the sin of unmarried sex. Sex wasn't something she could understand, even thinking the word made her uncomfortable. She found men disgusting and disturbing. And she'd seen several visiting males leer at Mary with a longing that revolted her. Mary really was too pretty to be trusted on the street.

Julia waited while Mary spat up the last of the vomit. She handed her a handkerchief and patiently rubbed her shoulder. She knew Mary would plague her with relentless questions.

"For the love of God, how many are there?" Mary clung to Julia's arm.

"I've lost count. But, there are other chambers."

Julia regretted lying. She knew exactly how many trips she made down these corridors, sent on a hushed mission by the nuns.

"So all the stillborn babies come here without burial?"

"Yes, but it ain't just stillborn babies."

Mary brought them to a stop, she covered her mouth with the handkerchief, her fingers dug into Julia's flesh. "No.

Don't tell me. Don't you dare tell me all *them* sick babies are down here too?"

Julia didn't bother answering. She bobbed her head and carried on walking. There was no way she'd take any of the blame and was about to say so.

"We have to tell someone. This isn't right." Mary pulled her to a stop again.

"Who? Just who are ya gonna tell? Father O'Leary? The milkman? Perhaps you can tell the Garda the next time the nuns let you out of their sight?" Julia wrenched her arm free.

"Julia. Listen. This isn't right."

"And what da ya think ya know 'bout it? If ya tell anyone, the sisters will see ta it that ya end up in Ballinasloe madhouse, or they'll ship you to Magdalene. Is that what cha want?"

Anger simmered on Julia's lips. She shouldn't have allowed Mary to accompany her.

Had she not been caught in a weak moment of self-pity, she would have said so. Before Mary trapped her, Julia had been deep in thought, rehashing the argument she had with Sister Martha and the harsh words that cut her like a dagger.

You're worse than a Home baby.

In the home, the children, the orphans, the women were treated based on an invisible scale that the nuns ruled with. It stung Julia that despite dedicating her life to serving the nuns, they still regarded her like dirt.

No mother ever shed a tear for you, I can tell you that. You were left like trash at our doorstep. If it hadn't a been for the mercy and kindness of the sisters in Tuam, the rats or a pack of dogs would have had you for breakfast.

Sister Martha was no one's favorite nun. She was mean and didn't allow anyone to forget that she was. She towered over Julia, and seething with fury, Sister Martha's brought her face within inches of Julia's. She loomed so large and close that Julia could count the hairs sprouting like a goat's from her upper lip and nose. She stank of garlic, of copious amounts of black currant wine, mixed with last week's sweat. If Julia had been younger, the angry nun would have smacked her, and all because Julia suggested that one of the new nuns take the dying baby to the sewer they called the crypt.

Julia was exhausted from it all. When Mary caught up to her again, she knew better than to stop her in the middle of this chamber of horror. Inclining her head toward Julia, she whispered and wove her fingers into Julia's hand.

"I'm sorry, Julia. I didn't mean to imply you've done anything wrong. Never that. But this just isn't right. Is there nothing you can think to stop this, this madness?"

Julia exhaled her exasperation. She had to put an end to this. This strap of a girl had no business sticking her nose in a pile of rot that it didn't belong in. If, and big if, the Garda or health ministry shut the Home down, just where would that leave her and those poor babies? She'd never known any other place but Tuam. And were the sisters and those orphans who graduated to becoming servants, not doing the best they could under the circumstances for these girls, who had fallen from the grace of God, and these tainted unwanted babies? Was there ever anyone pounding on the front door claiming any of these women and making them into honest wives and demanding that the babies be released to them? Not once in her nearly forty years in servitude to God and the nuns was there a man who demanded to see his child. Once, in all her time at the home, there was an altercation. A burly cousin arrived and demanded that his younger cousin be released from the laundry. It surprised everyone that the sisters complied, but behind closed doors, the sisters quickly explained that the cousin wasn't right in the head. That they were giving in only to protect the others.

This time, it was Julia who brought them to a stop.

"Mary. I warn ya. T'is the last you speak of this. To me, or anyone."

"And what are ya gonna do? Yes, the sisters can threaten me with the Balli madhouse or have Sister Martha beat me. It can't possibly be worse than this, this madness of hiding babies in a sewer chamber. And I know for a fact that Sister Hortense sold Eileen's son Robert to some foster family without her consent."

"I swear if ya breathe a word, I'll have Sister Prue take you to the washhouse and scrub the hide off ya pretty face."

"Well, I'm gonna tell all the girls upstairs as soon as I can. There's nothing you can scare me with. This…" Mary gestured toward the dead infants stacked like freshly split wood on the stairs and overflowing, "this is the gateway to hell. And if there is a God, do you honestly think he'd support that?"

"These girls brought this sin on themselves. Ask the sisters. They'll straighten out your moral compass. What them girls has done is a sin?"

"Julia? Do you even know how babies are made?"

"Doesn't matter. It's nowt to do with me. I ain't the one who done wrong."

"I know that. You and I are here at the mercy of the kindness the nuns and the church bestow on us. And Ireland is right in washing itself of British rule. But don't you think it's unfair that the men aren't held accountable?"

"No, I don't. The Archbishop decides what is best for the Irish people. End of story. And you should listen to what that is. Not the idle chatter of wayward women who are now paying the price for the immortal sin they committed."

They stopped before the heavy metal door, and Julia jangled the keys, feeling more than looking for the largest key on the ring. Mary's insinuations made Julia uncomfortable. How the conversation had switched from dead babies to sex, to accusing the sisters of something, and to the Archbishop, and back to the seedy subject of sex, was like a bad pair of shoes: painful. Julia had no idea what sex meant. She couldn't picture participating, and she never wanted to be near a man as she had been to Father O'Leary. What some of the other girls indecently whispered about what he had done or tried to do in the confessional bordered on lurid facts that the nuns would whip from anyone's hide.

"Julia. This isn't right." Mary followed Julia closely up the stairs and back to the dormitory. It was close to lights out, and even though Julia wasn't *a wardling* any longer, she had her own set of rules to follow, and she was too tired to think.

"Go wash. Or Sister Evangeline will cuff ya behind the ear."

She left Mary on the landing and headed toward the attic where her own room was beneath the eaves. Besides, Julia had a ritual to perform. She fingered the locket of hair in her pocket like a rosary on a broken chain. The last one was born with a shock of red curls, just like its mother.

Outside, the wind was kicking up a fuss. Julia couldn't ever remember hearing it howl so viciously in the forty years she'd been at Tuam. She stopped on the landing and looked out into the garden, toward the orchard. The trees were bending sideways, trash flitted through the air in funnels, and rain hammered the window panes. She was afraid the storm would smash the glass to smithereens.

Alone in her room, the wind howled through every crack; she pulled the quilt from the bed and wrapped herself in it. Down on her knees, Julia felt for the loose floorboards. With her deft fingers, she lifted the hatbox she had stolen from the trash. Nestled in tissue paper, her fingers played with the downy strands of hair. These were hers to keep for walking dead babies. Come what may, and she'd never allow anyone to take these precious silky locks from her. She was afraid of what Mary would do with the information; it could have grave consequences. But what was worse, at the moment, was the howling wind. She pulled the quilt closer and nestled the newest lock among the others. And then she heard the crash, the screams that followed, her door opened, and Sister Martha yelled above the noise of flying roof tiles.

"Get everyone downstair!"

There wasn't time to hide the evidence; Sister Martha had seen it. A small glare dictated that Julia would pay for the secret she harbored in the box— if they survived this storm.

"Into the cellar. It's a hurricane."

Although Julia wasn't fast, she efficiently managed to get everyone into the basement to safety. When the storm ended, she was the first to climb over the rubble and survey the damage.

Her small attic room had been taken away by the wind; the fragile strands of hair were blown across Ireland. Over the years, she lost count of the number of babies notched into the rafters, but she would remember them—the dead babies.

I closed my laptop and took a drink of cold tea and sat back. As a writer, I borrow and steal elements from real life to create fiction, leaving me with a responsibility I hadn't bargained into the cost. This story is complicated to tell as it happened. Even Stephen King would have difficulty competing among these lines of horror. Not that I'm competing with Stephen King.

I gather the notebooks, the almost unreadable scribbles that have both exhausted and consumed me for weeks. A cold cup of tea won't rejuvenate me. Mostly, I'm so sad and also ashamed.

The Irish government is still grappling with the horrific fallout and trying to bury the truth for another 75 years, under the cloak of the Bill of Retention Act. Through exploring this incredible and cruel story, I tried to give life to the women, girls, and babies as they might have been. An orphan by the name of Julia, in the care of the nuns in the Tuam Home for Mothers and Babies, existed. Her name really was Julia, and for 40 years, she obeyed and walked many of the babies into the septic chamber where the babies still are today. It is incomprehensible to me how anyone survived; I assume none did so unscathed.

A hurricane ended the empire of abuse and neglect in the Tuam Home for Mothers and Babies, but not in Ireland. In my mind, I walked the corridors, listened to the lament of the women whose babies either died or were stolen from them. I grieve with them. There are no words in the English dictionary that can ever give justice to the suffering these poor souls endured.

It wasn't until Catherine Corless published her findings in 2014 that the roof blew off and revealed the devastating truth the nuns left behind and created. What is true is that the Bon Secours nuns orchestrated the shameful disposal of 795* babies without a proper burial. I will never be the same person because of this discovery.

Just as demeaning was the horrific treatment of these unwed and pregnant Irish girls and women who suffered a grave injustice from the dominating church who should have, under God's love, cared for these victims. The willfully blind Irish society, the state's ignorance, and the families who turned their backs on their daughters defy explanation. Children born out of wedlock were also, that is, if they survived the horrific levels of neglect and abuse, sold in a massive child trafficking ring, while others were used for vaccination experiments.

These conditions were repeated throughout Ireland in eighteen institutions. From approximately 1922 to 1998, this was the state and church's regime. Their negligence and abuse are now under investigation by the Commission of Investigation of Mother and Baby Homes.

The death toll is a breathtaking sample of abuse of the highest order; the injustice and cruelty a perfect match to pure evil. Image if these women and children had instead been showered with kindness, love, and compassion, as they deserved.

Run from the truth,

... but you can't hide dead babies forever.

*795. While this number fluctuates, every baby deserves to be remembered and mourned.

About the Author

Monika R. Martyn is retired, married, happy, and a minimalist. She enjoys traveling and has been published in print and online. Her debut novel, The Lucky Man—An Act of Malice, is scheduled for publication in March 2021. She is currently the Canadian Culture editor at BellaOnline.com or visit her at https://monikarmartynauthor.wordpress.com/

Molding

by Jessamyn Violet

Frankie wasn't sure when exactly she'd lost the moment, but that "slip under" sleep space she'd felt earlier had long passed. There were things on her mind, sure—terrible old things, but nothing triggered insomnia quite like setting an alarm for the next morning. She tossed from side to side, seeking the secret position to seduce slumber. One more thing about Frankie— the more anxious she got, the more her mind used alliteration to soothe itself. It was an OCD thing. But obsessing and horizontal positioning weren't her only problems. Her sheets also reeked of mildew and the upstairs neighbors were on a bona fide bender. It was a full-on second-floor shitfest up there, and it was stressing her out.

Frankie felt a fizzing inside, something close to annihilation.

"Why're all women the worst with directions?!" some drunken idiot was slurring from the porch above her bedroom. "Seriously, why're all women the *worst* with directions?"

No one answered. No one seemed to care. She supposed that was what heavy drinking and hard drugs bought: The ability to be unaffected by incredibly stupid and/or depressing surroundings. Frankie had endured those years. They didn't help her tolerate the second-hand scene any easier. The spectrum of her stereotypical 20s mistakes had concocted a large "keep-calm-and-carry-on" cocktail that she was trying to sip slowly from a comfortable distance in her 30s. She couldn't afford to be "that girl" anymore. No more shots or bare-knuckle bottle slugging like so many perfect-looking movie stars glamourized in-scene. Sure it looked sexy for the camera, but Frankie knew exactly how bloated their beautiful faces would be if they really drank like that. She had learned that there was no hope for people who didn't simmer down with time. Frankly, Frankie found the forever-partiers hard to look at and harder to listen to, especially *these days*.

These days, humanity was in a rough place. Society was in shambles. Everyone was on the brink. There was little left to lose.

These days, Frankie's patience was a thin membrane seeking sharp edges.

"*Stop!*" Someone shouted from upstairs. "Too much!" A drunken shriek. Some laughter. *That's fucking it.* Frankie began to curse out loud in the dark bedroom to no one but her cat. The arithmetic of the night was adding up to a desire to do troublesome things. Things that had landed her worse places than she'd probably ever admit to anyone—

Thoughts cut loose by a thud. The crowd quieted. Low murmurs and the unmistakable sound of a body being dragged down the narrow steps outside her bedroom door. Frankie ignored the buzzing in her head and dialed 911 immediately to report the situation. The operator promised someone would be there as soon as possible, which in Venice Beach translated to *we make absolutely no commitment to getting there in time to do anything.*

A car started. The dull clomp of a human head hitting against metal. Shouting. Doors slammed. Tires squealed. Feet tripped down stairs. Muffled sneakers on the pavement. They were scattering. The crapulous clowns were taking to the streets.

"*She's naked,*" came a hiss from outside the window. "*Get her out of the street!*"

Adrenaline laced through Frankie's veins as she heard a woman wailing in the distance. The warbled, nonsensical vocal flow invaded her soul like a horror film score. She held herself in a deep cringe at the looming disaster.

But the break squeals never came.

In fact, everything went eerily quiet. Not one car drove by for what felt like a long time. She waited for the emergency evacuation hormone to work its way out of her body with little aftershocks. Adrenaline: *An earthquake of a drug.* Frankie strained to hear the waves crashing a short ways from her apartment. They were there if she listened hard enough, faint yet steady reminders of the passage of time and inevitably changing tides.

She'd just slipped through sleep's sticky lips when the sound of a car door slam jolted her back awake. Her heart beat staccato reverb in her ears as a shadow made its way up the steps, flashlight cutting across her bedroom through the side window. A man announced himself as the police and knocked on the door of the apartment above. Waited. Knocked again. No one answered. No surprise there. The response time had given them enough of a window to get to Mid City. Footsteps made their way across the upstairs hall, knocks repeated on doors. Finally, they stopped.

Then: A loud knock on the back door and Frankie nearly shed her skin. She reached for the first thing to cover herself—her pink kimono hanging on the doorknob—and stumbled to open the door. There stood a tall, thin cop in his early 50s, mustached and squinting in the moonlight. He gave her the once-over.

"You the one who called in?"

"Yes."

"You live here?"

"Yes."

"Alone?"

"Yes," Frankie said grudgingly.

"I checked upstairs. I don't hear or see anyone."

"Yeah, they took off a while ago." Frankie made sure to flaunt her exasperation. "I think someone was running around in the street naked."

He shook his head. "Daylight savings makes people crazier than usual."

It sounded like white noise, meant next to nothing. He raised his eyebrows and looked meaningfully out to the empty street. Frankie could swear she saw white powder rimming his nostrils. The officer sniffled and wiped his nose immediately. She tried to read his nametag but it was too dark.

"I didn't see anything on my way over," he went on. "Most of the unit is handling a big situation over on Electric. I tried to get someone to answer the call but after twenty minutes of no response I had to leave the station myself. I'm supposed to be holding it down over there."

"Sounds like you need more officers."

The cop shot her a look and sniffled again.

"We get a call about this building every week."

And there it was: The truth. Funny how it always had a different ring to it. Frankie had an urge to slap the man but instead went to her own defense. "It's not usually me. The older first-floor tenants are fed up. I called because it sounded like someone overdosed. I heard them dragging someone down the steps."

She expected him to at least alert the force. Bark something at someone in his walkie-talkie. Anything. Anyone helpful. *Anytime, now.* But the cop just ground his jaw and ran a hand through his hair. "This job is wearing me down. I'm supposed to retire soon. Been serving for 30 years already. I started young."

He winked and Frankie wished she hadn't caught it. Her mouth made a little "o" of surprise. In Venice, such midnight moonlit winks were doomed. Only foolish women accepted winks from strangers. Seasoned local ladies knew to keep their eye level low late-night. She felt trapped, and it was entirely her own fault. She'd caught the damn wink in the cradle of her stare and now there was a tear in the realm. The door was officially open. No matter that she had a 7am call time for a shoot in Pasadena. Here she was, stuck with a winking public servant in the middle of the night.

Of course, she did have to wonder—what *did* cops do when they retired after thirty years working in a batshit place like Venice Beach? Move to a retirement community in Palm Springs? Get a ranch out in Rancho Cucamonga?

He carried on. "I want to travel for a long time... Just take off by myself until I find a place that feels right. I have a lady at home, but I'm not sure how long that's going to work out."

Awkward... Frankie thought she saw a smirk under the (honestly, pretty clichéd) moustache. He seemed eager to talk about it, and certainly in no rush. As far as his demeanor was concerned, he didn't have a thing in the world to do other than chit chat about his lady problems. She decided to dodge the irrelevant info with a quick follow-up question. At this point, Frankie felt she was a prisoner of the law.

"I'm thinking Ireland. Or Texas. Where do you think I should go?"

"No comment."

He paced back and forth a little in the doorway. The full moon shone bright over the street, illuminating empty cars parked like a silent audience for late-night lazy cop theatrics.

Frankie thought she heard the wail of the naked girl in the distance. Maybe it was a dog howling. Or a canal creature yowling. Whatever it was, she was paralyzed by it.

"What do you do?" he asked.

"A lot of things," she said. "Industry."

"Actress, huh? What kind of films?"

There appeared a predatory gleam in his eye but he kept his face as straight as he could make it. His internal dialogue seemed particularly nefarious at that moment. Frankie envisioned the future in a flash: He would tweak their late-night chat into some steamy kimono porn scene for his buddies back at the precinct. She could already see him telling them the gory fake details in the drab, burnt-coffee break room.

She rolled her eyes. "All kinds."

"I could see that," he said, resting an elbow on the banister so casually that Frankie could swear they were at a bar. He grinned down at her as she squirmed. Everything felt dingy and tinged with sticky subtext. Her naked skin prickled under the thin robe and she crossed her arms tight.

"I have to get some sleep, now," she said forcefully. Enough standing out there. Maybe it wasn't really happening. Maybe she was dreaming. The thought didn't wake her, though. Bad sign.

"Well, I guess I better get back," he said. "Contact me directly if anything else happens." He pressed a business card to the wall and started writing on it with a ballpoint pen. When he held it out, she saw a personal email scribbled on it. "That's my direct line as well as my email."

At that moment the wail returned, immediately pulling every hair on Frankie's body to full attention. It was the wail of a wandering waif, a wench whimpering without words, wanting to warn others—*of what?*

She stood frozen in fear. "Do you not hear that?"

He watched her with suspicious eyes. "Hear what?"

The wailing came closer and closer. Frankie felt it swirling around her, smothering the musty marine layer with misery. It was all she could do to not cover her ears and curl up in a ball.

"Nevermind... Thanks," she said as she took his card, putting on her tired face. Apparently, he was a Lieutenant. Didn't take much, she supposed. Her skin grew tighter as the wailing grew louder and louder. Frankie pulled her robe so hard she heard a seam rip. She tugged at the decomposing silky threads that reeked of mildew and crinkled her nose. "Goodnight."

"Don't let the bed bugs bite," he said, somewhat sinisterly.

Frankie smiled flatly, shutting the door in his face. She supposed he would shrug it off, go back to the station, do some more blow and wait for another woman to call. She vowed to never answer the door in her kimono again.

She would not look at her ninja sword. She did not take it out, but as it lay in her hands, she had *the thought* that meant it was time to put the sword away and count backwards from 500 while standing against the wall. The wailing finally died down by 88. Everything seemed to die down by 88. Then she went into the kitchen to self-soothe through satiation. The cookie she'd wanted to finish had molded after only a day. Things had been going bad fast, lately. Something in the air was definitely making things funkier. It was closing in on her, closing in on all of them, and she didn't know how to stop it.

Tomorrow I'm buying a dehumidifier, she thought as she lay back down in her musty sheets. It was the same thing she'd said to herself for the last three weeks.

Her body was so perfectly bored of the line that she fell right asleep.

About the Author

Jessamyn is currently a writer and drummer living in Venice Beach, CA. Originally from Massachusetts, she graduated with a BFA in Writing, Literature and Publishing from Emerson College and then moved out west to work in journalism. She went on to earn an MFA in Creative Writing from California College of the Arts. Her poetry book "Organ Thieves" was published by Gauss PDF. She has short fiction published in Adelaide Literary Magazine and Little Break. For more info, you can visit jessamynviolet.com.

The Day of the Jaguar

by W. Royce Adams

I was told I must go, that there is nothing like it. So, one Sunday while on sabbatical leave, I visited Chichicastenango in the Guatemalan highlands. Little did I know what effect my visit was to have on my life and my future travels.

A few hours north of Guatemala City and home to one of the largest, most colorful native market places in Central America. Sundays and Thursdays bring together not only local Maya vendors, but scores of artisans from all over Guatemala hawking mixed-matched woven textiles in anomalous color combinations; ornately carved wooden masks and costumes depicting various Mayan gods and animals; pottery of various shapes and purposes; machetes, knives and other tools; exotic candles; incense; medicinal plants; myriad grains, fruits and vegetables; pigs, goats and chickens; and small eateries offering anything that would fit in a tortilla.

The thick air felt old and tired, swirling with greasy cooking smoke, mixtures of strong incense, and the residue of fireworks from rockets and firecrackers exploding periodically for no particular reason I could discern. The smells volleyed from putrid to sweet and back again as I made my way through the market, all my senses entertained.

I meandered through the city with my heavy-lensed camera slung over my shoulder at the ready, though no device could have captured my visceral enjoyment of the thriving foreign life and cacophony of languages and music surrounding me. There, at the top of the eighteen worn rocky steps leading up to the entrance, sat the 400-year old Santo Tomas Catholic Church that housed *Popul Vuh*, the sacred book of the Maya, before it was stolen years ago. Men and women in their vibrant indigenous native dress, some selling flowers, some waving burning incense and chanting, some burning candles, one scattering something on a small fire, together commandeered the steps as they meshed their thousand-year old traditional Maya beliefs with those the Spanish brought hundreds of years ago.

I started to climb the steps to enter the church, but had difficulty making my way through the crowd. Someone spoke to me in a melodic language I took to be K'iche' Maya, a soft, soothing sound. I smiled, not understanding, and attempted to continue through the mass. Halfway up, I was stopped by a native Spanish speaker who told me the Church was a sacred place, and that I could not go inside with my camera. Best to obtain a guide, he suggested. I looked around and sensed everyone on the steps was watching to see what I would do. I saw myself as a trespasser and turned back down the steps.

As I continued to roam the streets, an inexplicable feeling of apprehension and premonition came over me. I can't say why, neither will I try to describe it. But something compelled me to wander deeper into the narrow market streets as though on a quest. Like a magnetic force, I felt drawn to something yet unfound.

I stepped aside at one point as a procession of men, some dressed in jaguar face masks and spotted costumes, others in simple everyday clothing, marched by, a ragtag group, not particularly in step with the sounds of wooden flutes and drum beats. I almost started to follow them, but I held back until they passed. Moving on, I stopped at various stalls half-heartedly examining the offerings of each and became aware of the market's organization: all wood merchandise in one area; all pottery makers in another; condiments in another, and so on. At one point, a vendor, a small man dressed in simple dark pants and a white, opened-neck shirt, held out a small, plain pottery cup to me.

"¿Quieres una bebida?"

Taken aback, I peered into the cup of brown liquid he offered reminding me of the kava I drank in Fiji, a lightly numbing, narcotic-like drink.

"¿Qué es?"

"Una deliciosa bebida." He smiled, nodded and pushed the cup further toward me.

I looked at the drink, then back at him, my skepticism obvious.

"¿Qué hay en ello?"

"Una bebida de Maya," he said with pride." Ixcacao con guaro."

"¿Qué?"

"Ish-ca-ca-o." He gave me a wan smile. "Chocolate and sugar rum."

"You speak English?"

"Some." He continued to hold out the cup.

I examined him more closely. His face, dark Mayan chocolate itself, appeared as smooth as polished leather. Greenish-black, cat-like eyes seemed to search for something in mine. I felt a slight unease and reticence to accept.

"How much?" I asked, stalling.

"Nada, señor. An offering."

I didn't want to seem impolite and felt compelled to take a sip, even though all travel books warn tourists to be leery of such drinks.

Forgetting caution, I took the cup and sipped. A not unpleasant taste, I nodded approval and offered him the cup.

He gestured for me to drink more.

I felt sure I shouldn't, but sipped some more. Slightly sweet, yet peppery. My mind told me I would regret drinking this muddy water, but my taste buds encouraged me on as I wondered what this was going to cost me.

After a few swallows, I handed the cup back, feeling I'd finished my unnecessary obligation.

"Very...different. Graçias." I wasn't sure what I was supposed to say.

"Ah, de nada, señor. A pleasure."

I started looking in my pocket for some quetzals to pay him. "¿A como?"

He waved his hand. "Nada. Nothing, señor."

Odd, I thought. "Well, graçias again."

I started to walk away wondering when I would begin throwing up, when the vendor called back to me.

"Señor, I show you something?"

Of course, I thought. Now comes the reason for the drink. What does he want me to buy?

"I don't know," I hesitated. "I need to get back to the city before dark."

"I promise, not long takes. And never you forget what you see."

Before I could answer, he offered his hand and name.

We exchanged a loose handshake.

"Sorry, say your name again?"

He repeated his name. Ish something. It did not sound Spanish.

I still had trouble understanding him, and decided the closest I could come to pronouncing his name was to call him Ishmael.

"Follow please," he said as he slipped into the crowd.

Things were happening too fast. I thought he wanted to show me something in his stall. Where was he taking me? Should I trust him and follow? I hadn't felt comfortable around him, yet here I was being led to…where? And to what?

I trailed behind him through and around many vending stalls, almost losing him on occasion in the crowded streets, then realized we were leaving the market. I caught up with him as we headed across a clearing and up into a wooded area. "How much farther?"

"Soon."

Whoa, wait, I told myself. You're walking into a trap, stupid. Turn around. Some gang is in the woods waiting to take your camera, your money, your clothes, maybe your life. I tried to shake off these negative thoughts and noticed I was feeling a bit lightheaded. Was it the mountain air? Fear? Or, maybe it was something in the drink he gave me. Of course! He's drugged me!

I stopped walking. He noticed and looked at me with a face that offered no surprise, no danger, no threat.

We caught eyes.

"You hold fear."

"Yes, I have fear." I wasn't about to pretend I didn't.

"Si, entiendo su posición. As I would, tambien."

"What do you want me to see? Where are you taking me?"

We stood in quiet a moment. I still felt a bit dizzy and my tongue felt tingly.

"Did you drug me?" I blurted out; then felt a little silly. I must have sounded pathetic.

"Señor, how to tell…no quiero hacer daño. No hurt do I make you."

His face seemed innocent, but those deep, cat-like eyes….

My mind raced. Should I believe him? Who is he? I should go back. Be sensible. But if I turned around now, what would I miss? I might never have an occasion to witness something off the tourist track like this again. Is my paranoia unwarranted? I'm physically bigger than he is. But if there are more of them in waiting? Oh, come on. Ease up. You're being overly cautious. Go with the man! Maybe this is that expectancy you felt earlier.

I nodded. "Okay, okay. Let's go."

Showing no emotion, he continued walking, his footsteps seemingly soundless on the dirt path.

I stayed on my guard as we went deeper into the woods, never seeing another person. He stopped at a small clearing just outside the opening of a small cave entrance at the rise of a mound and pointed to the remains of a fire. From my various readings in preparation for my travels, I learned that Maya shaman used fires for all types of sacred ceremonies, believing fire is a living, breathing organism, some saying fire is God itself. Shamans make a circle of sugar or grains around the ring of the fire and divide the circle into various parts, placing items like incense, corn, cocoa beans, copal, or whatever they deem useful for a particular ceremony. Four tall candles representing the four directions are often placed within the circle. Then smaller candles of different colors are placed flat around the center of the fire. Yellow candles represent peace; red, love; green, earth; white, purity and so on. No doubt I was looking at a recent ceremonial fire, certain of it when I noticed some small feathers around the circle of melted candles burnt to the ground and dark spots I assumed to be dried blood.

The grey ash still let off an occasional bit of smoke. As I stared into the ashes, I thought I saw the lively, crackling fire, the blood of the sacrificial fowl being dripped into the sugar around the fire, the melting colored candles oozing into the wood beneath them, a shaman chanting something. A vision. I saw it all, but understood nothing.

His voice brought me back from wherever I was.

"You have stood here before."

"What?" In a flash I awoke to where I was. "Here? No, never. This is my first time in Guatemala."

"Si, you here before," he insisted. Then he said something unintelligible I assumed was K'iche. "I told to bring you back here."

I breathed a nervous laugh, but the way he said it made me shiver, and my skin felt pricked; my breath skipped. What kind of deceit was this turning out to be? I looked around and saw nobody. What was he talking about?

"Who told you to bring me back?"

"The I'x-Balan spirits."

Right. Spirits now. Spirits ready to jump from the woods and attack me now while drugged.

We just stood there, each of us looking down at the ashes. No spirits or human bodies came running at me out of the woods or the cave. Baffled, mesmerized, really, I just waited for his next move.

Slowly, in a low voice, eyes closed, he again started to mumble in K'iche or whatever. He repeated what sounded like sound, "Ish. Ish." He kept blowing his breath into his hand. What was that about?

He's got to be setting me up for something. Why did he say I'd been here before? Spirits told him. Does he expect me to believe that? The only spirits are the ones in the drink he gave me, and I foolishly drank myself into a world that's playing with my perception.

While my mind groped for normalcy, I remembered my camera. I needed pictures to prove this incident was happening.

I started to take a photo of Ishmael standing by the fire, but he stopped mumbling, raised his hands and shook his head.

"No."

"Why?"

"Sacred place. No take." He pointed at my camera.

"Well, can we go in the cave? See what's in there?"

"No. A shaman must cleanse you first."

"A shaman? What's in there?"

"The spirit of the jaguar."

Now I knew this was all a con of some type. Can this get any more preposterous?

"Well, can I take a picture of the outside?"

"No."

I relented, too baffled and annoyed to argue.

Through my travels, I had learned to take hip shots of people who didn't want to be photographed or who wanted money for a snap shot. Never raising my camera to focus, I just aimed the camera from my hip which self-focused when I clicked. And I wanted proof of what was happening to me, so I managed to snap six pictures of him and the area on the sly as I questioned him.

"I don't understand. Why do the spirits want me here?"

"They have reasons."

"But why me?"

"You are of the number twelve of the Day of the Jaguar."

I knew the jaguar held a special place in Olmec, Aztec and Mayan traditions. In many of the places I had traveled, Chichen-Itza, Palenque, Uxmal, Tikal, jaguar symbols were etched in stone, formed in ceramics, temple mantles and wall paintings. A totem animal, the jaguar represents power, confidence and energy. It has the ability to live not only on the flatlands and the mountains, but also in the trees and in the water. No other animal can kill it, only man. Its spirit, Maya believe, can enter a person and give that person power.

But it was his reference to the number twelve that caught me up. My birthday is December the twelfth. How could he know my birthday? Just happenstance? Maybe no connection at all. I wanted to know more.

"What does that mean, the number twelve of the day of the jaguar?"

"Is one of the 20 days of the sacred Mayan calendar. You are of the Day of the Jaguar."

"How do you know?"

"The Spirits."

This fiasco was getting nowhere. I shook off the idea I was drugged, and felt in some way duped. Unsatisfied, yet intrigued, I wanted him to get on with whatever scam this was leading up to, curious as to why he picked me to bring here. He could not know my birthday. This was one mysterious carnival con, and I was more than ready for it to come to an end.

"You must allow the Nawales to enter your being, or you will miss the core and become depressed, angry, mean, jealous. You no find road to wisdom. Look. Up that tree. A black jaguar looks at you. Accept her spirit."

I looked up where he pointed. I saw nothing. I searched the trees around. There was no jaguar black or otherwise in the trees.

"I see nothing."

"Allow it. Then you will."

Unsettled by Ishmael's insistence the Spirits wanted me, I decided I'd had enough. His clever deceit pushed my discomfort button. I began to feel a touch of panic. "I think you have me confused with somebody else. It's getting late. I need to get back to the city."

In a steady voice of confidence, he said, "The jaguar sees you. You will see if you allow."

"Sorry, I'd like to see a jaguar, but I don't."

His eyes and face held a look of disappointment in me as his body slumped. Yet, he did not seem to want to hold me there. He nodded, looked at me sadly, and turned to go.

We started back to ChiChi and I followed. He didn't look behind as we walked, but seemed to read my mind.

"No photos."

When we got back to the buzz of the market, Ishmael disappeared into the crowd. I tried to find his stall again, but it was impossible in the market melee. Who was this Ishmael? Why had he picked me to dump all that business about sacred Mayan ceremonial places, spirits, a jaguar in a tree? I felt confused and unsatisfied, even used.

On my way back to Guatemala City, I tried to convince myself that I'd been entertained in some way, but had no idea why I had been picked to participate. And participate in what exactly? Then I began feeling foolish that I was in such a haste to get away and wished I had stayed and asked more questions. I'd missed an opportunity – for what exactly I couldn't be certain. I'm certain now he never wanted money or planned to rob me. But I realized it too late. I was left with the impression I'd cheated myself of an inexplicable experience through my anxiousness to get away.

Over the weeks, as I finished my travels in Latin America, the experience vacillated in my mind between a lost sense of adventure and an acceptance of being seduced by a clever Guatemalan, whoever he was and for whatever reason. That is, until I got home and examined my collection of photos. Curiously, while every single picture I took on my trip revealed their subjects, the six forbidden hip shots I took at the "sacred place" in Guatemala were all solid black. Never one to believe in the supernatural, I admit the black, not just blank, six photos gave me pause. Coincidence? Perhaps. Still, my mind failed to make sense of it.

My confusion was further tested a few months later when I was on a night safari in Botswana, and I took a photo of a leopard sitting in a tree. Because of the poor lighting at the time, I wasn't certain the picture would reveal much. But in the enlarged photograph, the leopard's shining eyes seemed to be staring directly at me, and I shivered when an unanticipated image of Ishmael came to me. Instead of a spotted body, the animal in the tree appeared in the photo as a black jaguar. In fact when others, not aware of my story, viewed the picture, they assumed it was a black jaguar.

Maybe I'm making too much of these oddities. But taken together, I'm still having trouble making sense of my encounter with Ishmael, because in a way he was prescient. As he predicted, I never will forget what he showed me. The forbidden photos had not been permitted. His mysterious reference to the number twelve, my birth date, still puzzles me. And I eventually did see what looked something like a black jaguar in a tree.

In an awakened, spiritual, metaphorical way, as I write this, I find myself returning to that sacred place in the hills near Chichicastenango and wishing I could relive my meeting with Ishmael. Who was he? Himself, a shaman? I realize now that he sincerely wanted so much for me to "see" something that I turned my back on. Obviously, the episode continues to haunt me, and I worry I missed an opportunity to be made aware of …what? An enlightenment or insight of some kind? I need to know what he offered me that I passed up. My moment was lost by my own narrowness and fear of something I didn't have the openness to explore.

I'm coming to believe that my travels have mostly been superficial. I ask myself what I have learned or personally gained by visiting other countries that couldn't be found in travel books. Yes, I've immersed myself in other languages, learning bits of words and phrases, witnessed a variety of dress styles and customs, listened to musical styles and instruments, stayed in the recommended hotels and inns, eaten a variety of culinary treats, visited the historical contents of museums and art galleries, climbed the steps of ancient ruins, relaxed on sandy beaches, hiked exhausting mountains, shared space with wild animals, moved about in taxis, vans, buses, planes, boats, on horses and foot, and come with souvenirs. Sometimes traveling was exhausting, a strain, only to arrive at my destination wishing I were home. That's not to say there weren't times of pleasure and unexpected excitement. Of course there were. And I've been privileged to be able to travel. But it seems my experiences are nothing more than those gained by following a trail made by others before me, a collection of information for yet another Lonely Planet edition. And if I add it all up, is there much difference between a traveler and a tourist?

How many "days of the jaguar" have I squandered in my worldly travels? What really do my collection of travel photographs say about me if photos of places and people are nothing more than photos of places and people? Look, see, I was there at one time.

But something in those pictures is missing, and I can't help but feel that given a chance, Ishmael might have lead me on a path to formulating an answer.

Forgive me, Ishmael.

About the Author

W. Royce Adams, emeritus professor of English, has published over a dozen college textbooks, several academic journal articles and juvenile novels. He won the Haunted Waters Literary Magazine's 2016 Grand Prize Short Story Contest, Honorable Mentions from Glimmer Train and from Winning Writer, and for a notable essay of 2016 by Best American Essays, 2017. His works have appeared in The Rockford Review, Black Fox Literary Magazine, Catamaran, In the Depths, Coe Review, Chaffey Review, Adelaide, bosque and others. He lives in Santa Barbara, California.

A Moment in Time

by Taylor Boughnou

It was just before dawn, and the feelings were so many, and the thoughts so profound—that Jeffery Higgins was awakened by his active unconsciousness. But he didn't get up, only turned over and continued to lay there in bed thinking, staring off into the darkness or perhaps into the beyond. Who could ever say with any degree of certainty? Had he been wrong? he thought. What mistakes did I make? And where and at what point did I? All these questions and many others presented themselves to his mind.

He looked at the green-lighted electric clock that was across the room on the dresser. Out doors it was cloudy, he could tell because it was in June, and at a quarter to five o'clock in the morning it should have been more illumination, penetrating through the shades than there was. Though as it were, the room was almost completely dark. He really didn't know why he'd thought about it; it was really no surprise: it had been forecasted to rain for several more days. He was really so unlike himself: he felt sluggish; and he did not want to get up to go to the athletic complex to workout as he usually did with an abundance of enthusiasm. His energy and focus just wasn't there. The weekend had passed in a sort of swoon. He had stayed indoors the past two days with the shades closed and for most of the time lying in bed as if he were deeply depressed. And now it was already Monday morning, and there had been no *absolute* resolve.

Susan had confirmed on Friday night—after talking to her briefly, in the most uncouth and ill-respectful of ways, he thought, by telephone: that after eleven months—that she could no longer be in a relationship with him. It had hurt him. Perhaps in his pride most of all, mainly. But then, it was intensified, in the fact that all their contact had been by telephone, and not in person ,which he could have better lived with, after the fact.

When he wanted to see her, she had something pressing, some tedious issue, that was only urgent in her eyes, that prevented her. But then that thought was perhaps a bias in his mind. And when she wanted to see him, he allowed his pride to deter him; it was now payback time—a sort of justifiable vengeance; though it was just foolish stubbornness that served only to make his sufferings more acute. But what did any of it matter now: when after eleven months he was back where he started? And for all he knew, she had reconciled with her husband, whom she had only been separated, and that was where they had begun, right before the actual divorce process was started. Either way, not any of it mattered, he thought, turning over and starting at the ceiling fan that was now coming visible, in the sparsely lighted room, that he had only up till now felt its enlivening breeze and heard its revolutions. And all that mattered to Jeffery now was that the sensations of absence was overwhelming. This discomfort was like nothing he had ever experienced.

Still yet, he knew all-too-well that there could be no finger pointing; no blame game. That would've been only a superficial cover-up; a denial of his inner-most feelings. But moreover, it would've been an affront to something that had been, for most of the time, and for him—something most wonderful.

As it were, he had already planned to move. He was not going to do it impetuously—those kinds of moves never seemed to work out well, for any one. But he had resolved within himself, over the course of the weekend that passed seemingly unnoticed, that in one year's time, it would be when he would start over fresh. For that part, and beyond his disappointment, he felt rather triumphant: for having allowed sound-reasoning to decide it for him. Anyhow, there was so much that had to be done. The emotional, mental, spiritual and physical strengths had to return. There had to be an all-around sense of well-being. Slowly, over the course of the coming year, there had to be things discarded. There was no place for sentimentality; no feelings of sorrow for himself and wallowing in self-pity and, certainly no denial. So that if it were to be done right, so that his orientation on life's outlook was to be anything along positive lines and healthy—a year then, was a good and logical goal with which to aim.

Yes, he got up and went over to the window and parted the shades and looked out, it was as he had thought: cloudy. It was a dreary early Monday morning. It was not raining now. But must have rained during the night; all the cars were wet, the grass, the streets glistened and water dripped down from the leaves. But not any of it was he really aware in a deeper sense. He saw it, but that was the extent. His mind shut itself down completely. He went back over to the bed and he lay down. And there, exhausted and wearied by thought, fell into sleep and began to dream, and when he woke he remembered it clearly, perhaps because it was simple.

There was chaos everywhere, and he didn't like it, but he was in the middle of it all, not fighting for survival—but as witness. It was as though all peace and order was gone and people ran here and there, and there was fighting, chaos. It didn't frighten him when he woke, because he knew the works of dreams, and with a quick analysis he knew that it was his own unknowing, which in the frame of the dream-work became chaos. And like in the dream, he could but only be a witness to the decision that Susan had made. He couldn't prevent it, and he couldn't convince her otherwise. Her decision had been so final. It reflected in the emphasis and inflections of her words. He had pleaded with her to be mindful in her thinking, but that was all he could do. He had felt an overwhelming sense of helplessness, a by-stander of his destiny; destiny being no more than the moment to moment shaping of one's life. And in that brief place in time, he had no say. So the vulnerability of his waking life had manifested itself into his unconscious life. And he had to confess that in this ineptitude; he felt so helpless in the shaping of his own future.

It was hard to believe that after so much time and that for no particular reason given, he and Susan were indeed through. While part of him would have so readily welcomed her back with arms wide open, in heart, mind and body. Though now a growing segment of himself, and he knew this because he felt it, and had begun to cultivate his mind away from it, would soon—so very soon overtake the welcoming part, for leaning in another direction, and to be far far away from where they loved and dreamed so together of the future. It was really simple: his circumstances had changed, so his life and living had to change along with it.

The one positive thing that he had going, was the rain. It had begun to rain again. And the rain somehow always settled him down, providing the gentleness that was needed for both healing and deep reflection. Could there ever be change? he asked himself, softly aloud. Did people ever change, really, for the better? Was it a trait innate that made one resistant to taking an inward look into themselves; seeing the horrible as well as the pleasant? All those questions and many more that would take a lifetime, and, an objective consciousness beyond the simple subjective perceptions to answer, demanded answers now. But he had none. He had only recently just begun to even realize how very complicated was life—speaking of his very own.

The rains continued to fall, with brief periods where there came only mist. It was cool for June, the sky one mass of gray.

In the not so distant past, just to know that Susan was out there, that they had each other, had always managed to solace Jeffery, and she had once told him that it did so for her as well. But now, that seemed like a lifetime ago. His head was spinning with thought and confusion. What about now: how was she feeling after her decision? Though he had only had her word then on that; and now, after the seemingly quick and easy way that she moved on—he had tremendous misgivings even toward that.

But one thing that he did know for certain, beyond any doubts, was that he could not even begin to answer anything while existing in his current mode of fast-paced life of the northeastern states. Where the mainframe to living was but hustle and bustle; and to which he was but a country tourist from another time in space and truly so very far from any place that might have resembled any home. And where to him the inhabitants always appeared so desperate, and malnourished for what, he knew not. Perhaps it was owing to the living of life that so eluded them, and the encroaching of the beyond that so frightened them as a result, which could have only been appeased by living; not existing to work. What was it to labor so after a career, without much enjoyment? he considered. He had to depart, and soon. This he knew, felt it most virile inside of him. While a year to heal would have been ideal; ideals were what caused his troubles, he believed. There was simply nothing that anyone could've said that might've relieved his tension; only a long stretch of time and trying to live past it could ever accomplish that. But then, he had to admit that he had been left in the lurch, with yet another scar that he would have to live with, that was much a part of him now. For him it had all been all too real. Now he was depleted at the core and exhausted. Even if they hadn't discussed every single one of them, he had built many wonderful, fruitful dreams in his heart for them together. He felt nervous and jittery as he lay.

They had entered into a committed, faithful relationship as adults, and in goodness and honesty; her yet to be divorced never waned that belief. His only regret being that they did not clear the air of any doubts on the part of that trustworthy commitment that had been made between them, on their way to parting. It would have simplified their lives here on; most definitely his. And owing to the suddenness of the break, for his own part, he had suspicions that he would have to forever live with.

He was at a loss. Because he had always placed greater value on human feelings and emotions, as to exist so transiently as others did in their comment to him, in word and deed. So negligent was Susan, particularly lacking in thought, to just wander away from someone in whom she had pledged to care so genuinely. Where were the compassions and understanding, in life now gone to? he thought. Or had that also been just some illusion belonging to some ideal? Jeffery shook his head back and forth on the pillow in the most profound disbelief, which was almost like disgust. True, there was a fading belief in others rising up inside of him; yet, slowly seeping to the surface, there was a sense of utter certainty about himself that heretofore had been unknown.

Then he thought, as he was getting up to get ready to go off to the athletic complex to have some well needed movement and exercise, that would perhaps serve to soothe and begin the healing process of his deeper emotions and mind:

Susan, I wonder—if she understood just how much it pained me? If she were ever really capable of feeling or knowing what it meant to me having adoration for her, and to hear her confess that she felt the very same way for me? And I will always wonder, if it were really legit, the feelings that she said that she had, and that I was not just some insignificant thing, just a piece of flesh, really—to just take her away, for a brief moment in time, from the seething loneliness of starting her life over, he considered. And then, for a brief while, he thought nothing at all. Then:

No, it had been no more than a moment to waste—rather than one to enjoy and treasure, said Jeffery Higgins softly aloud to himself, shaking his head, in a final decision of absolute resolve, that he could now live with.

Unfinished Sympathies

He had always, rather without a second thought, placed Michelle's desires and needs before those of his own; without the slightest afterthought that there was some wrong in doing so, or, even that his behavior should be in any other way. They had shared, he thought, an equal amount of adoration and affection as it were, and this made it all natural to him, perhaps instinctual even; and they seemed to get on well with things having always been as they were. But now, Alexander could not believe that after four, terrific, amicable years that the relationship was really truly over forever, it now seemed. The day to day considerations and thoughtfulness and instinctive cares, that he had stood for, and which to any passersby, would have seemed, really, quite noble—had been rejected. So what did that say, of the modern world? he thought. He was inwardly destroyed. And now after four years, he was back at the beginning, sitting along the Riverway, back in Davenport, staring at the upper Mississippi River, hoping for answers, perhaps when there were none. But what else was there to do, when he found himself at an impasse: but to return to the beginning of where he had first discovered his way?

Every thing now, was changed, for this Covid-19 pandemic. And this increased his loneliness. In fact, perhaps it was the great change that had now come into the world as of lately, that had caused changes in Michelle, and was the cause of their relationship ending. But he could only surmise. He had seen so much now. And he'd rather think that it was the stressors of this pandemic that was the cause, if he had to think about it at all, rather than not any reason at all for their split.

It was a bright, sunny morning in early fall, resplendent; the air was perfumed with that crispness that is so common to that time of year. October was in its second week, and nature was just at the beginning of her subtle stages of gentle transformation of the season, where the mornings came into energetic life by the cue of sun filled, flawless blue skies at daybreak; and where the very days themselves seemed to be motivated by this theme. It was that time of year that everyone seemed at their best for whatever be their wont. The leaves were turning and bursting into their myriad shades of red, yellow, and patches of rustic orange and blends of other colors that were so magnificent that they were beyond descriptions, so were better left to just enjoy; it was a wondrous time. If he could but see objectively with patient eyes beyond his troubling cares, the vastness of possibilities that lay beyond this moment, that he viewed in this epoch as so final; to just enjoy this time itself, it might have made every small difference. But the almost feral look in his eyes appeared to have no boundaries—no bounds to how far gone he truly was in his mind for what he deemed to be the greatest tragedy he could ever know, even in the midst of this earthly crisis. Then in his brain-fogged mind, somehow, he mustered a moment's clarity to bring forth a worthy, poignant consideration: how many relationships, love-affairs and even marriages were not now ended for the uncertainty and fear-stricken effects of these times. . . . ?

From the distance of where he sat under the gazebo, the water, rushing past with its sweeping currents and counter-currents, looked silver and alive with an ever-changing dynamic and a living, pulsing life-force of its own, with the way the fall sun reflected, sparkling on its surface, and the way the light wind pressed at it. But none of it did Alexander recognize how it really was. He could not focus his mind on a single point. Everything seemed to whirl about him, surreal-like, as though he were existing in some strange dream-like world, and any clearness seemed ages ago: since he actually sat down with a consciousness to look with as much clarity as was possible into the core of his being, if ever he had. There was so much to recollect because there had been so much ending and pain; somewhere there had to be hope: he hoped—if only he could discover it so that there might be another beginning. He tried with all his effort to focus. And for the strain of it all, seeming to drain from his very life-force, he wanted to give up. How did one simply give up?

It was peculiar, he thought, trying desperately to recollect that last month when he stood in his little apartment in Beacon Hill, packing his effects, reliving what had transpired between Michelle and him; that once he had rejected another's affection only to find himself in this phase, being the one now rejected. Such were the sagas of life, he thought.

With that in mind, he left for Davenport; believing that if there be any place that could heal his emotions from all those unfinished sympathies—home in the Quad Cities would be that place. He called them unfinished sympathies, because there was so much that needed to be said that he had wanted desperately to say: but he had not been given the chance. Michelle refused his every attempt at contact. And that within itself was most defeating of all. Because it left him very little in the way of closure and the recovery of himself; and he was consumed with a kind of longing and achiness that strangely had some sweetness in it. Yes, he was hurt and hurting: most definitely—but then there had been no true closure, only memories and disbelief. It was as if Michelle held onto possibilities of reconciliation that was her own secret. So it made him in some place deep within, where perhaps he should have been healing, hold onto hope through good memories, and the belief in what had once been was powerful, and influential enough to somehow reunite them, when the pandemic was ended and life all reset could begin where it was once.

He stood and descended the few steps of the gazebo, and began walking along the Riverway. Being back at home did not offer the comfort and solace that it always had—the place and the surrounding country were lusterless in emotional healing stimulation—as he had believed it would; he could find no meaning being there. He felt something strange, deep from within—within his chest and in his head, like a significant change, a gateway leading him away from whom he had been, something though that was honestly necessary. He walked. Perhaps he *was* coming to: maybe even getting over Michelle. Was that what he wanted? Or was it self-preservation leaving him no choice in the matter. . . .as it did when one was perforce by circumstances that involved another who was unwilling to be changed? He could not make any sense of it. There was a throbbing, pulsing sensation in his head, like something knocking. He walked on. The people walking, jogging, and biking along the Way seemed at this stage of the season to be much more settled, and focused, than when he had first arrived a month ago. Perhaps the desires of fall were more substantial than the loose, wild aims of summer, he thought, in his wavering mind, that he was sure was coming clear and to again. He, himself like the people he passed was beginning to feel more effectual or so it seemed. The thoughts he now had of life, of being more productive, emerged in intermittent flashes as being sensible, no matter what would happen from here on. But his coherence was tenuous at best, fading in and out blending in with that knocking sound in his mind.

He missed Michelle dearly, with honest sincerity. Why had she denied him his say? He'd never know. He walked on reliving all those times that they had strolled in the historic, yet ageless

Boston Common, on days much like this day. She taking hold of his arm affectionately, as they would walk the short distance from Cambridge over the Longfellow Bridge—that was known to most as the Salt-and-Pepper Shaker Bridge with its admirable stone central towers that looked like salt-and pepper shakers—and the Boston skyline hovering in the distance just a little ways beyond the Charles River. Reminiscing, this was the one solitary thing of which Alexander could see all so clearly now. Then as they would descend the bridge and onto the street level and entering Beacon Hill, they would sometimes stop in at the notable Savenor's market, once a favorite shop of Julia Child, where they would pick up a few items to make a meal after class at the college, where they had first met and fallen in love, four years ago, and he feeling so delighted that she had taken his arm, and she, for her part—rather confident that she had done so. And he thought of all the things that they had planned to do, now that they had graduated, but would never happen now. But no, he had hope: it would turn around. It had to turn around and work out; and this ill-conceivable Covid-19, had to go away—it just had to: at some point, right? If only the intense pulsing in his head might subside so that he could think more objectively about the whole matter, he was certain that he could make sense of it all. Down the river, somewhere, he thought he heard something knocking. Always now this knocking sound. What was it knocking so! But it wasn't anywhere down river, it was inside him. He put both his hands to his head as he walked on for a moment, his eyes partially covered, existing in the surrealism of it all—he was frustrated; he was scared and alone; confused to the point of numbness, maybe the sounds were only in his mind, he tried to rationalize. Still the cursed knocking, and in back of this knocking a darkness rising. An unfathomable, seething darkness like a madness wanting to take hold. He sat down on a bench along the Way. He was distraught; almost blind against all calls of reason, but he did not desire to become comfortable with this terrible uneasiness, lest he should want it to be germane to him always. He shook his head, wanting to get clear. Still, this knocking!

He looked around in dismay, as the season of change was manifesting just as much from within as it were from without. The grass was starting to lose its color, the leaves, beautiful, yet changing and some were falling. The baby's-breath now bobbed with the last of the season's pant in the light breeze of the flowerbeds around the gazebos, seemingly without care. He was once that way, without heedful care; not because he was in any way thoughtless or insensitive, or thought himself ever incapable of more—but due to his youthful outlook on life and his adoration of Michelle and what they felt for each other, and what they would accomplish together, because he had unconsciously thought, no—instinctively believed, that it would last forever.

He stood up and began to walk again. At first, everything whirled about. He stopped to steady himself. He was fundamentally weary. He when on. In deep thought, and trying to clear his mind, before he knew it he had walked over the Centennial Bridge to Rock Island and the District to look among the shops and all that was familiar, to see what changes had occurred since last he'd been home. After some time, he began the walk back to Davenport. And no sooner than he began, at the highpoint of the bridge, to his great surprise and happiness—there was Michelle. Ah. . . .relief took him. There was a great pang and the strange knocking, thumping sound that he was most certain now had been in his head subsided, along with all the up to now cares and troubles and doubts that now vanished. It was all true—there she stood as real and true as the day itself.

She looked so fresh and radiant in the mid-morning fall; even lovelier than he'd ever remembered; which caused him to look around and about himself; he imagined he looked a disheveled messed for all the worrying, doubts and misgivings. He began to brush at his dark hair with his hand, and rearrange his shirt to make himself more presentable to her, for up to now nothing meant anything. Her smile, her long brown hair and enchanting blue eyes beckoned to him, at first he could not believe it, and then he increased his pace towards her as she was coming nearer to him. Seeing her suddenly appear in one way was a surprise, but in a more profound way, none whatsoever. Because she had gone home with him many times before and had seen his favorite spots through his eyes as he toured her around. Her embrace that he thought he should never know again, so precious it was, immediately restored him. They walked, and it was all so familiar. Michelle took hold of his arm in the same way as he remembered her doing when they would stroll through the Common after leaving class. It was so wonderful! They were so young; and in love; and they had their entire lives before them now, once and forever again.

"I'm so sorry," she said. "Truly, I am. Will you forgive me— not just on the surface, but deep inside where it really counts?"

"There's nothing to forgive," he said. He was just overjoyed that she was all right, and that she was there and that they were once again together, and that they were all right together was all that mattered.

"But I hurt you," she said. He could see in her eyes that were welling with tears that she was hurting for having hurt him. "Just tell me you'll forgive me; and mean it, when you say it."

"You were just afraid," he said. "Mature commitment, beyond what we had at college, is sometimes frightening—I know. It's serious. I forgive you, honestly. And then, with this pandemic who can rationalize anything: we're all afraid, all of earth. Yes, I forgive you and I mean it, truly I do."

"You felt it too?" she asked, relieved, as a light smile was taking away her tears. "You too were just a little bit afraid?"

"Yes. I did," he said. "I was. Somewhere I still am. But we'll get beyond it."

"But you didn't make a fool of things as I did," she confessed." To this he gave no verbal reply—but began fumbling at his shirt again and brushing at his hair with his hand, as if to say that to worry one's self into a distorted figure when there was truly nothing to worry and stress about, nothing at all, was even more foolish.

"We're together now," he said, enraptured by it all. "That's all that should matter. Say no more about it."

She embraced him tenderly and kissed his face and lips. In a timeless, stillness, they held each other ever so closely. Even closer and more tenderly than he had ever remembered. It was true—the separation had made their hearts fonder. They went in for some time and loved, and it was as it had always been between them.

After spending the day together around the Quad Cities, and as evening was coming on and the sun was lowering on the horizon, they took the Channel Cat water taxi to the dock of the village of East Davenport with its quaint little shops, taverns and cafés, the neighborhood where they now lived. They came home and she prepared them a nice fall supper of quail and cherry sauce, wild rice, and asparagus which they enjoyed with Bordeaux. And for dessert, they had a pear and rhubarb cobbler. It was the same meal that they had shared at the Casablanca restaurant in the Harvard Square on that fall night over four years ago when they had decided that they would see no one else but each other. The meal had been on special, and they had shared it; this made it proper in both fare and in ambiance. It felt good to be at home and to enjoy this reminiscent meal. It was the start of their mature lives together. But that too, the thought of the Casablanca was ironic, a chapter in another life—as it no longer existed now owing to the turbulent times manifested by the pandemic, it had been shuttered and with it a part of them.

Alexander stood at the highpoint of the Centennial Bridge, staring at the surrounding country: Rock Island, where he had just come from, and Davenport were he was now headed and where perhaps he could begin anew, and then down into the ancient and foreboding waters of the Mississippi River below that had seen so much. Here, at this precipice—it would be the easy route to just give up. But in that instant, another frame of mind took wholly possession. And somehow he just knew from a feeling, that everything would be all right—he just needed to shake himself completely free, clear his mind. Then he smiled an honest and infectious smile to himself, that was almost laughter, knowing that he didn't want to shake completely free just now. Let this be a well-learned lesson in love, he thought: and, in that wavering illusion that had appeared so life-like, bringing him to the brink, he knew well enough, that he had partaken in the last supper of that life. But there was still the greatest hope for his future up ahead.

Chapter II

Courtship at the Lavender Crest Winery
(A tale of Masculine and Feminine)

There was a bright yellow sun shining down from the cloudless blue backdrop of space, in an accentuating contrast, that was so moving and so profound, enhancing this picturesque day to almost enchantment, giving equally such sensations of delight and anticipation, both to the moment and times yet to come. There was a feeling in the atmosphere that inferred so much to the imagination of the heart. In the distance, a lone Blue Heron coasted in what appeared to be contemplative circles in the sky. Growing, in back of the winery was a thriving, fertile field of corn, whose tall stalks bobbed and swayed sprightly, as far as the eyes could see. And a lush green lawn lay smooth like so many aisles of carpet all around the spacious place. There was a white gazebo, with an assortment of festive colored flowers in flower-beds on either side that resembled small English gardens, with a little picnic-table just for two, at its center, that was erected in the middle of this exceptionally green lawn, just this side of the corn field, not too far from the patio, dotted here and there by evergreens. Where to the right there was a vineyard, and next to that a fair-size grove of blueberry bushes. There was a gentle breeze, blowing now, but the day was still quite hot. It was now the month of July. Much of the patrons that had come to the Lavender Crest Winery from all about the Quad Cities for lunch, were pretty much now gone. But a man and the young woman that accompanied him, seeming under no restraint of timetables, remained. They sipped casually at their chilled white wine at intervals and looked subtly across the table in admiration of each other and out across the enormous expanse of this midwestern countryside.

And although it was hot, they had been served their lunch out on the covered patio of the winery, instead of dinning inside in the coolness, shielded from the intense noon day sun, they were, by the covering overhead. All in all they seemed content enough. Which to the eyes of any passersby, simple meant—that they were a cozy and charming looking couple, displaying all the signs of flirting with love. They smiled at each other often; they talked and even when they didn't utter a word, it was evident that they were much aware of each other in some daydreaming of things to come, and this gesture attested to how authentically together in a deeper sense, they were. Now this was a true poignant sentiment: that made them truly so utterly so charming: that even in their own secret contemplations of each other, or, the world that hummed all around, they appeared content, void of the strain that too often seemed to plague those who are uncertain of themselves. They seem to feel each other beyond normal sense perceptions. It was displayed in their bearings and manners of being, that spoke thus: that each sincerely, without pretext—valued the other's presence.

Not too far from where they sat, there was a small stone fountain that was continuously welling up, giving off a serene and peaceful, tinkling sound like a flowing brook in a pristine forest deep in a secluded wood. The couple, the mood and the setting, the time and place was a recipe for so much,—so much that so many in this modern time denied themselves, and that was: living each moment to its fullest in the actual presence of another living-being; as opposed to some remote fashion that was but a passing trend, so void of any aspects human.

For Mason Benoit, there could be no greater triumph than to be back at home in the Quad Cities—none greater anywhere: for him. And even if he never uttered it, in his heart and mind he felt it and knew it. So many times he had felt himself to be a modern day Odysseus. He had been out east, at Boston, Massachusetts, for twenty long years. He had come home to visit as often as he could, of course, but to be here now living again, is what counted. For the absence and longing for it were now gone. That past now, so very unthreatening, was no more than some reference point in another space.

He had taken a place in the Harrison Manor, exactly where he had always envisioned in his mind's eye that he would live when he should return. Mason saw the time away, and the difficulty in getting back for good, as one might see a detour on a road. It took him out of his way, but looking at it now the journey of it revealed to him, that it had been a beautiful route to come to know himself—that inner-man, that he had only ever imagined, he had now become. And for that triumph: he was proud of the man who stared back at him in the mirror. He was tactful, poised, cultured, extremely well-read, understanding and oh so grownup and above all, so patient. Patience he discovered, now thinking of the young woman with him, was virtuous, indeed. But if there was one thing that he felt had been lost in all that in between time, it had only been the social and romantic aspects of his life, he saw as having been neglected. And now, well, it wasn't something he could view so lightly. Because he knew that in order to have gain, and he did gain a lot; that there was always a tradeoff. And to the extent of that episode's lasting effects: he knew not. Only that time and living would reveal, and then more living and time beyond that, would remedy it.

They finished their lunch, and then Mason and Jennifer went the short stroll across the lush lawn to the gazebo. He was carrying a wine bucket, filled with ice, chilling their bottle of chardonel.

"Is this pleasant enough—you're not too hot being outside, are you?" asked Mason thoughtfully, in a tone that was full of affection.

"It's a hot day, but I'm fine," said Jenny. "Besides, gazebos are always much cooler." They sat closely on the little crescent shaped bench of the gazebo. It was no denying it: it was hot out, but under the gazebo it was at least fifteen degrees cooler. And if anyone had trouble with the heat it was more Mason than Jenny.

"So," said Jenny, "this is your first full summer being back in awhile—how are you adjusting to the heat?"

"I'm coping," he said. "But I'll adjust quickly. Remember, this is my home." After years of being in New England, where the summer weather could barely be called summer, in comparison to the Middle-West region, her concern was valid. Not that he couldn't handle it, but for the initial unpleasantness of it.

She touched his very strong, masculine hand that lay on the little table next to the wine bucket, then she touch his face, and then placed her hand on his, but she did not say anything, only smiled. Mason was about six feet tall, with well-sculpted shoulders, and a remarkably defined v-shaped back and fit waistline and toned musclcular arms and thighs. His dark hair was cut close on his head, and he was always clean-shaven, so that it exposed a chiseled chin. He had the look of men a hundred years ago when men's faces were manly and angular and personable. Not like the round shapeless faces that had become so prevalent nowadays. And she really was enrapt with him and his appearance. And his reaction to this tactile contact was as one might have expected, from someone who had lived for a long time in another place; a place were affection always seemed more calculating and conditional than it ever did natural. He looked at her soft very feminine hand on top of his, and his eyes lit up and he delighted in a smile, looking up from where her hand lay unrelenting on his, and into her eyes. He did not like the strained, slow reaction of his responses, and certainly not with Jenny. In feeling he was slowly returning to what he had once been: sensitive and thoughtful, engaging—so in touch with being able to feel liberally, and to react to the stimuli between a man and woman, without censure, trusting in the senses; and void of the haughty and cavalier pretense that he had been perforce by the very nature back in New England to be an unwilling participant. Which already, that long span of time was, in this six months' time beginning to truly fade from memory; but he knew that it would take time. And to return to what he had once been, was exactly what Jennifer Thompson was so deserving of Mason Benoit to be. Because as it were, she was a young middle western woman just now twenty-two years of age, and budding to fall in love. For a time she lean her head with so much certainty against his shoulder, but no words were spoken between them. They simple lived in the moment, trusting in feelings. And this was a good place; for it was all about feelings—to be able to feel after what you desired, so much so that it had no other choice but to become one's very own reality, was the universal power-force of everything.

There were no ifs and buts about it: it *was* so true, Mason now thought, that whoever said it first, stated it most accurately: that before a man was ever capable of knowing and loving another—he had first off to know and to love himself: by becoming the man he was meant to become and not shrieking away from it, due to external beliefs of a world outside himself. In fact, it was a chief duty. Otherwise, he lived sort of like a scoundrel: never able to commit to anyone or thing, in a deeper sense. And those that came into the life of such a man, risked completely losing everything, certainly the women he pro-claimed to adore, and certainly the years that they could never again retrieve. And he had decided, with this knowledge in the very heart of his consciousness, and that was some time ago now, that come hell or high waters, that he was going to be true to himself, first; abiding by his own "golden rule" which was: he would never squander himself, by lowering his standard of who he truly was to accommodate others; so that they could relate to him. And in doing so, perhaps never disappoint another, and thereby become the kind of man in whom he could be pleased. No, anyone that wanted to relate to him would have to raise *their* vibration to where he was, at that given epoch. It was awful, he thought, sitting there underneath the gazebo with Jenny, truly awful, that so many never fully came into their own owing to that fact, that they never allowed growth and change to take place, for fear that they would not be accepted or understood or have anyone that liked them. Like them! he smiled cynically to himself, inwardly, at the notion. How absurd, he believed, to squander all one's potentiality on this wacky premise. He shook his head. It was a gesture profound enough that it got Jenny's attention. Up to then she had been sipping at her chardonel and watching out into the forever-ness of this middle-western landscape.

"Oh no—what's the matter, darling?" Jenny asked. "Is it the heat? I know you're my strongman and all," affectionately she put her hand on his shoulder, "but still yet, even so, this heat can be oppressive when you're just reacclimating to it—I know, because I felt so drained and uncomfortable last year when I went to visit dad, at New Orleans, after not going down for some time." Even though Mason had been unaware, he had drunk most of his chilled chardonel. She poured him another proper glass. And he took note of ever detail of her elegant arm and how taut yet supple was the skin, and the hand that was so compliant and dexterous, and fingers that were so caressing, as she raised the bottle from the ice bucket and began pouring the wine from the wine bottle in to his glass. He was pleased, too, that she knew how, for etiquette's sake, to what level to fill the glass with the wine, as opposed to stopping only because the glass could not hold anymore. And he had known such beastly people. He saw himself a lucky man now and he doted on her every little, authentic bodily movement. For her physical appearance Jennifer Thompson was a lovely young woman. She was regal and tall, very elegant, buxom, with a soft, vibrant complexion. And for her heritage: she was French and German and Shoshoni. And her hair that was long and dark, and straight, came almost at her waist. Her appearance was at once a phenomenon of natural beauty and sophistication. She was wearing a fashionable pair of white palazzo and a soft peach colored blouse and stylish brown sandals. She was well put together; and he saw her as the most impeccable woman he'd known. Yes—my patience is rewarded, he thought, as he continued on admiring her. She's young, lovely, chic and vivacious, and not yet too jaded, and so high on living. We'll work.

"Thank you," he said, taking a sip, and then setting his glass down. "This really is nice sipping wine—isn't it? It's still cool too." He stood up and went over to the railing, and looked down into the flower-bed, and then, turning back to her: "No, it's not that—I can manage the heat. In fact, it feels pleasant enough under here. Don't you think?" He smiled to her, and her wondrous blue eyes that were so full of expectancy flashed coquettishly back at him. And she stood up and came up to him, and kissed him without embracing, and went back to the little table.

"I really enjoyed our lunch," she said, now pouring herself a proper glass; "did you?" They had desired to eat something

very light because of the heat. So they both order the salad consisting of grill chicken, romaine lettuce, walnuts and tangerine
slices with a light peppercorn dressing to complement their
chardonel. "And yes, I think it's pleasant enough under here,"
she said, gesturing with her hands. "It's amazing the difference
under gazebos, isn't it?"

"Yes, very much so," he said, his eyes fixed on her now.

"I must admit: the winery was a nice choice," she said,
thinking of all the places, that in such a short-time since they
met, that he'd introduced to her. And the maturity of Mason, age
notwithstanding, she really admired, without taking it for granted,
or his masculinity lightly. Because she was well-aware that some
people never grew up; and that some males feared being manly.
She was now feeling herself a real-woman, in all the feminine
sense, and she was proud feeling the thrust of a natural-woman
pulsing. And for a moment, in contrast, she thought of the boys
back at college, and it repulsed her. She was so relieved, though,
that the monotony of college life, that'd so wearied her, was over.

"I'm glad you approve. I've always thought it nice here."

"And you've come often then?"

"Not every time that I came home, but every few times.
And they used to serve dinner, nightly, but I believe only on
weekends now."

There was a look of excitement brewing in her eyes:
"Should we do dinner here some time—perhaps in the late
summer and go blue berry picking over there?" she pointed
toward the blueberry bushes where a signed mentioned picking
blueberries. "I think I'd like to do both?" Jenny's excitement
and romanticism about simple things, made him eager about
life and living, and their sentiments together, reveled in the
repose of the vibration of the masculine and the feminine that
pulsed ever so between them.

"Yes, we have to," he said. "And we will."

For a few moments silence ensued while they took refreshing sips from their chilled wine on this hot afternoon.

"Mason," she said, in earnestness and quite lovingly, "after eight months, since we first met, and six months of being committed, and after all the time we've spent together—are you okay with this, with us, are you satisfied—with me?"

Moments passed, and he said nothing, not because he didn't have a response, but for the nature and timing of her inquiry: which was a valid one. And he respected Jenny for braving it. He had known so many women over the years who were much older than she who had not the wherewithal to ask, but simply assumed.

"You don't answer," she said, a look of so much uncertainty now replacing the oh so contented expression that had made her face glow up to then.

"I'm sorry, sweetheart, for my hesitancy," he said, seeming to her a perplexing response, and it frightened her; it was the first time since she met him that he appeared this way; "I am just disappointed in myself."

"Disappointed in yourself?" she asked. "I don't understand."

"No. You wouldn't. And that's why I'm disappointed in me."

"Tell me: would you?" she said, almost pleadingly.

"I'm not upset with your question. But for the fact that you had to ask, in the first place—where we are; where we stand. It brings back to my mind so many bad memories accompanied by unpleasant images. Where I spent many times on tenterhooks, because I always had to wonder where I stood with another. And I had vowed that I'd never do that to anyone. It's the most wretched of feelings, and quite cruel to be made to feel that way."

"I didn't at all mean to upset you. Never would I want you to have to relive the past of things unpleasant."

"And you didn't upset me. I upset me: because at some point, I didn't reassure you."

"I know, that for twenty years you had a lot going on. This much you've told me. And then to not only weather it, but to find a bright spot in it all: was noble. I'm so glad that you never quit. You could have so easily, at any moment threw down the gauntlet that life laid before you, and come home. But you didn't. And I'm proud of you. So much. Because had you not endured, you would not be the man I meet and every day become more enamored."

"Jennifer," he said, "I'm more than okay with us. You remind me of the very reason that I never just came home when there was so much unpleasantness. I grew faithful that some day my princess would come. And now here I am holding the reality of my faith in my arms," he said, sealing his commitment with a kiss. And for the time being she was reassured and soothed.

The time had come for them to go; they had had enough heat for one afternoon. Mason took up the lead and descended the two little steps down from the gazebo back on to the earth, but he was still shielded from the sun by this little structure's overhang. He turn to extend his hand to Jenny, but when he did she wasn't immediately right there. She was turned askance from where he faced her staring out beyond the forever-ness of this land. Another breeze had come up, and it raised her hair; to his mind came the affinity of Jenny and Botticelli's "Birth of Venus" painting. He was so enthralled and enlivened and quickened at how his courtship with Jenny was proceeding. It was so remarkable that he had trouble at times of believing it. But although he was pleased, there was some doubt that so frightened him, really. And that fear and trembling, was in himself. Have I been to damaged by a long and barren life back there in the east? he thought. For so very long, I told myself that a relationship with one person, beyond sexual gratification, was something that was no good—no good for me. Have I whored too much to be of any good for one deserving woman? Oh, God I certainly hope not! He felt his manly chest tighten with panic. Granted, he thought, I said that monogamy was no good, to not allow myself too much close contact back there. And although I knew that it was but psychological manipulation, after years of saying it—it became a kind of live by proverb, before, during and after every encounter. But I'm not there now; true, he said softly to himself. But can I get beyond this once necessary mental and emotional rampart, that became an internal commandment? I do not know, I hope though that I can; for both our sakes'. At least, heretofore, I thought I had already overcome it. Jennifer deserves that I have overcome it. Just give it up. Don't let some wayward pride dominate you. He turned from his lovely young lady and looked in the directions of the fountain and the winery.

He was not alone. Jenny too, although entirely different than Mason's, had some misgivings. She, as she stared longly with ever increasing intent, was concerned about her little ex-perience in real romance. She wondered if she could live up to what it meant to be 'really' involved, and present, day after day. Oh, my, she considered, standing there at the wooden railing on the opposite side of the gazebo, looking beyond the agile fields of corn, out into the future: this is real, and serious, she turned briefly to face Mason, and she smiled but he didn't see: for he was consumed by thought peering in the other direction. He is tall, noble, and erect with such wondrous piety, and he exudes confidence, he's strong and oh so charming; every thing that I might've ask for,—so why would there be any doubts in my mind, just now, at this point; where I feel it, sense it, and know it inside all my being, that we're just about to push forward into that next phase? If only I knew, for absolute certainty, that I could live up to what he expects, and should have. Who am I kidding?—I expect this of myself. To be the best companion that he could ever have dreamed, during all those years that he did just that: dreamt. Am I me, or am I what he really did, actual dream into existence, by a very persistent will of the imagination. . . .does it matter—does it really matter at all? 'I think, therefore I am.' She took the few strides across the girth of the gazebo to the steps. And as if by magnetic attraction, he turned as his arms and hands simultaneously reached up and out for her. He took hold of her at her trim, taut waist and lowered her ever so gently back on to the earth. There was a smile in their eyes. They were on the same vibrational frequency, just now. And she had to admit to herself, that she felt so good with him, and together they were good; and they felt equally good about each other, separately, inside themselves. And now, for the immediate time being, they were at an armistice—safe from the troubling cares of the uncertainty that loomed furtively in backdrop of their contentment: and perhaps their great challenges that lay ahead—that of overcoming their individual doubts and misgivings, about their worthiness to each other, beyond the sublimity of what was, for now.

About the Author

T. M. Boughnou was drawn to the writers and thinkers of the ninetieth and early twentieth centuries. After years of a dedicated reading and writing regimen and journal-keeping of his thoughts and observations of his daily routines and personal travels, he began to write. He splits his living-time between Davenport, Iowa and Boston, Massachusetts. He works as a wellness specialist.

A Secret for Uncle Teddy

by Edith Tarbescu

Ted McCullough opened the door of the B&B to greet his sister-in-law. He was surprised to see her, but happy to take a break. He noticed Fiona's black jersey dress pulled tight across her breasts and open-toe heels, both inappropriate for the rainy weather in Belfast. Did she wear this outfit for him? he wondered.

"Where's Bobby?" asked Ted.

"Identifying birds in your backyard for a school project. He'll be along in a moment." She lingered between the inner and outer doorways. "Aren't you going to invite me in?"

"Sorry." He held the door open as she entered the sitting room. She chose the sofa and leaned back, reminding Ted of an artist's model. The thought caught him off-guard as he seated himself opposite her in a leather recliner, but he didn't want to get too relaxed. He eyed Fiona's outfit again while she looked at him and smiled. "You've made a lot of changes since I visited a fortnight ago. I love the new rugs, by the way."

"Earth colors were your idea," he said. "I never had a chance to thank you, by the way."

"You're welcome, love." She leaned forward, palms touching. "What else do you need to buy?"

"A few paintings."

As she crossed her legs her dress rose to lower-thigh. "We could go to Hillsborough, if you'd like. I'd be happy to go to art galleries with you."

"I was thinking of driving down to Dublin. I'll also look for rare books while I'm there. "

Fiona's face brightened. "We could go shopping in Dublin and then have raw oysters at that pub on Grafton Street." She stopped abruptly as she watched the expression on his face change.

Ted bit his lower lip. "I don't think so."

"I didn't mean to impose. I suppose you're meeting someone."

"No, that's not the reason." He picked up a glass paperweight with a miniature lighthouse inside and turned it slowly as he studied it then put it back on the table. "Peter dropped by on his way home from work last night."

"No surprise about that. He's your brother."

"In name only. He wants you to stop helping me refurbish the B&B."

"I'm an adult in case you haven't noticed."

The dress, the high-heels, the perfume, yes, he had noticed. Trying *not* to notice was the problem. Ted leaned forward. "I'm not one for quoting the Bible, but I don't want a reenactment of Cain and Abel in my living room."

"And who would you be, Cain or Abel?"

"Either way, I would be a doomed man."

Fiona crossed the room and looked out the bay window. A lorry drove past, nearly drowning out her words. "I'll collect Bobby and take him back to my shop with me. Don't worry about us not going to Dublin, I'll get over it." She fiddled with a strand of pearls as she waited for an answer.

"I've had to get over a lot of things. It's Peter I'm worried about."

"I doubt it's that bad between the two of you."

"I haven't told you everything."

"That's kind of you," said Fiona. "Your Mum once told me that you were the sensitive one of the litter."

Ted winced. "Before I left for America mum told me, Teddy, don't forget she's your brother's wife."

"Your mum was one for dramatics, too."

Ted shook his head. "Not in this case. Peter suspects we were intimate when he went to France on business years ago."

Fiona walked back to the couch, picked up a velvet throw pillow and hugged it to her chest. "You left before daylight each morning."

Ted leaned forward. "Listen, love, somebody saw me leave, a neighbor perhaps. Peter also told me he tried to talk Dad out of leaving me the B&B if anything happened to him. He didn't want me coming back from America."

"What did you say? About the time he was away, I mean."

"Cheap talk, I told him. That's all."

Fiona walked to the window again, rested her shoulder against the frame as she watched the traffic on Lisburn Road. He moved towards her, hoping his timing wasn't off. "Bobby's changed a lot now that's he older." He moved closer until he was only a couple of inches from her. "Who's his dad, Fiona?"

She whirled around and faced him, eyes blazing. ""What nerve you have. Peter. Who else would his father be?"

There was no response from Ted and Fiona broke the silence by asking, "You don't think it's you, do you?

"I'm not wanting to think that, but I'm beginning to."

"You're a conceited bugger."

Ted instinctively stepped back, afraid she might slap him. "It's not just the physical resemblance. There was an entry in my calendar from that time that I'll never forget. Peter away on business. Nights with Fiona. That was nine months before Bobby was born."

Hands on hips, she stared back at him. "Don't you think I also had sex with my husband around the same time?"

Ted winced and reached for his glass of leftover Guinness. "Sex with Peter did not produce Bobby. He is nothing like Peter. Bobby's a genius or close to one."

"And you? What makes you so special?"

"I'm not missing half my brain cells from too much whiskey. Tell me love, have you noticed the birth mark on Bobby's neck? Or the mole on his cheek?"

"Coincidences," she said. "Nothing more than coincidences."

"You were hoping I wouldn't come back, weren't you? Dad once told me, I don't know why Fiona keeps saying, Ted is doing so well in the States. Encourage him to stay there."

Fiona stiffened. "Your dad was one for the bottle, too. Bobby is not your son. He's Peter's." She took a deep breath then exhaled slowly. "I'd better leave. I'll collect Bobby on the way to my car." She retrieved her purse from the couch and hitched the leather bag over her shoulder. "I feel guilty. That's what's troubling me."

Ted blocked her from moving. "How do you think I feel?" He rubbed his eyes and added, "But it's too late for that. I don't want Peter hurting you. We both know his temper, me as his brother and you as his wife."

"Peter is acting strange since you're been back in town. I don't know why. But I can take care of myself." When she reached the hallway, Ted followed and ended up beside her. "Let Bobby stay a while. But in future, it would be better if you asked Peter to collect the boy on his way home from work."

When she didn't move, Ted put his arms around her. She leaned against his shoulder. "It hasn't been easy remembering," he said.

Fiona lowered her head. "It's not easy for me, either. Since you've come back, I've been dreaming about stone walls. That's what I've surrounded myself with so I won't get hurt." She glanced at her watch. "I really should go. I promised my friend Bridget I'd visit her in hospital." She reached up and kissed Ted's cheek. He was about to lean over and kiss her on the lips when Bobby called out.

"Mum, Uncle Teddy, look at the book I used to identify birds." He held up a hardcover book titled "Birds of Northern Ireland." Meanwhile, Fiona slipped out from under Ted's arm while he turned abruptly and faced his nephew.

"That's wonderful," said Ted. He hadn't heard the door open and wondered how long Bobby had been standing there. "You've quite a good book there," he told him.

"I'm proud of you," said Fiona. She faced her brother-in-law. "Bobby is getting good grades in school, too, you know."

Bobby took off his glasses, wiped them on his shirt then smiled at his uncle. The boy's blue eyes appeared watery as usual, as if he had just pulled himself out of a pool.

"That's true," said Bobby. "I've no friends, though."

"You will," said Ted. "I was bookish like you, but I eventually made lots of friends."

"I've been waiting for friends my whole life," said Bobby. His mother and uncle laughed. "And it's been a long life, too, hasn't it?" said Fiona. "All of twelve years."

"I've another problem," said the boy, facing Ted. "I don't know what to call you."

"What do you mean?"

Bobby kept his hands cupped together as if he was about to accept a treat. "Should I call you Uncle Ted or Uncle Teddy?"

Teddy licked his lips. His mouth was dry from the stale beer. "I call myself Ted, but I'm still Teddy to our family. When I was your age, I was Teddy Boy, especially to your Granny."

Bobby pushed his glasses onto the bridge of his nose with his index finger. "You like to walk in the woods, don't you, Uncle Teddy?"

"I do."

"And you like bird watching?"

His uncle took a deep breath and nodded. "Sure, but why are you asking?"

"I've been thinking since you came back that I'm more like you than my dad."

Ted stepped back, nearly knocking over a lamp. "I'm your uncle, you know that."

Fiona moved next to her son. "What's going on?" she asked.

Bobby laid his book on the table next to the glass of beer as he faced his uncle. "Mum and Dad were arguing in their bedroom late last night. And I heard my dad say, "Why don't you leave? Go to Teddy's house and take Bobby with you. He's the boy's *real* father."

Fiona spun around and faced her son. "Bobby, listen to me: Arguments in our house are not Uncle Teddy's business." Her face suddenly turned pale and she appeared visibly shaken. Teddy held out his glass of beer and said, "I think you need this." She accepted his offer and drank quickly. "Bobby looked from his mother to his Uncle Teddy and said, "I know, but my dad doesn't love me. He never did. He's always punching me in the arm and saying, "Aren't I right, Bobby? Aren't I right?"

Ted caught Fiona's eyes. He wanted to ring her neck. Peter's been acting strange lately and she doesn't know why? That's what she told him just a little while ago.

"Don't exaggerate," Fiona told her son. "Your dad's just being playful."

Ted turned to Bobby. "Would you please step outside for a moment. I have to talk to your mum." As soon as the boy was out of earshot, Ted turned to Fiona. "You lied to me. You know why Peter is acting strange." Fiona covered her eyes with her hand. "I considered telling you earlier about last night, but I couldn't bring myself to repeat the awful things he said while he was drunk And he was plastered." She hesitated before adding, "I'm sorry."

"Sorry?" Ted answered. "It's too late for that. Too late for a lot of things. When did he fall off the wagon? After I got back?"

Teddy clenched his jaw and spat the words out in Fiona's face. "Drunk! Just another excuse. And what about you? When are you going to leave the abusive bastard? He just totaled your car. Wasn't that enough?"

Fiona twisted the silver bangles around her wrist. "I can't."

Ted starred at her. "It's not the church holding you back, is it?"

Fiona shook her head. "No. It's the fact I have two children."

"That's an excuse, too..."

The door opened and Bobby called, "Can I come in?"

Ted nodded as he moved closer to his nephew. "I want you to know, Bobby, that what your dad said to your mum isn't true."

"And you're not to repeat it," said Fiona.

Ted suddenly developed heartburn. It wasn't from the stale Guinness, either.

"Listen, Bobby," said Fiona, kneeling in front of her son. "Your dad was angry. He wanted to hurt me so he said something nasty."

"You don't have to cover up for him, Mum. He's not fooling me."

"Remember how nice he was when he stopped drinking? I wish he would stop again," said Fiona. "And I'm sorry you heard us arguing."

"You're forgiven, Mum, but there is something odd," said Bobby. "I look more like Uncle Teddy than my father. I've thought so for a long time."

"Nothing odd about that," said Ted. "You're my nephew."

Fiona rubbed her forehead, then glanced at her watch, twisting the leather band around her tiny wrist as she spoke. "Time to go. Visiting hours at the hospital will be over soon." Nobody moved. There was the sound of a lawn mower next door and a fly buzzing near an overhead light. Teddy walked to the window and slammed it shut. For a moment, the air in the room seemed to stop circulating.

Bobby stared at his mother. "Why are you all dressed up, Mum?"

"I told you I'm going to visit my friend in hospital. I chose this outfit to cheer her up."

"That was a grand idea," said Teddy. "I'm sure she's nothing else to think about."

"Why don't we talk?" said Bobby.

"We are talking," said Fiona. "That's why I'm late to visit Bridget."

Bobby's wire-rim glasses slid off the bridge of his nose again. "I mean a real chat." They moved into the sitting-room. Ted seated himself on the sofa near Fiona. Bobby sat opposite them, his feet dangling from the chair. He appears short for twelve, thought Teddy, but he'll probably catch up. All the McCullough boys did. Poor lad. His father pisses whiskey and his mother feels trapped. Ted glanced at his sister-in-law. She was tugging on the sleeves of her jumper.

"Shall I hang up your jumper?" Ted asked.

"No need," she said, laying it on the sofa. "I won't be staying long. I'll either visit Bridget in hospital or go back to my shop. I've customers coming to pick up dresses."

Ted smiled at Bobby. "What would you like to talk about?"

"We're alike in a lot of ways. I want to know something. Are you my dad?"

Ted uncrossed his long legs, nearly kicking himself in the shins. "No, I am not your dad. Do you realize what you're saying?"

"I do. And at first I was mad at my Mum. "

Fiona shook her head, as if unable to speak.

"Well, no reason to be mad at your Mum. I'm not your dad. I'm your father's brother, his youngest brother. Sometimes, nieces and nephews look more like an uncle than a parent. You're a bright boy," he said, raising his voice. "Can't you understand that?" He stopped abruptly and said, "Sorry, I didn't mean to shout at you."

Fiona knelt in front of her son, then reached up and grabbed his forearm. "Listen to me, Bobby. Your dad was angry. Even grownups say things they don't mean."

"I always say what I mean," said Bobby.

"No, you don't." said Fiona. "Remember this morning? You called your brother dumb because he spilled milk on his shirt."

"He is dumb."

"He's younger than you and can't read your books or do sixth form math. That doesn't make him dumb."

Ted was starting to sweat as he watched the boy staring straight ahead.

"I have an idea," said Bobby. "I'll have a test when I'm older. I read about that on Google. And I'll ask my dad to take one. You, too, Uncle Teddy."

Ted shook his head as if he hadn't heard correctly. "How do you even know about such a thing?" He ran his fingers through his hair. Of all five brothers, his hair was the thickest and darkest. Peter used to tease him by saying that was proof he was the black sheep of the family.

Fiona sat facing Teddy biting her lower lip. He wanted to stroke her cheek and whisper, "Everything will be all right, love, everything will be all right." He remembered her telling him once when Peter was drinking heavily and passing out, "People can die from lack of touch." She didn't say that she could die from not being touched, but that's what she was implying.

Bobby caught his eye and said, "You've been gone a long time, Uncle Teddy. You don't know that I'm in the gifted class in school. And I read on a college level."

"Your mum told me," said Teddy. 'I'm very proud of you." Fiona traced the outline of her upper lip with her index finger before speaking. "I've been thinking. It's not too late. I can still visit Bridget in hospital, even briefly." She turned and faced her brother-in-law. "Do you mind if I leave?"

"Yes, I mind. You should stay. This concerns you, too."

"I know, but poor Bridget is looking forward to my visit."

Bobby brushed a smudge of dirt off his knee. "Go ahead, Mum, don't worry about me. I won't discuss paternity tests with Uncle Teddy again, not for another six years, when I turn eighteen."

"Good," said Ted. *Very good.* He'll have sold the B&B by then and moved back to New York out of his brother's reach.

"Sure, go ahead," said Ted, facing his sister-in-law. "If it's that important, Fiona, visit Bridget in hospital. Bobby and I will be fine." She got up and kissed Bobby's cheek. "Be a good lad," she told him. "And try not to beat your uncle at chess." She was standing at the front door when Bobby caught up with her.

"Your jumper, Mum." She smiled as she threw the sweater over her arm and walked out the front door.

As soon as it was quiet, Ted watched Bobby walk to the bookcase and scroll his fingers across a row of books. "You've a lot of books, Uncle Teddy."

"I do. You will, too, one day." His nephew was still dressed in his school uniform: blue shorts and white shirt. He looks ordinary, thought Ted, like any other boy on the street. What price bril-liance? he wondered. "Listen, Bobby, a lot of children think they were adopted, or imagine they ended up with the wrong set of parents. I was certain I had been stolen from a king's palace."

Bobby grinned. "Maybe you were. Let's figure out the odds of that happening. Do you have a calculator?"

"Not handy," said Ted, reaching for his Guinness.

"Here's something interesting, Uncle Teddy. I'm teaching myself physics."

"That's wonderful."

"It is. I love math. I do equations in bed at night, especially when I want to shut out the sound of Mum and Dad arguing." Ted downed the rest of his drink. "I'm sorry to hear that. Anything interesting happen in school today?" he asked, hoping to change the subject.

Bobby looked up and smiled. "An author visited our class. She told us she's staying at a B&B. Is she stopping here?"

"I don't know. Describe her for me."

"She has yellow hair."

"In addition to yellow hair, how would you describe the woman who visited your school."

"She has a funny accent. I can't imitate it. She told us she's from New York."

"She is staying here." Ted took a deep breath as if he had just remembered to breathe. "Speaking of authors, I'm having a poetry reading here tonight. Can you help me arrange the chairs later?"

"Sure. Can I stay?"

"Sorry, old chap, it'll run past your bedtime." Bobby shrugged. "All right, but what shall we do today?"

"I can read to you or I can finish telling you the legend of Finn McCool."

"I like legends. But read today and finish the story of Finn McCool next time."

"It's a deal. Same book?"

Bobby nodded, then pulled a copy of *Beowulf* from the shelf. A leather bookmark protruded from the middle.

"I've a secret," Bobby said, seating himself opposite his uncle. "I sometimes pretend I am your son. I make believe we go to Dublin and buy lots of books and I keep some of them hidden in my room. My father wants me to spend less time reading and more time playing sports."

Ted smiled. "You're my favorite nephew, Robert Dennis McCullough. And if you want to *pretend* you're my boy, that's okay with me."

"I like that word, o-kay. Did you like living in America, Uncle Teddy?"

"I did."

"Did you come back because Grandpa left you the B&B after he died?"

Ted nodded as he shifted his weight deeper into the soft cushion. "You're a curious lad, aren't you?"

"I'm not a lad. I'll be a man soon. And. I'm going to start calling myself Robert." The boy bent down and adjusted his knee socks until they were even. "I have one more secret."

"What is it?"

Bobby's face brightened. "I am your son."

"Stop saying that. You heard your mum. Your dad was angry and wanted to hurt her."

"You said I can pretend."

"As long as you know the truth. You do know the truth, don't you?

There was silence for a long time before Bobby said, "Of course." As he brushed his hair back, his cowlick remained at attention, refusing to obey. "All right, we won't discuss the subject any further."

The boy took off his glasses and squinted. "I'd rather have you for my father. I sometimes wish my dad would leave and you would come and live with us."

The sitting room felt familiar yet strange. Despite its large size Ted felt claustrophobic and his forehead was sopping wet even though it was cool in the room. He should have sold the B&B after the reading of the will and returned to his flat in Brooklyn.

Bobby coughed. "You can start reading, Uncle Teddy."

Ted leaned back and took several deep breaths. "It's been a long day, painting and scraping, it's hard work refurbishing a B&B."

"Close your eyes and rest," said Bobby. "That's what my Mum always tells me when I don't feel well. I can read to you, if you'd like."

"Give me a moment, I'll feel better." The color drained out of the room and Ted heard a buzzing sound before he suddenly slumped forward, hands splayed on his knees. When he opened his eyes, the room zoomed back into focus and Bobby was handing him a glass of water.

"Uncle Teddy... Uncle Teddy. Open your eyes."

Ted stared at his nephew.

"You scared me. I kept calling your name, but you didn't answer. I think you blacked out from all the hard work you've been doing."

"I did," said Ted, accepting the glass. "It's going to be all right," he murmured. *It's going to be all right, Son.* But he could never say that to Bobby. He could never call the boy 'Son.' I am the black sheep of the family, thought Ted. If I stay for the boy's sake that fecking brother of mine will probably try to kill me one night when he's drunk.

"What are you thinking about, Uncle Teddy?"

"How grand it will be for us to go birding together. You've a pair of binoculars, haven't you?"

"Of course. Mum bought me a pair a long time ago."

"And," Teddy continued, "when you turn eighteen _if_ you want a paternity test…"

"I don't really need it," said Bobby. "I can imagine the results. I'll tell you the results if I ever get them, but I'll never tell my dad, it would be a blow to him." He bent down and readjusted his socks. "You know, Uncle Teddy, he hasn't been all bad to me. He encouraged me to take advanced math." The boy's right eye started twitching. "But poor Mum, we'll never tell her the truth." He brushed the cowlick down. "Did you hear me, Uncle Teddy?"

"I did. No, we won't tell her," he said, picking up the book. *No need to tell her, he decided. She knows.*

"Come, sit beside me," said Teddy, patting the cushion next to him. "We'll tackle *Beowulf* together.

About the Author

Author of four books for young people, published by Houghton Mifflin, Barefoot Books, and Scholastic (2) as well as a produced playwright. My mystery titled ONE WILL: THREE WIVES will be published by Adelaide Books. You can read about me at: www.edithtarbescu.com

Celebration

by Magdalena Blazevic

Darling, my days are mournsome. The morning began with a rotting southerly. The street was empty, just wet leaves and plastic bags. The bare park was strangled in water. The windows across the street were asleep. Only one was yellow at the top of the building, cut in two by a taut clothesline. A black silhouette of a female, arms raised high. Pointy antennae tearing the sky.

The room is stale with alcoholic fumes, my prints are missing from the cold bed.

He sleeps on his back. His mouth half-open, black.

My forehead is pulsating sharply.

The pill is bitter, the water tasteless.

Nights are quiet celebrations. You always come at the same time. As festive as this one now. I close my eyes and the rain is drumming. Copper lights flash in the crystal flowers. You're in the armchair, taking a forceful drag of your cigarette. A gentle spasm on your face. The shallow, gentle hollows become deeper and go darker. You exhale terrible shadows into the air. Your muscles relax slowly and only then do you look at me. Lust contained in the gaze.

The light quickens my step. French toast and mugs of milk on the table. The marmalade jar half empty. The windows are wide open, the curtains swaying to and fro. The smell of crumbs on the child's fingers. In the mornings his body is slow and clumsy. His eyes are misty and bloodshot. Some of their fire returns when he uses his pet name for me. Psycho!

The door slams. The clock ticks, the dishes clatter. The chest pain weakens, and tap water runs warm.

Look around you and you will see that nothing here is yours. Keys and a leather wallet in the bowl under the mirror. Untied shoes in the hallway. Always in the same place. A few ironed shirts in the wardrobe. They smell of white washing powder.

All your things I carry with me.

At your touch the radio makes a loud noise. I make a face and cover my ears. You laugh and turn the black dial in a kaleidoscope of sound. Quiet music emanates, as fragile as delirium. It overpowers our bodies. The crystal bouquet above us is a diffused eddy.

During the day, things are proud and bright, and I deflate and decay. The steel pad is sharp under the skin. Like frost and thorns. Flaking nails. On the dining room table, I've placed a bouquet of garden flowers. From yellow to red. I bought it at the market today. The woman's face was grey, her fingers red.

They'll last you all week. You won't regret it.

The paper in my hand rustled. The white bag stretched. Two large pomegranates in the plastic bag. Healthy and ripe. Fresh meat. In the other, a child's hand was trying to break free. On my squeeze it responded with scars, as thin as a razor.

I bought a newspaper on the way. The threatening headings remained spread out on the table.

Oh, how nice it was when we met today by the department store. My heart drove me crazy. It fluttered. At one point our coat sleeves brushed against each other. I don't know if you noticed.

The child was crying nervously. I sat down on a bench and watched you walk away. Your collar raised against the wind. Hands in pockets. You turned left into Radnicka street. Your flat at number 53, on the third floor. I waited for you to come back, but you didn't. I'll be there again tomorrow.

I hurried home. The child's legs could barely keep up.

In the hall, the smell of beef stock mixes with a current of cold, stale air from the cellar. I never go down there, but from the top of the stairs I look at the broken handrail like a seductive river eddy. You only need to bend over far enough. My neck would probably snap, my shoes fall off. I would lie there with my eyes closed. My hair spread all over the place. The doors to the flats would creak, women scream. And what would you say then?

Nothing in the mail box from you. Just long envelopes with bills.

At twilight, a familiar sound on the parking lot in front of the building. The motor falls silent, a door slams. Pots brought to the boil. The pasta's been overcooked. The lids are red hot. On the table, the spoons shine. In the haze, atoms of grease stick to the walls. From the window I can see his black coat and the whitish mist rising from the parking lot towards me. As thin as the smoke of your cigarette.

His kisses are snotty. I scrape them off with my sleeve. He raises the child high in the air. He screams loudly. A spasm of fear on his face.

The night is still a long way off.

The glasses on the table next to us are empty. The tapping on the tin window sill gets weaker. We lie down and pull the covers over our heads. Can you feel the darkness?

Your breath is sweet, and your skin is woven with silk thread. Your fingers find me.

With the darkness, my steps become silent. My voice is a lullaby. I remain lying in the child's room, in the dark. I don't have to wait long before I hear his rough breathing. Torn like a rag.

My steps are quiet.

I sit before the mirror and comb my hair for a long time. In the reflection, his suit is thrown over the chair. Limp limbs. I don't dare move it.

I see you out at the break of dawn. I've swallowed my tears. Go, you mustn't be here in the fateful moment.

If we meet today, we may speak to each other. I'll ask you if you dreamt anything. You'll rest you hand on my shoulder while talking. Your eyes would be bronze.

If you're not around, I'll greet the twilight and patiently wait for night.

About the Author

Magdalena Blažević (1982) is a short-story writer from Bosnia and Herzegovina. She was born and grew up in Žepče, a small town in Central Bosnia. She studied English and Croatian Literature in Mostar where she lives and works. Her first short-story collection "Celebration" was published this year.

Hunter's Cabin

by Donny Barilla

Through the drooling jaws of Summer, I swerved and dashed my way to the great, ancient oak which held the branches as a canopy, holding thick arms, loosening few droplets of rain and motioning these trickling beads tender and chilled across my long chestnut hair. As the chill of the surmounting clutch of falling night, tapered through the sweetly scented groom of the earth, and soil of the earth, I felt a gushing patterned splash of heavy rain as each wave of the winds shifted upon the loosened floods, rising in both drench and deepened valley. Swift and hurried, I sprinted through the cold, flooding water and ran for the pine woods which rested and haunched upon the mountain groves which spread in far distance and spoke, held the banquet for the rising sun.

As the reach of the rising path which lay coated and pressed in a thickened layer of shatter needles and a calm spread of cones, chipped and crunched fractures of the depleted wooden curves, I sat upon the currently dry gesture of the passed tampering rain, I curled beneath the evergreens and slumbered in the prison of my own flesh and vessel of a fragrant cluster of saps and greens.

The winds slowed and depleted at the base of the coats of sweat as my green and towering cliffs smoothly held a draft of the tensing breath as this morning hour brought me to the thickness of the burlap poncho which held me in a warming grip.

I last saw him upon the tallest cliff of the mountain pass which drove one in madness as one would if that person attempted the dusty and level groove upon the deep of the earth. 'Hickory Cliff' held the climber of the sheer face which grew more difficult by the tensions of each muscle, pulled muscles stung it's way upon me. His name, 'Sandol' left himself to hold furiously on Hickory Cliff, where he found food and drink from the gushing spring and berries and nuts upon the scattered trees. I slithered my way on to the mad clearing on the tallest cliff which left me panting and gasping for air.

With measured time, I stood and looked upon myself with the absence of the poncho. My thin cotton shirt was pasted in a translucent pressing sweat. Every inch of these khaki pants clung to my twitching, trembling and weakened legs only to motion to the cool fastening air. Here, I stood and looked upon the thick, green pasture and glen and so slowly, every grassy spear waived with the snip and soft breeze of the flourishing wind. I watched the sun pass the crest of the mountain reach and intensively, I saw the shadow of the dense, wild groove where the wealthy spread of the forest sulked upon the approach of powders and their ivory coat. The trees hung and frowned in defeat and floundering sorrow which soothes the frost of the woodland soil and patter of the calming of the dust.

Having restored my breath to a steady press, I looked on the cliff top and saw the smaller pine trees only to grow taller and thicker by size as I wandered the dusty clay surface of Hickory Cliff. In a tense and eager moment, rays of the pounding sunshine groomed their way past the forest and shot a large grip of the mountains which cherished each evergreen pine and warmed from weed to tall trembling tree branches, hosting the Autumn breath.

I reached the trickling spring which sponged into my emptiness and parched leathery tongue, only to drink in heaving gulps and fill the goblet of my stomach and basin of my jaw. Upon taking a deep breath of spirited air, I returned to the endless valley of the caverns Hickory Tree which motioned with the direction of the winds, only in a wild madness which did not need direction only the passion of the pulsing company which trembled through each leaf and crooning sound of the bark.

"Eko, Eko, I wait for you by the Hickory Tree. I breathe your arom and hear the patterns of your footsteps. I have waited for you for a tremendously long time. The Hickory Tree seems eager and excited to see you. Perhaps you could bring me a drink of fresh water? I miss you and I need to see you," Sandol spoke with tenderness and an arousal of an all but forgotten crawl of this early Winter.

There, I found him resting beneath the tree and crouched with the face and withering stature of an old man in a very old majestical place. Wearing a thin tan colored shirt and a woven pair of leather pants, he held his feet in a slip of old sandals. He wore dozens of necklaces and medallions around the frailty of his neck. Nearby, he rested an old hiking stick which held the dark color burgundy and came near to matching the color of his years of burnt flesh. As I looked upon his loosening, receded hair, each thread rested upon his scalp the blankness of the color of white.

"Hello Sandol. I hope you haven't waited for too long? I anticipate the smash of Winter , will groom and caress us soon. The woods grow weary and I see floods on top of floods. With each ounce of speed, I ran as a cat from the plains. I felt your anguish and age reach me. What can I do for you Sandol?" spoke Eko to the aged one beyond the woods.

In a steady reply, Sandol said, "Winter, as you stated, comes near. I need to reach the vast and heavy woods one last time before I leave and undergo the realm of the spirits. I once, years past, lived in a series of caverns and a wild man attacked me and took my most loved possession. I held this relic in a burlap satchel. It was a series of bones which made the Winter time tolerable and suitable for living. The wild man in mention lived in the Towering Mountain Chain many miles to the north. With a new eon arriving with the beginning of this Winter, all which will remain are the bones and peeling flesh of us who live upon this cliff, woods, pine mountains and fields."

Sandol sat in stillness and in silence for a great length of time. Slowly, I spoke to him and said, "What type of bones held so much power?"

"I have aged here and far beyond the woods. With or without the bones, I will not live past this Winter. I am weak, frail and ready to encounter the spirits which have spoken to me for so long. I think of death and I tremble. I think of an endless Winter and I shake in madness. Please, Eko. These creatures live on the top of those great mountains and live in caves. Follow the route to the northern valley and you will be very close. If you hurry, you will arrive in time,

Bring the bones to me. I know you can run, so please, do so." He spoke with passion curling like a spirit off his wilting tongue.

Calmly, I spoke to Sandol and said, "I will leave in a moment. If I do not survive, I want to spend a few moments with you."

The flexing fog which thrives upon the Autumn breeze suckled across the dusts and pebbles which scattered beneath the threading steps of my nimble feet. Several hours past and I headed north. I reached a cabin mostly used by hunters. Upon trying to see if anyone lurked beyond the old wooden door of the old wooden cabin, I struggled to defeat as the fog grew thicker and higher and dragged a threading of calm mist.

I listened and heard the popping of shuffled feet which scraped across the gravel on the woodland path. In the dash of a moment, I felt cool, sharp steel against my neck as a large, heavy man stood before me. I stood motionless and all revealed. The man before me wielded a thick large axe and grinned as the person behind me covered my head in a satchel. I panicked and felt the breath I took begin to dwindle.

The agony continued for a length of time which I will never forget. With the thick joust of penises, I began to vomit a heavy measure of blood as every moment felt like ages. Now, in the moment when darkness shrouds the light, I moved freely toward the nearby creek. I washed my mouth and brought myself to a more decent position for running, preferably as the speed of a cheetah. Needing to focus, I desperately tried with great effort to reach the Northern pass and scout vigorously for caves.

I felt my legs tighten and immerse themselves in a quickening height of speed. As I motioned closer to the mountainous caverns, I solemnly thought of Sandol and our many years of most tender friendship. He remains the last of a long line of Spirit Dwellers which finds him as a companion of the chanting moans of brethren and fellowship. I stayed as his companion for as long as my memory would allow. I tossed my other companion aside and things such as the hunter's cabin which I thrashed through my weaving memory in an effort to ignore and defy. The longer I strode across the vastness of the mountain chain, the more passion surged through my legs.

In the distance, I smelled and saw the threads of smoke which arrived in their cave as a chunk of meaty flesh and noisy people which seemed to celebrate, something.

Upon making a closing distance to the entrance of the cave which clutch to the lowered and sprouted on the mountainside, I crouched tenderly behind a large boulder which seemingly once rested for reasons I could not discern. I stayed in a hidden position and will continue to do docsso until the hours grow darker and the cave becomes more silent, much more.

Hours passed and the fullness of the moon crept beyond the clouds which meshed in a shade of marble gray and heather gray. Billows of thick smoke reached to the width of the collapsing dome of the sky and the growth upon the earth halted beneath me in a fumbling frost which coated the soil in these mountain chains. Shaking from a heavy dose of fear and the madness it will take to enter the deep of this cavern, alive with the wild people Sandol spoke of and most likely feared. I felt the odds stood as insurmountable and gripped me with fear.

I shifted slightly and peered into the cave which held about three dozen wild people and all seemed thoroughly asleep. In the back portion of the cave slept a woman who most probably played the role of the medicine woman as she laid painted in the color red and held various hues and shades. She held a look of antiquity as she poised in a needled breast and hosted many tattoos and gripped a sack in the grip of her left hand. I removed a knife from my well gripped satchel and I made way for the medicine woman who looked near death herself. I moved as a cat would move and silently motioned upon the slick and cluttered floor of the cave. The fire had been doused and all seemed silent. I wept for what I edged forward to do. Reaching the edge and curve of where she slumbered, I swiftly sliced her across the throat and watched for a moment as the blood gushed and coated each inch of her body. She could not breath and died without making a sound.

The bones rested in the bag. I turned and witnessed a thickly compact scattering of bodies which lay motionless and seemed to sleep far into the deep of night, the conquering quest of morning. Upon having left the deep of the cave, I pressed my feet on the pebbled road and in a sliver of a gesture, I ran with speed I might never duplicate.

Reaching near the cabin which I dreaded passing, I looked at the haunting place which struck me with lathering terror and a grip of madness which I held for the duration of the passage. I almost reached the thin trail which would eventually take me to the cliffs which held the Hickory Tree. I saw, out of my corner of my eye, the man with an axe which threw the weapon. I fell to the earth and drifted to the spirits of the forest deep. I wandered and felt the passions of my brethren and the endlessness which now courts me to the deep and depth where I assemble in trembling bliss.

About the Author

He writes avidly and reinvents his poems with renewed enthusiasm. Topics such as the transitions of death, intimacy,
sexuality, mythology and nature find their way upon his page
with invention, intense imagery, metaphoric thought and the
enigmatic relation of man and nature which coat the background of his poems and flood the pages from his creative
palate. From poem to poem, each image and blending sounds
as the words fluidly possess the reader, one finds oneself in a
sweet and delectable arena of literature, an open captive wade
into the ocean of turning pages. With the demanding pulse of
heavy language, these poems embody the spirit of trembling
phrases and beautiful metaphors.

FINALISTS

Melody Sinclair

Impersonating a Civilian

Anne woke to Scott rustling in his nightstand drawer, probably looking for that horrible orange gum, the sex gum. He unwrapped the wad, masticating with slurping and sucking noises, like what Anne imagined a greedy nursing baby would sound like. She pulled a pillow over her head and held her breath against the fermented fruit of death.

"Wanna?" He rubbed his hand on her naked hip.

"What time is it?" she asked.

There were a thousand questions she should have asked instead. Since when did they wake before the sun? Why did he chew gum that smelled like carcass when they had sex? Why did he confine their lives to this suburban hellscape? But lately, Anne only questioned if she was certain she could handle the answer.

"It's early," he mumbled into her neck as he rolled on top of her. His body was softer than she was accustomed to, bone and muscle slowing receding into doughy flesh. She missed his hard edges but knew that other women found his dad-bod and silvering hair appealing.

The gum's complex musk assaulted Anne's face as she twined her legs around Scott's back. Her mouth betrayed her, saliva pooling and running down her throat. Scott chewed and suckled rapidly, finishing before Anne, and rolling away. Since he started chewing the gum three months ago, Anne became a sperm receptacle, the fruity rot obliterating her chances at orgasm.

Scott nestled into his pillow, his eyelids heavy, the gum resting like a tumor in his cheek. "Marry me, Anne," he said, before sliding into deep breathing, as if asleep.

He'd been asking since they moved here, always after sex, and the question was so routine that it no longer held any meaning. Anne rolled over, facing a framed picture of them in the black sand at Punalu'u Beach. It was back when they owned a duffel bag of clothes between them and traveled on stolen money. They were alive then, rich in spontaneity that extended to their income, location, and especially sex. Anne could maybe grow accustomed to living in one place and working an honest job, but she'd never acclimate to their boring sex life. They used to make love during thunderstorms on beaches with the ocean waves crashing dangerously close. Anne missed coupling in sticky bathrooms in remote locales, behind hidden waterfalls, in empty cornfields, and by frostbitten lakes. Never once had Scott breathed artificial citrus in her face and requested that she enter a lifetime of lockdown.

His hand slithered onto her belly, and he whispered. "It's amazing to think this could be the beginning of life. We could have our own miracle. Plus, having a baby would bring your dad back around."

His premature paternal joy sent shivers of revolt through Anne. She bit back the truth that threatened to escape during moments like this: there would be no baby because she hadn't stopped her birth control. Never would.

Anne swept his hand away and sat up, suddenly remembering a Men's Health article about sexual conditioning that Scott had shown her months ago. The author argued that Pavlov's classical conditioning experiments, getting dogs to drool when they heard a dinner bell, could be used in humans' sex lives. He recommended using the same scent during each sexual encounter, like a candle, or cologne, *or gum*. At the time, Scott had rolled his eyes and declared it ridiculous, but now Anne understood that she was being conned.

"Have you been—"

"Think the contractor's going to show today?" Scott interrupted. He was jokingly referring to his best friend, Gary, who was also the contractor.

Anne struggled to think of a response, but couldn't care to comment. The house was *his* dream home, an abandoned horse property nestled on the edge of the Colorado prairie, straddling the border between suburbs and wilderness. With the help of his parents' money, Scott's house-related passions varied by week. When they first moved in, he fought against the encroaching backcountry. He hatched plans to eradicate the native yucca, sagebrush, and wild grasses in favor of stamped concrete, decks, paint, plantings, and border walls. Scott then learned about sustainability from a gardening class at the community college. He ripped out the newly planted hydrangeas, turf, and roses, citing water conservation and prairie-management. He replaced the lawn with magnificent swaths of a twenty-foot grass called Giant Reed. The next week Scott seemed devastated to learn that Giant Reed was an invasive species that reduced wildlife habitats, fucked with the floodplain, and increased wildfire risk. He called Gary back, opting for the original plan of stamped concrete wilderness, and moved on to picking wallpaper for the foyer.

The only house-adjacent activity that Anne enjoyed was standing among the hollow canes that impersonated native plants. She surveyed the Front Range peaks as they stabbed their snow-tipped daggers to Heaven and estimated how many people happily died hiking to the top.

Anne palmed her phone and scrolled to the analytics page for their blog, LuxyLifestylers, turning on the bed to hide the screen from Scott. The last spike in visitors had been back in Florida when she'd posted that hot picture of him. Now the blog was dead, and checking the numbers every morning amounted to poking the carcass with a stick. She rummaged through the duffel bag at her bedside for clean clothes.

"When will you unpack that nasty green thing?" he asked, running a finger down her spine.

"I thought you liked Army green," Anne said, stroking the bag like a pet. "You liked Sergeant's rainbow straps." Her face burned. Resurrecting the bag's nickname was a mistake.

"The empty dresser's yours," he said, stiffer now. "Closet's waiting. Dump Sergeant in the trash when you're done—that thing's festering with all kinds of germs and bad juju."

Anne dressed, thinking about how to fight back, but Scott's newfound sense of morality was impossible to penetrate. Her refusal to unpack and live in the honest home that Scott's trust fund had made for them probably seemed ridiculous. But no matter how many weeks drifted by, she couldn't bring herself to view this as a permanent situation.

She posed in front of the full-length mirror, pleased that she was still slim, that her raven hair was full, and her eyes bright. It couldn't last forever, though. Scott was the kind that would leave the moment her face wrinkled and find a pliant girl resembling a younger Anne.

Scott's sly attempt to lure her in only aggravated her already frazzled nerves. He bought her gifts like blenders, monogrammed towels, bathmats, and spatulas. There were gadgets

Anne didn't understand like cherry pitters, panini presses, and shoehorns. How did Scott know to need such things? He held a frightening and hidden domestic depth, only exasperated by his ticking biological clock. Anne had plastered on wooden smiles when presented with such gifts. She would thank him, but never unbox the items. Perhaps soon, Scott would understand that her silence spoke volumes.

"Smell that?" she asked, pulling back the drapes.

"Smoke," Scott said, jumping out of bed and running to the window. "Holy shit, wildfire!"

Both of their phones chimed an emergency alert, and Scott fumbled to read his screen. "It's an evacuation order," he said, his voice quaking.

"Voluntary," Anne said, checking her own phone. "It's not that close." She wasn't lying, but she was omitting information, which was next door to a lie. She didn't share the facts that she knew, that the wind could shift at any moment and put them in grave danger, that a voluntary evacuation was a baby step away from a blazing inferno. A warm glow radiated through her chest.

Anne had never seen Scott so pale or frantic. As he scrambled to dress, he fell to the floor, one leg in his jeans and the other treading uselessly at the cream carpet. It was difficult to reconcile that this was the same man who'd run with the bulls in Spain, swam with sharks in the Bahamas, and pickpocketed titans of industry at five-star beach resorts without breaking a sweat. Shame tightened her chest, and instead of watching him struggle, Anne descended the staircase. She weaved through the cavernous house until she reached the sliding doors to the back.

As she stepped outside, a jackhammer pulsed, pleasantly rattling her from the feet up, sending bits of broken concrete into her uncombed hair. On the horizon, maybe a mile away, an orange line of fire engulfed the crispy prairie, spewing black pillars of smoke into the wind.

"Gary's working during a wildfire?" Scott yelled from behind her, the odor of rotted orange gum still overpowering the smoke. "He won't even work when it's raining."

A gust of hot wind sent the smoke spiraling. The distant flames licked higher, nearly touching the helicopters that dropped water and powdery retardant. Gary jackhammered, seemingly oblivious to the approaching inferno. His forearms and face jiggled, giving him a blurry appearance. Anne walked away from Scott's shouts of warning to the back of their property, trying to get a closer view of the blaze. Small rodents scrambled over her tennis shoes to escape the flames.

The distant roar of the fire and the jackhammer's pounding brought to mind the same chaos as the Grand Bazaar in Istanbul or surfing in Australia. This wasn't quite the same as a half a million visitors haggling with merchants. Waves weren't hurtling her against the rocks of Bondi Beach. Still, a dead piece of her reanimated in the face of the destruction. For the first time in months, her legs no longer itched to move.

Anne sat on a pallet of stone at the edge of the yard. The jackhammer's vibrations tickled up her sit bones and through her spine. Scott ping-ponged between her and Gary, yelling, "It's too hard to breathe. How can you breathe?" She ignored his useless questions and studied the firemen protecting her as if she were a real civilian, someone worthy of their sacrifice.

For decades, Anne's civilian title wasn't in question. Her dad, a single father, and a retired police officer had started each day by kissing her goodbye. He hitched up his uniform pants under his beer belly, loudly proclaiming, "Got to go protect and serve my favorite civilian." Anne grew up understanding that a civilian wasn't about absence, someone who *didn't* serve in the military, police, or fire department. A civilian was worthy of help from others, someone to be guarded and protected. The last time she was a civilian had been in Florida.

"One more big score to keep us afloat. Give us more time for the blog to earn money," Anne had said, squinting into her computer screen.

Her tank top suctioned to her back, hot and wet in the unforgiving sun. They'd been lounging poolside at the Four Seasons near Disney World for hours, arriving early enough to avoid the pool staff and their snooty questions about room numbers and keycards. Like all of their "pool days that pay," as Scott had termed it, they had to wait hours for a suitable mark.

"Let's get enough to get the hell out of Orlando. Hate it here," Anne mumbled, removing her wet top. "What are you feeling next? International again?"

"We don't have enough to go abroad. Montauk, maybe Nantucket," Scott said. "Or I could ask my parents for money." He scooped pool water into his cupped hand, rubbing it over his oiled torso.

"Let me get a pic," Anne said. "Your abs are popping. Move, so the palm tree's behind you. Stand by the Four Seasons sign."

Anne snapped the photo from her computer and opened the filtering app. Scott was delicious clickbait on his own, but a little enhancement pushed him over the top. She posted the doctored photo to their social media platforms with a cute caption, adding the hashtag of their blog, #LuxyLifestylers.

"We don't need to rely on your parents so much. I wouldn't say the traffic to our site has spiked," Anne said, toggling back to the blog statistics, "but slowly climbed is accurate. We should be getting noticed, getting sponsored."

Scott ground his teeth, jutting his jawbone forward in an unflattering way that made him look malnourished.

"Spit it out," Anne said. "And stop making that face. It's horrible."

"This is the last time," he said, running a hand through his shaggy hair. "My parents bought the property for me in Colorado. I'm tired of hurting people—"

"Of course, they did," Anne mumbled. "We don't hurt people! We take money from rich assholes that can afford a loss…" She trailed off because of the pinched look on Scott's face. It was a look that informed her that *he* was a rich asshole that could afford a loss. He'd only joined Anne in her cons because he'd been bored with college, bored with his fraternity brothers, bored with marriage-track sorority sisters, and bored with his family's second home in Aspen. For Anne, this was a way of life, but maybe a decade of stealing was starting to bore Scott too.

She pulled her hair off her neck. "Besides, the blog—"

"The blog's not going to do shit," Scott interrupted. "It amounts to a cute scrapbook of our world travels. That's all it'll ever be." He laced his hands behind his neck and leaned back, the cocktail waitress openly stared. "Don't you want something more stable? We're getting too old for this."

Anne received the words like a punch, bending her legs onto the chair to hug them. They were in their early thirties, but she suddenly felt ancient. "Too old," she repeated quietly into her knees. He didn't outright say so, but Anne was sure that Scott was referencing their last mark in Sarasota. She'd been tasked with seducing and distracting the gentleman while Scott took the mark's bags. Anne had done everything short of strip, but the man remained too alert, almost annoyed by her advances. "Sorry, ma'am," he said. "I don't date older women."

Anne scanned the pool area, pretending to forget about Scott's insult. "There," she said. "That's our mark. Easy."

Anne nodded toward an obese woman with three children and armloads of pool toys. The smallest girl was bald and wore a t-shirt that read, Make-A-Wish Hero.

"Really?" Scott groaned. "I told you I'm not down with stealing, and you want to take from charity?"

"It's your turn," Anne said. "As you've pointed out, I'm getting too old for this."

"That's not what I—"

"Plus, you know they're not total charity cases," Anne said. "Why are they staying at the fucking Four Seasons? Look at that wad of cash she's flashing for drinks. You're up, Mr. Charming. We'll talk more about your new moral code when we have a room and a shower."

The kids jumped into the water, and Scott approached the mark, snuggling up in the lounge chair next to her. Anne marveled at how these broken women uniformly believed that he was interested in them. Scott's smarmy voice layered fake praise so loudly that Anne could hear it from across the pool. The mark sat straighter, giggled, and batted her lashes. Sometimes that voice was all it took. Other times, Scott touched their arms or their faces, literally grabbing a mark's chin to direct their attention to his eyes. Occasionally a kiss was in order, usually, at the moment Anne snatched their belongings. It created in Anne an exhilarating high with notes of righteous recrimination. Hopefully, a monetary loss would shatter the delusions of these disgusting women.

Scott stroked the woman's curls while Anne stole the bloated purse and a duffel bag that looked like Sergeant, same rainbow handles, and everything. She exited the pool deck with both her bag and the mark's, forcing a leisurely pace as she strolled down a never-ending sidewalk to the front of the hotel next door.

Scott took longer than usual to meet her. Sometimes these women were clingers, so Anne sat in the lobby and tore through the stolen purse hoping for enough money to leave fucking Florida. The purse was brimming with junk—granola bars, tissues, paperbacks, and stolen hotel pens. Anne fumed as she dumped the items in a nearby trashcan. It was rare that people were careful with their belongings, using the room safe as recommended, but it happened on occasion. She poked her head out and scanned the sidewalk, no sign of Scott, before opening the duffel that matched Sergeant. Mounds of hand-worn cash filled the bag. This woman couldn't have been a stripper, but Anne was hard-pressed to explain the rumpled ones and fives. She straightened the bills like a bank teller while counting.

Something in the bag poked her hand, and Anne removed a thick card with a cartoon picture of spaghetti on the front, the font made from the noodles: "Spaghetti Dinner! All donations support Lexi's Disney World dream!" Later, Anne understood that if she were going to feel remorse, it should have been then. Her mom had died of cancer before Anne could make memories with her—she should have a depth of emotion about stealing from charity. Instead, she operated as she always did. She remembered having read a stolen paperback, *The Fault In Our Stars,* by John Green. She'd failed to cry for the cancer-stricken lovers, but she did agree with one sentiment from the book. Disney World was a fucking stupid Make-A-Wish destination when the whole real world was at your fingertips. Did cancer kids have that little imagination, or had Walt Disney somehow strong-armed the Make-A-Wish people?

When Anne looked up, still thinking about the book, she barely registered a teary-eyed Scott standing beside her with two officers. She'd been traveling with Scott for years, and the only time he came close to crying was when he got sand in his eyes in Brazil.

"You hurt?" she asked Scott.

"That's her," Scott said to the officers. "That's the woman that took the bags."

Anne was too confused to flee. Instead, she gathered Sergeant and his twin to her chest, as if the officers were there to take her bounty.

Their remaining time in Florida slowed to a stagnant trickle. Scott hadn't been arrested because he cooperated and claimed not to have known what Anne was doing. It didn't hurt that the fat woman from the pool still believed they had a legitimate connection. Scott explained his betrayal as a benefit—it was better for only one of them to be in jail so one could help the other.

Anne shrugged off the deception but continued to question Scott's new remorseful persona. Why did he cry and apologize when he didn't get caught, when no one was looking?

Anne's dad flew to Florida to bail her out and hire a fancy lawyer that he likely couldn't afford. Her charges were reduced from robbery to pickpocketing. Because of the lucky-look-alike bag and no one finding the discarded purse, the fancy lawyer argued that Anne had a "good faith belief" that she was the owner of the taken property. Anne was sentenced to community service and fines. After the judge banged his gavel, Anne's dad issued an additional sentence.

"You're not a civilian anymore, Annie," he'd said, his skin sallow under the courthouse's florescent lights. "Criminals are a category all their own, breaking the law, working against civilians. You've broken my heart. Don't come home until you've straightened out."

Anne watched, as if from a great distance, while Scott cried and begged her dad for forgiveness. He blubbered promises about doing good in the world, creating a family, and settling down. Anne fought to feel as devastated as Scott, but the only emotion she could summon had been confusion. Scott had found morality at no cost and no consequence. Anne's price was her civilian status and her dad. Why was he making her problems part of his?

"Evacuation order!" Scott screamed, brandishing his cellphone. "Mandatory now!" He ran back into the house.

Gary seemed to have heard because he stopped the jackhammer and spit into the pile of rubble at his feet. "I still get final payment if she burns." He smiled at Anne a beat too long as if he expected her to laugh. "So…does he know?"

"Know?" Anne asked.

"That you hate him? I can see it plain as day on your face. Think Scott gets it?" Gary asked.

Anne inhaled the Sulphur deep into her lungs and considered the frumpy, but observant, man in front of her. "Hate is a strong word," she said. "I don't hate Scott. I'm just not finding him useful anymore."

"You know, I've been with him since high school," Gary said, wiping sweat from his forehead. "I'm going to tell him."

Anne was sure that she couldn't use Gary in any way, and even more sure that she was dealing with an amateur. A contractor was likely only the beginning of an army of household help. Scott would eventually hire gardeners, painters, cleaners, and more. She should take control now while it was still simple.

"Try. See what happens," Anne said in her threateningly soft voice. "The fact is, *I've* been with him all these years. *I'm* the one he wants to spend the rest of his life with." She brushed some soot from Gary's shoulder. "It would be a shame for the owner of Front Range Construction to face assault charges."

"What?" Gary's face turned a delightful shade of purple. "I've never—"

Scott stuck his head out of the sliding door. "Go! Evacuate!" he shouted at Gary, before yanking Anne's arm, pulling her back from the beautiful destruction, into the house.

"You pack the kitchen. I'll get the photos," he said.

Anne couldn't think of a single necessary item from the overdone kitchen. "Scott, this isn't a move. Just throw some clothes into Sergeant."

"What about the fish? Oh my God, the fish!" Scott ran to the tank in the foyer. Anne laughed at his idiocy—as if he weren't slowly killing the animals anyway with his fumbling attempts at care. A fire would be more merciful.

She rolled the backdoor open again, the wind had shifted, and the blaze was closer now, only one hundred yards away. Firefighters worked near the house, the flames gaining precious ground. Soot-streaked and earnest, the smoke-jumpers toiled, not realizing they were fighting to save criminals, non-civilians.

She climbed among the Giant Reed, listening to the crackling vegetation. The heat cleansed her face, and sparks sizzled against her skin. She willed one to lick into a flame and consume her deadened limbs.

Anne turned and studied the horrible house as Scott ran room to room, squirreling away his material goods. He talked aloud, grabbing throw pillows, table lamps, and takeout menus. He'd become wholly domestic in such a short time. Everything, including his bloated maggot-colored body, his need for a mortgage to tether him to earth, and his too-short fifty-dollar haircut, made him stand out as a mark. A flattering smile etched Anne's face as she walked back inside.

"Baby," she said, grabbing Scott's arm, slowing his frenzy. "You have insurance, right?"

"Insurance? Yeah. The Make-A-Wish event…we were supposed to host next week! I've got to call and let them know." He wrestled his cell phone from his pocket.

"They'll find some other sucker with a bleeding heart," Anne said, gently nudging his phone away. "Is there enough insurance to cover all of this?"

"More than enough. My parents got the...." He trailed off, his left eye crossing slightly before coming back to the room with Anne. "Yes, there's insurance," he said. His determined jaw weakened, his soft chins melting into his neck.

"Scott?"

"What?"

"Yes," Anne said. "I will marry you."

She slid her hand up Scott's back and marveled at how this broken man believed she was interested in settling down with him. Scott's gaze drifted toward the blaze outside, and Anne grabbed his chin to direct his attention to her eyes.

"Yes!" he said when her words finally registered.

He pumped a fist in the air and swung her into a hug. It created in Anne the familiar exhilarating high with notes of righteous recrimination. Perhaps down the road, Scott's loss would shatter his delusions of domestic bliss.

"I can't wait until you're my wife," he said.

"Me too," she said and moved his hand to her flat stomach. "I can't wait until we meet our baby. I have a good feeling about today. Now, go throw some clothes into Sergeant, and let's evacuate."

Scott moved toward the stairs, but Anne stopped him short, resting a hand on his arm.

"We have a lot of planning to do, but I was thinking... destination wedding?" she asked in her best impersonation of a civilian.

Insurance Against Extinction

Lee bit into his PB&J and watched Bono, the dominant Silverback Gorilla, knucklewalk from the back of his enclosure to the front. Bono stood upright near a puddle, reaching his full height of six feet. Even though Lee had seen him do it before on rainy days, it was still unsettling. Despite fitting every depiction of King of the Jungle, Bono also exhibited several endearing high-maintenance attitudes, like never allowing his giant hands to drag through the mud.

Bono sat by the glass closest to Lee's bench, his leathery face reproachful. Lee's tendency toward anthropomorphism was on point when it came to Bono; he believed he could read subtle emotions like awe and even amusement. Bono eyed Lee's sandwich slyly before looking away. Lee yearned to look his friend in the eyes but had learned to love the gesture instead. For gorillas, direct eye contact meant a challenge. Lee didn't want Bono to feel like he had to be territorial with him.

"I know, man, I'm sorry," Lee said around a bite of sandwich. "It's been what, three months? There was a pandemic, you know." Lee grabbed his face mask from the bench and waved it in the air. "Where's *your* mask?" Bono scratched his potbelly in lazy circles and focused his heavy-lidded gaze somewhere near Lee's shoes. "They're making me wear this damn thing all day at work now, as if business attire weren't torture enough." Bono slapped his thighs as if in agreement.

"Barely got in here today, you know," Lee continued, loosening his tie. "They're limiting zoo guests. Luckily, the season pass puts me to the front of the line." Bono foraged a sunflower seed from the dirt, letting it rest on his lip before pushing it into his mouth. Lee paused, looking behind him to make sure they were alone. "I've missed you, man."

Lee had spent every lunchbreak for five years at the bench by Bono's exhibit. His office, the only office he'd been at since graduating from college and since Sarah left, was just a short walk to the zoo. Lunches with Bono went long, but he preferred working later to make up the time he took midday.

He wasn't sure what made Bono take notice of him and join him for lunch each day. Maybe it was the same things that attracted his co-workers, the neighbors in his building, and the ladies from the dating app—because he was tall and wore dark suits, his hair had a slight wave, his smile was friendly, and his complexion clear. He looked like a young Marlon Brando. Lee laughed at his vanity, realizing Bono only watched him because he stood out against the gaggle of school-aged children on field trips. Lee only spotted Bono because he was a huge gorilla, big for even a silverback's normal standards, and how could you miss him?

A gust of wind ruffled the greying hair on Bono's shoulders. It wasn't the first time Lee found himself wondering if the aging gorilla was nearing retirement, or if he seemed older than his years. He meant to ask a zookeeper but didn't want to spend his entire lunchbreak fending off the advances of the women who worked the primate enclosure. There were five of them, each more aggressively single than the last.

Lee put down his sandwich, unable to continue eating it. The wind carried the smell of animal shit, and rainy days made the smell more intense. A new plaque stood out against the cinderblock next to Bono's enclosure. Lee stood to read the sign, drifting his fingers over the engraved script and an image of a gorilla that Lee didn't recognize.

"Meet Barb, the newest member of Bono's troop! Barb is a nine-year-old female, and she's ready to mate. Gorillas are critically endangered, and the numbers are staggering. Over 100,000 western lowland gorillas exist in the wild, with 4,000 in zoos; eastern lowland gorillas have a population of under 5,000 in the wild and 24 in zoos. Thanks to conservation efforts like captive breeding programs, gorillas now have insurance against extinction!"

Barb's plaque reminded Lee of the dating app on his phone, where pictures and biographies of possible matches were at his fingertips. Lee sheltered himself during the start of the pandemic alone, but that was nothing new. After Sarah left, he started a sexual quarantine for five years, but being trapped in his apartment had thrown his normal solitary life into the harsh light of reality.

A few weeks later, he downloaded the dating app with the name, *Love Fool*, and ended his celibacy period. Lee had been open to any type of woman—playboy bunnies with aggressive makeup, crafty women with sharp haircuts and heavy costume jewelry, granola gals with nose rings and natural looks, and muscled tomboys with thick thighs. He was never alone, but lonely all of the time, which made his thoughts drift to Sarah.

"You avoiding her?" Lee asked, nodding toward Barb with the other females in Bono's enclosure. They idled on the ropes while eyeing Bono. "The new one?" Bono yawned, flashing his yellowing canines that made Lee thankful for the glass between them. "I get it. It sounds counterintuitive, but quarantine kept my dance card full too. Women brave enough to come over were suddenly afraid of exposing themselves to the virus when it was time to go."

Barb slipped away from the group. She approached Bono from the side, slow and leisurely with uninterrupted eye contact while puckering her lips. Lee laughed out loud.

"Aww, man. She's into you. Doing those stupid duck lips and everything."

Bono broke eye contact with Barb, gazing out of the enclosure with disinterest. Barb edged closer to Bono, reached out and touched him, and a pang of worry twisted in Lee's gut. Would Bono hurt her? Did he ever act on that primal anger that tainted the blood of the male species, men and ape alike?

"Reunited and it feels so good!" a high-pitched voice screeched from behind Lee. He didn't know if it was the irritating voice or Bono's rejection, but Barb scampered away to join the other females.

"No, no, no," Lee whispered to Bono before turning around. "Cheryl," Lee said, grinning stiffly, "Good to see you. I was just ending my break."

Cheryl, the most sexually aggressive of the zookeepers, tossed her red hair and turned slightly to present her ass in khaki shorts. "Thank God we are open again. Glad to see my favorite boys are back together," she said.

Lee, astounded that she had the audacity to call him one of *her boys,* hurried to the trashcan and threw away his sandwich. He took too long waving goodbye to Bono, and Cheryl blocked his path out of the viewing area. Lee shuffle-danced side to side, trying to get by without touching her.

"Cheryl, I need to get back to—"

"—excuse us," said a woman, tugging her young son by the hand.

As Lee and Cheryl stepped aside and watched the woman pass into the viewing area, he was hit with sudden recognition. The woman was one of many rotating though his apartment during the haze of lockdown, during what he jokingly referred to as his "mating season."

The pandemic had made all of the women from *Love Fool* unapologetically ferocious, like Cheryl. Lee continued to swipe on the app. The women continued to appear, entering the confines of his apartment, needy, horny, and out of control. The threat of the virus seemed to tear away all of their inhibitions, and they scratched, screamed, and hair-tugged their way through orgasm after orgasm, just as Lee did.

Lee looked at the mother looking at Bono and tried to place her face. Erect nipples and wax came to mind. Biting. But that could have been anyone. Was she the one that refused to kiss? Refused to remove her mask? The musk of her sweat was at the edge of his memory, but she spoke, breaking the olfactory connection.

"Lee, right?" She took a step away from the boy and toward Lee. The over-eager look still simmered in her brown eyes, and it somehow didn't jive with being a mother.

At first, he'd loved the willingness of all the ladies on the app. He didn't have to hide the toys that kept him busy during captivity—his lightsabers, novelty bongs, gaming accessories, and action figurines. Hell, he didn't even have to shower, cook dinner, or watch a movie. They didn't care if he had a job, a car, or a 401K. It was all about sex.

After weeks trapped in his apartment with sex-starved strangers, he'd suspected he was courting melancholy. He waited until his dates made a trip to the bathroom to rummage through their purses, overstuffed shoulder bags, slim clutches, totes, and everything in between. Lee sifted through eyeliner stubs, condoms, lipsticks, gum, and credit cards, coveting clues of who these women were. For a few weeks, he'd believed the truth hid in the unusual items they carried. But the odd items he found in their possession, Scrabble tiles, butter knives, a lightbulb, and even the full calligraphy set, failed to penetrate the haze of sexual need that surrounded the women. None of it was enough to piece together a life or to hold a mirror up to his loneliness.

The person he thought he knew the most, without going through her things or exploring her body in a kinky way, was Sarah. He'd grown up across the street from her, had always known her, and planned to grow old with her. Sarah promised a life with him that seemed so comfortable and unremarkable that it bordered on boring. They would have careers, kids, dogs, and a house. The prospect of normalcy was exotic to them; Lee's Mom rotated through volatile husbands every year, and Sarah's Dad drank until he erupted with anger.

Lee and Sarah checked all of the boxes together, including prom, losing their virginity, graduation, college, and cohabitation. It was traditional, run-of-the-mill, and routine, but Sarah held extraordinary magic that made it into something else. It was a quality Lee tried to articulate, but something that dissolved under close inspection. Her magic was turning their shitty college apartment into a home without spending money, or how she could whip up gourmet pancakes out of nothing but was a miserable cook when it came to anything else. The heavy river of curly hair that trickled down her spine. The way her smile went crooked when she laughed. How she held Lee during thunderstorms. The way her body fit against his. Her magic was more than he could explain, made all the more mysterious now that she was gone.

The Jesus-looking guy in Sarah's senior writing workshop the semester before she was due to graduate would prove to be their downfall. On the day she'd met this man, Sarah's green eyes simmered with yearning, a look that Lee didn't understand at first, but later found repellent on other women. She spoke about Fake Jesus often, her breath quickening and her face aglow. Still, Lee naively chalked it up to admiration for the man's writing.

The day Sarah left she'd scrawled a quick goodbye on the whiteboard, as if she only went out to grab milk. Lee tried to put emotions like love, devotion, and heartbreak aside, which clarified his vision and made him wonder if he'd known her at all. The Sarah he thought he knew was dependable and wouldn't quit college so close to the end. The Sarah he thought he knew wouldn't leave most of her belongings behind. The woman he thought he knew wouldn't steal money from their joint account to start a new life with Fake Jesus on a bus. Since then, Lee had graduated and started his career, but he floundered to craft a personal life on his own. Instead, he created a solitary existence in which he relied on a captive gorilla for emotional connection.

Bono slapped his large hand onto the glass, something he rarely did. Lee moved closer to examine the almost-human appendage, the universe in the primate's fingertips, filled with unique loops and whorls. He pushed his own considerably smaller hand against Bono's. The glass was frigid, and for the first time, Lee felt culpable for supporting Bono's captivity. How healthy was it for an animal from the Congo to live in this chilly Colorado climate?

"Lee? It's me, Rochelle," said the woman holding the kid's hand. Lee stopped his racing thoughts of Sarah and about Bono's comfort. He turned his head toward the woman. Her teeth chattered as she hugged herself against the cold. Why did these women dress in so little? Lee fought the impulse to rescue her by giving her his jacket.

Nodding and waving hello, Lee began to recall who Rochelle was. She'd sent him dirty photos, but never typed a greeting or even an introduction. This was the first time they were properly meeting. But that wasn't unique among the women on *Love Fool*. Not all of them sent dirty photos, but every single woman started with physical intimacy, eschewing the societal norms of courtship. What was unique to Rochelle was that she wanted him to choke her.

They'd been in a naked tangle in Lee's sheets, Lee inside of her when she'd slapped his face. Lee stopped moving, his penis threatening to shrivel.

"What's wrong?" he asked, stopping and pushing his arms against the mattress to make some space between their bodies.

"Keep going, but choke me," Rochelle said, pulling at Lee's torso until they were skin to skin again. "Sometimes, it helps if I slap first, primes your anger. You need more, or can you be a man and choke me?"

In the split-second that Lee hesitated, he hoped she would forget about the whole thing. Instead, she slapped him again, harder.

"Now," she panted.

Lee put one elbow on the mattress, and Rochelle grabbed his other hand, clamping it around her tender neck, squeezing her hand around his. Torrents of uncharted hate flooded his system, unexpectedly intensifying his sexual experience. He mashed her neck harder between his fingers and bit his lip until the coppery taste of blood saturated his mouth. She rose her pelvis to meet his thrusting until the blue vein snaking by her eye seemed dangerously engorged. Lee stopped.

She gasped for air, and Lee rolled onto the empty side of the bed, allowing his primal rage to simmer and cool. Looking at the marks on her translucent skin and tasting the yeasty exhalations of her breath kept the confusing mix of anger and arousal roiling. Lee dressed and left the room.

"Lee?" Rochelle asked, bringing him back to the present. Lee looked at her neck instead of meeting her eyes and relaxed at the sight of bruise-free skin.

Cheryl, seeing another female approach Lee, asserted her dominance. "Ma'am? Need you to socially distance from Lee and me. See the X over there? Our patrons must stand that far apart," she said.

"You're standing next to him," Rochelle said in a whiny voice that Lee found irritating. "And you're not wearing a mask. Aren't zoo employees supposed to wear masks?"

Lee was vulnerable, caught between the two women, away from the safe confine of his apartment. Rochelle's son, who looked to be around ten, climbed the benches and jumped at the glass near Bono and Lee. He seemed numb to his mom's complaints, and screeched with each jump, looking to see if Rochelle had noticed. While Rochelle and Cheryl bickered, Bono slipped his hand down, made a fist and pounded on the glass, sending vibrations down Lee's arm. He took a step back.

It was enough to shock the group into silence until the boy pointed to the enclosure and yelled, "Gross!"

Bono hunched over, vomiting an oatmeal-like spew. When he was finished, he panted for a moment before shoveling handfuls of the vomit back into his mouth to eat.

"He's eating his puke," the boy said, laughing.

"What's wrong with him, Cheryl?" Lee asked, fighting the urge to vomit too. "He never does this."

Bono barfed again and started eating the vomit before Cheryl answered robotically. "They do that when they aren't getting proper nutrition." She stared at Bono, but then had the good sense to blush when she seemed to remember that she was responsible for Bono's nutrition. "It's hard to get the diet right for captive gorillas. They get the calories they need, but not the *way* they need them."

"What does that mean?" Lee asked.

"In the wild gorillas spend half of their life eating, but there's no need to do that in captivity. They're starved of the *behavior* they instinctively want so they eat their vomit, feces, urine—"

"They drink their pee?" the boy asked. He crouched on the bench, his delight looking explosive.

Lee slammed the glass with both of his palms. "I'm sorry," he said to Bono. He turned to face Cheryl. "Why do we get this privilege? We put him in a box and watch his life deteriorate?"

"Lee, don't get dramatic. You've known him for years. He's healthy and happy." Cheryl's face reddened to match her hair. "Besides, what's the alternative? What's your big plan, Lee? Release him onto the city? He's used to captivity now." Cheryl continued with the standard zoo-employee response about education, conservation, and sustainability, but stopped when Lee shook his head. "He has all he could ever want here—food, drink, entertainment, women," she continued. "We've freed him up for his real purpose, breeding."

It sounded reductive, especially for a woman specializing in primate care. Lee flashed to his claustrophobic apartment as it was during stay-at-home orders. Greasy take out containers, alcohol, the constant ticker of death tolls on CNN, and the revolving door of frightened, horny, women. Like Bono, he technically had enough to keep him alive. He was going through the motions of breeding in captivity. Still, he was missing his connection with Sarah, some soul-sustaining and vital connection.

"If this were all he could ever want, why is he eating his puke?" Lee asked. He hated that his eyes were tearing up, so he focused on Bono's silverback and blinked. Cheryl had already answered his questions, but he couldn't stop. "He's not the same as before the pandemic." Lee took a steadying breath, feeling disoriented and not remembering who he was referring to.

"It's expensive to feed gorillas a more natural diet. We're trying, though. We dice the food and spread it out. They forage what we can scatter—peanuts, seeds, dried fruits." Cheryl looked proud of her answer like she'd cured both Bono and Lee of what captivity had sapped from them.

Lee pounded on the glass until Bono looked up. For the first time, he gazed directly into his friend's caramel-brown eyes. They were ringed with creped skin, brimming with tears that trickled down his face, into his fur. If Bono felt threatened, he was too sick to care.

"He's crying!" the boy yelled.

"That's from vomiting," Cheryl explained, "when you throw up your eyes water."

A ripple of disappointment crossed Bono's face. Lee touched his own eyelids, unadvisable with the virus, and wondered what his stare revealed. He understood now that he possessed the look he detested; he was an unending pit of need. "I'm sorry," he muttered, backing out of the viewing area on stiff legs. "I'm sorry, man. I love you."

"Lee," Rochelle said, "I thought we could get together again?"

"I…I can't," Lee said.

"Are you seeing someone?" Cheryl cut in.

"I can't come back here," Lee turned to Cheryl, "I was starved of something, acting out of instinct."

"Your instincts were great," Rochelle purred.

"Cool down, sex kitten," Cheryl said, rolling her eyes. "He's comparing sleeping with you to eating his own vomit."

Lee backed away, ignoring the mating calls from the two unmasked women, their Botoxed lips puckering in disappointment. He considered visiting a less complicated exhibit, maybe the aviary where many of the birds mated for life. But the thought of caged birds proved just upsetting as Bono's situation. He could never return to the zoo and the comfort he had found in Bono's captivity. Before turning to leave, he made eye contact with Bono for the second and final time. The 500-pound silverback met his gaze, leaning his giant head to the side as if confused. The new gorilla, Barb, moved forward and started grooming Bono, over-eagerness swarming in her dark eyes. Lee turned his back, and a familiar need to feel Sarah's body against his returned like a slap in the face. He knew how it felt to be enclosed in a small space, how it eventually felt smaller and smaller until there was nothing left. But Bono had Barb now, and Lee had something now too, something he'd suppressed for months, and up until now, didn't know he had the courage to begin.

The Slow Breakup

Kelly's SUV is packed with seventh-grade boys going to their first school dance. Their bodies reek of too much competing cologne, a chemical stench that barely masks the greasy smell of their fast food dinner and puberty-induced body odor.

Lake, her son, sits in the passenger seat and shouts conversations to his friends in the back. He is jittering in his seat, buzzing with palpable excitement.

"Lake," Kelly says, placing a hand on his bouncing knee. "Calm down."

Kelly smiles at the memory of her and John picking the edgy name for their only child. They named him in the hopes of offering a uniqueness that his peers wouldn't have. The joke was on them though; now she chauffeurs kids named Ryder, Storm, Kale, and one pimply boy named Bronson Money, who shortened his name to Bro Money. Naming Lake after her husband John would have been the more unique choice.

After picking up Bro Money and stopping for fast food, Kelly still has a thirty-minute drive to the private Christian school the boys attend. She stops at a red light and examines their faces in the rearview mirror. They are such good kids, all joyfully doing the work of God through school-sanctioned service projects—feeding the homeless, caring for the blind, protecting animals, and never letting their manners drop by forgetting to answer with a "yes, Sir." All of these young men are primed to be better than the generation before them, to not repeat the mistakes of their parents.

"Aced my Algebra test and got the new Gucci kicks," Kale says, propping a new, but muddy, Gucci sneaker on Kelly's console.

"Sick," Lake says, stroking the laces. "I'm wearing a cologne that smells like the Gucci kind. Smell." He thrust his arm at Kale.

Not for the first time, Kelly is saddened at her inability to buy Lake the things he wants. This pack of boys collect brand names, live on sprawling horse properties, and carry two phones at a time for reasons she can't understand, even with their explanations.

The only saving grace is the school uniform; on regular days, the boys are starched into button-up shirts, blazers, khakis, and ties. Usually, everyone looks the same. It's strange to see them dressed in their own unique clothing for a school dance.

Kale must not have reacted to Lake's cologne the way he wanted him to, because Lake blushes into a deep shade of purple that Kelly had never seen before. He digs into the pocket of his cargo shorts and pulls out a hood ornament.

"It's from a Caddy," he says, brandishing the ornament for the boys in the back to see.

"Sweet! That pulls $40 on eBay," Storm says. "Jack like ten more of those, and you can get a designer belt." The boys laugh.

"Lake, did you steal that?" Kelly asks. "How did you—"

"Relax, Mom. I pried it off a junker when we were getting burgers," Lake says, dropping the ornament on the floorboard.

"You stole?" Kelly fights to remain focused on her driving. She clenches her jaw, the raw ache of her bad tooth forcing her attention on the road.

Lake shrugs and rolls the ornament under his foot. "It was just some junker," he repeats. "You gonna tell Dad?"

It sounds like a dare. Kelly doesn't reply. She hates the silent treatment, but finds it useful when dealing with Lake because the alternative is yelling at him. When he turned thirteen, like the flip of a switch, she was dealing with a new person—someone angry, insecure and unhappy with the blessed life he was provided. Kelly knows how to parent the tantrums of toddlers but doesn't know what to do with this adolescent angst.

"Guess you're not answering me now," Lake mumbles.

At the next red light, a frail man brandishes a weathered cardboard sign, waving it halfheartedly in their direction. Kelly digs change from the console and hands it to Lake, who rolls down his window. "God bless you, Sir," Lake says to the man as he gives him the change. Lake quickly grabs the Cadillac hood ornament and adds it to the man's bucket. "You can sell that for a few bucks," Lake says.

Kelly's fog lifts and her heart swells. Maybe she shouldn't worry. Maybe the material difference between Lake and his peers isn't important. What is important is that he's becoming a good person, someone who serves others and has a sense of morals, even if it takes practice to act the right way. She reaches across the console and strokes Lake's soft jawline. He slaps her hand away, the loud pop hanging in the air.

"You said you wouldn't embarrass me," he hisses.

At the same time, Bro Money yells in the backseat. "Fuckin' lowlife's gonna spend that on booze."

"Sorry," Kelly says to Lake.

"That's okay," Bro Money says. Kelly hates how it sounds like she is apologizing for donating to the homeless man, but the moment passed, and she can't correct Bro Money now.

Lake's green eyes curve into an annoyed squint, just like the face he made as a baby, like the infant face of his sister before him, the baby Lake had never met. Kelly wonders if the girl resembles her brother, with dark curls and long, elegant fingers. Maybe Baby Girl has Kelly's green eyes, the only physical feature in common between Kelly and Lake. The baby would be eighteen by now, probably out on her own at some fancy college, but not too far from home, because she might miss her parents. Kelly imagines they would have a close relationship after a happy childhood. Honking abruptly interrupts her thoughts, and she realizes she was holding up traffic at a green light.

"Shit, Mrs. Sterling," one of the boys shouts, "You slowing the whole damn lane up!"

Kelly twists in her seat to face the laughing boys in the back, angry that she'd let the bad language slide earlier. She probes at the aching molar with her tongue, considering what to say. "What goes into your mouth does not defile you, but what comes out of your mouth, that is what defiles you. The things that come out of the mouth come from the heart, and these defile you. Matthew fifteen—"

"Mom!" Lake says, grabbing her arm. "You said you'd be chill tonight." The unexpected contact, the warmth of her baby's hand on her arm, stops Kelly from reciting the verse number. She remembers how Lake used to hold her hand in the school hallway, his slightly sticky fingers rhythmically squeezing hers.

"Sorry, Mrs. Sterling," a boy from the back calls, and then quietly adds, "My mouth is going to defile Sadie Jacobs tonight." The boys laugh, and Lake shoots Kelly a warning look.

"It's bad enough that you wore *that;* you don't need to be so *momish*," Lake says.

Kelly glances down at the t-shirt that Lake had made her in Kindergarten. A series of his handprints form a flower on the front, under which his crooked handwriting spells, "Happy Mother's Day." The shirt is threadbare in places, as are the maternity pants that she still wears because the waistband is forgiving of both post pregnancy stomachs and middle-aged sprawl. She suddenly wonders how John could still be attracted to her, before a more horrifying thought presses.

"Are you embarrassed by how I look?" she asks Lake.

"Hey, Lake! Annabelle or Annemarie tonight? Get that candy—they're thirsty AF," someone from the back shouts, before Lake could answer.

Kelly fights to remain quiet, but she hopes they are talking about literal food and drink. She can't imagine her sweet baby, just a few years out of Spiderman Underoos, doing anything sexual.

"Don't know, can't tell them apart," Lake says.

The boys laugh, and Kelly whispers to Lake. "Are those the Robertson twins?"

"Yeah."

"If you choose to dance with one of them, be respectful. Learn to recognize the twins as individuals. Remember, leave room for Jesus. Your arms should be—"

Lake turns up the volume on the radio. Kelly trails off and pokes at her throbbing tooth with an index finger. Her eyes blur with tears, a byproduct of the excruciating pain that now shoots up the left side of her face. The fuchsia lipstick she'd smeared on in a rush this morning stains her finger, and her thoughts jump to Baby Girl's father, how they'd made out in the back of his car in eleventh grade, his face and neck smeared with the same signature shade of lipstick.

"Lift your ass, *Kelby*," he'd said, his Dorito breath hot on her face. "You're getting the seat all wet. My dad will kill me."

Kelly, her jeans and underwear around her ankles, had been too stunned at the misnomer to fight back. They were neighbors, she was literally the girl next door, and he'd known her since Kindergarten; there was no way he didn't remember her name. Kelly knew it was a tactic he used on the less popular girls to put them in their place, but never on her. She pushed her shoulders against the seat and lifted her butt. He wiped the leather with his t-shirt and hissed the wrong Dorito-flavored name into her face again, "Thanks, *Kelby*."

The boys howling with laughter at something on Bro Money's phone snapped Kelly back from her reverie. She wonders if she should pull over and see what they are looking at, be a reliable chaperone. But the thought saps all of her energy and she suddenly wants them out of the car, wants this ride to end. She knows this dangerous headspace. When she is this exhausted, this sort of weary, she wants the truth to come out.

She glances at Lake, his midnight hair shining in the ambient light from the dash. Baby Girl was born with the same mass of raven hair, despite Kelly's mousy brown coloring, and despite having a different father than Lake. Kelly shakes the thought, afraid that Lake can read the premarital deflowering on her features and report them back to John.

Kelly had met John during their freshman year at Wilson, the small private Christian college where women enrolled to find husbands and men attended for more serious degrees that promised careers. John had believed Kelly a virgin, and she didn't correct his assumption. He wouldn't have been able to handle the truth of Kelly's high school experience; he'd wilt at the notion that Kelly joyfully fucked the popular boy until he remembered her name and shouted it in the middle of orgasms. If Kelly confessed that she'd become pregnant her junior year, carried Baby Girl to term and gave her up for adoption, John would deem her unclean, even though she'd refused an abortion like a good Christian girl. Sometimes doing the right thing didn't stain you as much as doing something wrong.

"Holy shit! It's The Box," Lake says, cranking the volume on the stereo.

Kelly reprimands him for his language, but she can't hear herself speaking over the music. The console screen displays the song that plays, The Box by Roddy Ricch. It seems to be playing from one of the boy's phones in the back, not from the radio.

She's only ever heard the radio edited version, and even that was a bit risqué for middle school boys. But she promised to go with the flow, so she clamps her mouth shut as the boys rolled down the windows and shout the explicit version into the wind.

"Took her to the forest, put the wood in her mouth
Bitch don't wear no shoes in my house
The private I'm flyin' in, I never wanna fly again
I take my chances in traffic
She suckin' on dick no hands with it
I just made the Rollie plain like a landing-strip
I'm a 2020 president candidate."

Kelly's chest burns like she'd smoked a pack of cigarettes—another habit she'd hid when she met John. She'd read somewhere that having a son was like going through a slow breakup, and suddenly she understands. Lake still looks like the infant that had depended on her, his baby-fat cheeks smooth to the touch, his long eyelashes, dark and full, fluttering against his face the same way they fluttered against her skin when she cuddled him. He's still her baby, but now the rosebud mouth that she nursed is shouting, "suckin' on dick no hands with it." He's pulling away, had been the whole time.

She'd known other slow breakups. At first, Baby Girl's father had seemed unbothered by news of Kelly's pregnancy. For weeks he'd been even more attracted to her, probably because of her swollen breasts. He didn't offer solutions or make plans with Kelly beyond the carnal. As her belly grew, he called less often, slowly leaving her to understand that her body housing the baby in between them wasn't sexy anymore. The last time she saw him was in the mall when she was seven months pregnant. She was gripping her lower back and fighting off nausea from the variety of food court smells. He walked toward Kelly with an arm draped around another girl, a rail-thin freshman.

Kelly stopped and stared, barely resisting the urge to shake the girl and warn her away. He didn't bother to wave, only made brief eye contact, and dipped his head, a minimal nod of acknowledgment to the mother of his child.

Kelly turns down the music and clenches her jaw, sending jolts of pain through her face. The boys quiet as if suddenly stunned that an adult had been driving the entire time. They examine their phones without talking, but even this action irks Kelly. She suspects the boys are talking about her via text, and each new chime puts her on edge. But hadn't she grown accustomed to that as well? The small town she grew up in was a hotbed of gossip, and becoming a pregnant teenager sent whispers roaring around her.

Hadn't she made big mistakes, learned her lessons early, and turned out okay, despite everything? Kelly pushes her chin to the side to crack her neck and reminds herself that her mistakes never stopped haunting her. When she first met John, she'd used all of her extra energy hiding her experience, hiding her past. She'd been a mother pretending at virginity. The fear of getting found out by John had waned over the years, but obsessive thoughts about her lost Baby Girl stalk her nonstop. She doesn't wish these obsessive thoughts onto Lake.

"Have fun at the dance," Kelly says, pulling into the school parking lot. "When it is over, I will be at—"

"That girl's wearing a half-shirt and a mini skirt!" Bro Money interrupts.

"T and A," Lake shouts. The boys in the back laugh as they exit the SUV.

"Lake!" Kelly says, grabbing his arm. "Where did you learn that?"

"God, Mom!" Lake says, shaking off her hand. He watches his friends run up the sidewalk and into the gym. "You're such a hypocrite."

"What's that supposed to mean?" Kelly asks.

Lake assumes his most annoying sarcastic teacher voice. "Hypocrites appear good and virtuous, but it's all false. You're concealing your *real* self behind all this Jesus bullshit."

Kelly is momentarily proud of Lake's knowledge of the word hypocrite. "How do you know that?"

"It was a vocab this week in Language Arts. I'm not an idiot," he says.

Kelly drums her fingers on the wheel before pushing the child lock button. For once her overprotectiveness works in her favor too.

"This is bullshit!" Lake yells, tugging at the door handle.

"Your internet time is gone. After your behavior tonight, the punishment should be much worse," Kelly shouts, spittle flying.

"I already found all I needed anyway," Lake mumbles.

A powerful tingling runs through Kelly's hands and feet, as if they suddenly fell asleep. Could he know about his sister? She fights to swallow, but her mouth is too dry. She tries to convince herself Lake is talking about something different.

"Are you looking at porn?" Kelly asks, even though she knows he wouldn't do that.

Lake rolls his eyes, the whites flashing in the dim light. Kelly clamps her jaw shut, focusing on the pain shooting from her tooth and up the right side of her face; it is somehow more bearable than the confusing look on her son's face.

"I sent in one of those spit tests for science lab. A DNA test," Lake says.

Kelly floats somewhere outside of herself, somehow not even feeling her tooth anymore.

"You register online, and the results show all of your relatives. Turns out I have a half-sister," Lake says, "and there's no way Dad knows."

He looks triumphant and smug, and for maybe the first time ever, Kelly wants to hit him. It's pointless to deny that she's been lying to John. Lake knows his dad and his strict values just as well as Kelly does. Instead, she exhales hard and leans back.

"Your breath smells like shit," Lake says. "Get that rotten tooth removed." He makes brief eye contact and dips his head, a minimal nod of acknowledgment to the mother he's disgusted with.

The echo of the familiar gesture infuriates Kelly, and she pants with rage. "I've lived lifetimes before you were born," she says, "and you only know about one of them. You might think you're worldly and that you understand things that are larger than you, but you don't. You're still just a kid."

"A kid with power," Lake says. His eyes are hard, and his jaw set in a way that Kelly has never seen before; she's staring at a stranger. "I want a phone and a later curfew. Don't make me tell Dad."

Kelly studies Lake's traitorous face, and despite her anger, her hand drifts up to softly stroke his velvety earlobe, as if she's making sure he's still there, that she's not dreaming the whole encounter. "Did I do this to you by hiding my past? These demands, the way you're coming at me, it's so vile. I've never known you capable of blackmail. You must be very upset because you are normally such a sweet—"

Lake slaps Kelly's hand away for the second time that night. "Don't make me tell Dad," he repeats.

Shaking, Kelly studies Lake's infuriated green eyes, eyes that he had the audacity to steal from her. She wonders again if Baby Girl has the same gaze, but more understanding. She feels a hot tear trail down her cheek and hides her face in both hands.

"Mom?" Lake whimpers in a way that would have made Kelly hug him minutes earlier.

Kelly removes her hands from her face and pushes the master button, rolling down all of the windows. She waves Bro Money away when he steps out of the gym and looks toward the car for Lake. With a shaking hand, Kelly turns the radio up loud enough that the parents with their children on the sidewalk stop to look at her, dismayed. "Let's go home," she says, suddenly exhilarated. "*I'll* tell your dad."

About the Author

Melody Sinclair graduated from the MFA program in Creative Writing at Regis University in Denver, Colorado. She has been published at Adelaide Literary Magazine, Heavy Feather Review, Bull: Men's Fiction, Avalon Literary Review, Adanna Literary Journal, Prometheus Dreaming, and more. She's won the Denver Women's Press Club Unknown Writer's Contest and is on the Fiction Reading Committee for Carve Magazine. Melody lives in Highlands Ranch, Colorado, with her husband, dog, and two kids. www.melodysinclair.com

Viswanath Gurram

Crazy For Coffee

Here is a question for you - do any of you know who in history is anecdotally supposed to have died uttering these last words: "Just one spoonful, just one more spoonful?"

The answer is the French emperor Napoleon Bonaparte. After losing the Battle of Waterloo, he was exiled to the Greek island of St. Helena. Greek coffee is famous for its rich taste, and the coffee from St. Helena is said to be particularly delicious and excellent in flavour. No wonder then, that our king fell passionately in love with this beverage and died craving for just one more spoonful.

Welcome fellow toastmasters and invited guests!

The title of my speech is "Crazy for Coffee" – and I assure you, I am not being funny - it is an accurate description. I am addicted to coffee, obsessed with coffee, and I cannot live without coffee. Perhaps I was Napoleon at one point in time, in a past life …. who knows, eh? My teammates at work do say that my behaviour is sometimes Napoleonic!

Where I was born and grew up, in the ancient city of Hyderabad in South India, tea is more popular than coffee. A recent Uber Eats study showed that twice as many people there drink tea. The same was the case in the city of Chennai. But in the city of Mumbai it is just the opposite – more people drink coffee there! This study was appropriately called the Battle of the Brews!

So where did my love for coffee come from, you might ask. Well, let me tell you the story. I am told by my mother that when I just was a newborn baby, my father was standing by the cradle drinking his hot coffee. He took a small spoonful of coffee, blew on the drink to cool it, and then gave it to his baby. And the baby lapped it up hungrily and happily. And that is how this love affair began.

But like all love affairs, there have been some tragic moments. A few years ago, it was my first day at work in a new job. My boss's office was on the 9th floor of the building. And on the ground floor was a Second Cup. Across the street was a Tim Hortons. And in a side street was Starbucks. Speak about a plethora of choices! In the interest of time, I just picked up a large Second Cup coffee and went up to meet the boss. She welcomed me warmly, I sat down in front of her. And placed the cup on the table. And as I began to talk and made animated gestures with the hands, the inevitable happened. I hit the cup, it fell to the floor, splashed hot coffee all over the carpet and furniture. My friends, it took an hour for me, our admin, and our janitor to clean up the mess. You can imagine my severe embarrassment. People say that even today, after all these years, a faint smell of coffee emanates from that office!

Here is another problem I had to face with coffee. When I was working in Human Resources, the biggest challenge had to be conducting interviews, offering coffee to a candidate and them replying, "Sorry, I don't drink coffee." Now tell me, how could I put aside that horrible fact and still give them the job?

But I had to put aside my chagrin and had to do it. I tell you, my friends, life is not easy!

When it comes to entertainment, any movie, television show, song – anything to do with coffee appeals to me. A favourite movie is Barbra Streisand's A Mirror Has Two Faces, where coffee plays a good role. I will leave you with the words from her famous duet with Bryan Adams in that feature film:

> *It started over coffee, we started out as friends;*
> *It's funny how from simple things; the best things begin…*

The best day does begin with a little cup of coffee. Wish you a happy and caffeinated Day!

A Journey Home

"As soon as man does not take his existence for granted but beholds it as something unfathomably mysterious, thought begins."

—Albert Schweitzer

Attending a friend's funeral is disturbing at one extreme and traumatic at the other. There's death in the air and a chill in the bone. There's a stampede of memories, and nowhere to run, for you are standing at the edge of a precipice and an abyss beneath. You can only look up at the stars, wondering if your grandmother's placid words were true, that the stars were people gone by. You hope she was right, so you can shine there one night - a distinct speckle of light, light years away.

Leaving the funeral invokes a very different range of emotions, from general relief to general sadness. Relieved at being away at last from tears, from other depressed friends, from many more morose strangers and from the gaudy streak of children's laughter. Sadness at going away from that very group of people, united in the valiant efforts of coping with life in the shadow of death, or death in the heart of life.

The train gathers speed and you feel you are gaining distance from death. And yet you are moving relentlessly closer, every minute, and every second. You get to wondering whether the velocities of the departing train and approaching Death would match, whether they would collide...You shiver involuntarily and catch the eyes of the curious co-passengers. You manage a weak smile and wipe a sheen of sweat. "Are you all right, sir?"

"Yes... I am...okay."

"Shall I order some coffee?"

"Yes, please. And - thanks."

The coffee boy turns up, thin, dark, greasy, merry and blest with a vigorous voice. His steel drum sparkles and catches the eye. Almost everyone orders a cup of the steaming, tasteless, life-bestowing brew. People sip slowly and open up like flowers. Conversation starts flowing easily. The coffee boy had dispensed life, all for the price of two rupees and fifty pice.

So many threads, silver and gold; so many stories, leaf green and indigo blue; so many vibrant voices, so many vibrant languages, so many exquisite textures; so many threads, binding the hours together, like precious pearls.

At the end of the journey you are no closer to immortality than before, but there is now an active appreciation of life. So many contacts have been made, fingers meeting in the dark and holding fast. You come alone and die alone, but that doesn't matter anymore, for there's a gleaming realisation that while on this earth you are a part of an ever-pulsing, evergreen adventure. And when you do pass over, you are one among a million stars, twinkling at each other and whispering eternal tales.

You step down the train and move along with the multitude, the humanity, the creation.

Train travel in India bustles with colour, noise and adventure. Life bubbles and sparkles in the air, and people mingle in beautiful camaraderie. There's many a lifetime friendship born, many a valuable lesson learnt on a train chugging away across the sub-continent...

Physics, Mathematics, and a Twist of Fate

Ahmedi Siddiqui was majoring in Astrophysics. Her daily round was a triangle, her hostel, the classrooms and the library being the three invariable vertices. She sometimes felt trapped, but her innate love of the stars made her forget her ennui.

She glanced down from the library window. The protest against the fees hike was in full swing. She had signed all the forms which the student leader had put in front of her, but herself was too tired to actively participate in banner bearing and slogan shouting. Right now she was annoyed with the noise. She could not concentrate at all. And there was an exam scheduled for the next day. She left the library by the back door, planning on sitting for a while in the lovely park of the Lucknow University.

She had hardly breathed a moment of silence when a voice hailed her. It was Surjeet Singh, a student of Quantum Physics. Ahmedi was pleased by his appearance. Partly because he was her good friend, but also because she needed help with certain differential equations. Surjeet patiently explained the solutions to her, and soon they laid aside the books and chatted about their future. For Ahmedi it was imperative she find a job. Surjeet boosted her confidence with his cheerful optimism. She realized it and was grateful to him. Later he left her in front of the women's hostel and wended the way to his own.

Ahmedi was pleased to find her room locked. She wanted to be alone for a while. And her roommate Jamili was a real chatterer. Sipping tea Ahmedi considered her feelings for Surjeet. In his presence she felt safe, comforted, protected and there was also a sense of peace. Was she in love?

On the way to his hostel Surjeet encountered Chand Muneer, who dragged him to a nearby cafeteria. Over hot buns and burnt tea Chand described a new girl he had met while his group of protestors had gone to paste posters in the nearby Shaheed Bhagat Singh Engineering College. Chand was a casual mathematical genius. His obsession was women and his intentions definitely lusty! Surjeet had to bear these daily rounds of sleaze and often berated himself for being such a good friend! But he recognized the innate simplicity and honesty of Chand's existence and loved him for being himself, without a mask. Chand's mind and heart were as simplified and uncomplicated as a mathematical concept. And Surjeet patiently heard him out.

Later, in his room he lay back in his easy chair and allowed his mind to wander. Even though every single girl in Lucknow University had been lavishly described by Chand he had never mentioned Ahmedi Siddiqui. It's a blessing, thought Surjeet with a smile. She was very dear to his heart. He began a letter to his mother. He wrote about a wonderful friend called Ahmedi.

They had finished their final examinations and were busy giving final touches to their project works. After a hectic day gathering references in the library, Surjeet relaxed in the park. The summer colours were dazzling, despite the dust that clung to every single leaf. He wiped the sweat off his face and thanked the trees for the lovely shade. He hoped to meet Ahmedi; it was a long time since he had chatted with her. She must be busy. His sleepy vision perceived Jamili approaching him. He waved a hand. After a few minutes of casual talk, Jamili said quietly, "I'm afraid you won't like this news, Surjeet." Ahmedi and Chand were engaged. Jamili left Surjeet wide awake and yet in a strange daze.

Years later he was visiting an ailing friend in Hyderabad when Surjeet came across Ahmedi in the Toli Chowki market. They greeted each other warmly and he apologised for having been unable to attend her wedding. She smiled and said that apologies were unnecessary among friends. Both Chand and herself were now professors in the Osmania University. Surjeet had found employment in his alma mater, the Lucknow University. They decided that there was an enormous amount to catch up on and fixed up a rendezvous at her place the next day.

The friends had a lovely evening topped off with Ahmedi's wonderful cuisine. Chand still talked sleaze and mathematics and Ahmedi still talked stars. Nothing seemed to have changed. Later that night Ahmedi stopped brushing her hair and gazed unseeingly at her reflection in the mirror. She was remembering a gentle elderly Sikh lady who had visited her once at the Lucknow University with a certain request. She had obliged in the generosity of her character. She wondered at the twist of fate. Surjeet himself had never married.

About the Author

Viswanath Gurram is a poet and a writer who spent his formative years in the multicultural milieu that is Hyderabad, India. He is fascinated by the little stories that occur in people's lives every day, and tries to capture the soul behind those stories. He currently shuttles between United States and Canada doing human resource management which gives him more insights into human nature. As a young student in India he published several short stories and poems in major Indian newspapers, and one of his stories was published in "Sulekha Select: The Indian Experience in a Connected World." His book, ""A Young Couple in Bombay" and Other Stories" is available on Amazon and features eight stories that are alternately exhilarating, whimsical, dramatic, tragic, joyful and melancholic: A Young Couple in Bombay, On Coincidences and Jaunts, An April Night, The Papier-Mâché Buddha, HAIL VICTORY!, A Journey Home, That Rainy Season... , and Ramkali.

Steven Markusen

The Warrior

"This we know: the earth does not belong to man, man belongs to the earth. All things are connected like the blood that unites us all. Man did not weave the web of life, he is merely a strand in it. Whatever he does to the web, he does to himself."

—Chief Seattle, Squamish 1854

He walks toward me across the prison compound. You can tell a lot about a man by the way he walks. He carries himself ramrod straight, radiating power and confidence. His movement is fluid with the relaxed grace of a mountain lion. As he draws closer, I see twin lightning bolt tattoos down the left side of his face from brow to chin. He makes eye contact, gives a respectful nod, and passes. Without realizing, I tensed up. I exhale and relax. This is the story of a warrior who against all odds changed his life, and hopes to change the lives of his people.

His nickname is M-town, a Native American from Red Lake Indian Reservation, Minnesota. The lightning bolts symbolize a warrior willing to fight and die for his people. To the left, and paralleling the bolts, are seven blue dots representing the Ojibwa Grandfather Principles: wisdom, respect, courage, honesty, truth, humility and love. His finely featured face with small nose, pointed chin, and high cheekbones reveal his French Canadian and Native American Heritage. His head shaved, neatly trimmed goatee frames his mouth. Brown eyes, almost black, shine with intelligence. Tattooed on the top of his head is a Mohawk, "agichidaa": the warrior; on the back of his head is his war shield surrounded by two eagles, "gana", for protection in battle. Above his right eye is a symbol of his people: the Ojibwa, one of the larger woodland Native American Nations.

In 2009, sentenced to a 20 year term for drug law violations M-town found himself in the medium security Federal Prison at Oxford, Wisconsin: a melting pot of violent offenders and gang members where leaders with strong personalities used other inmates as pawns; a place where you always watched your back and your mouth.

Facing a long sentence, M-town needed to make a name for himself. He emerged as one of the leaders of the Native American Brotherhood. Every day the inmates marched into the prison yard where potential violence lurked. A struggle emerged for power and control between M-town's Native American Brotherhood and a gang of Native Americans led by a five-time convicted rapist serving a twenty five year sentence. War broke out in the yard when M-town drew the leader away from his gang and attacked. Eleven members of the Brotherhood fought fourteen members of the rival gang. M-town and the Brotherhood crushed their rivals, but at a cost.

M-town grew up on the Red Lake Indian Reservation in Northern Minnesota, the most poverty-stricken and crime-ridden reservation in Minnesota. He was the oldest of five brothers, two of which died within 90 days of childbirth. He grew up in a crime family. His earliest memory, at two years old, was pulling himself up to the top of the kitchen table seeing guns and a pile of marijuana. His father never told him and his brothers he loved them. M-town's father grew up hating his father who beat him, his brothers, and his mother almost to death. When he was young, M-town was a momma's boy, but that relationship changed growing into manhood. He felt his mom hated him. She said, "I wish you were never born," or "I wish you were dead." This cycle of violence and abuse was not unique to M-town's family, but repeated over multi-genera-tions of Native Americans and reservations across our country. Understanding requires a lesson in Native American history.

In 1879, Captain Richard Pratt founded the Carlisle In-dian School in Pennsylvania to "civilize" Native American children. Pratt held the conviction and wrote, "Indian cultures were worthless relics which must be destroyed." The Carlisle Indian School became a model for other institutions around the country. By 1900, there were more than 300 Indian Schools across the country with a combined enrollment of 22,000 representing ten percent of the Native American population.

Children age six to eighteen were forcibly taken from their homes. At school they received "American" names. The boy's long hair was cut—a traumatic experience. They were forced to wear uniforms, adapt to a strict military regime, forbidden to speak their native language, and discouraged from mentioning their background. Their diet was drastically changed and abuse, both sexual and physical, was rampant. A bounty was placed on children who escaped. When captured and returned, they were severely punished. In the original Carlisle Indian School, half the young children died within the first three years.

It does not take a psychologist to realize this experience in social engineering was crippling. Children learned to despise everything they held dear: parents, relations, culture, the white teachers that daily tormented them, and most importantly, themselves. No wonder thousands of Native Americans sunk into apathy, alcoholism, and despair creating cycles of abuse, dependency and self-destructive behavior.

In first grade, M-town met Pinkie. Later in life, they became best friends. By the time M-town was 14, his parents had divorced. His mom couldn't handle him so he moved in with Pinkie's family. Pinkie's mom showed him love and affection, but it was not enough to change his life. M-town brought his gangster ways into Pinkie's life and influenced him in a negative way. After high school, M-town married his high school sweetheart. When M-town first went to prison she had an affair with Pinkie. When Pinkie was locked up, M-town slept with Pinkie's ex-girlfriend evening the score; a cycle of love-trust-betrayal.

Separated by three years, M-town was "soul mates" with his younger brother nicknamed Poe. When Poe turned eighteen he received a sum of money from the reservation. He purchased a Springfield Arms, 1911 style, 45 caliber handgun. Poe was a wildcat, respected, but feared. He would shoot his gun into the ceiling at parties, the booming clap of the 45 silencing the room. He pointed his gun at people's feet making them dance.

One night at his dad's house, M-town and Poe were drinking and drugging. Poe wanted to go to a party at the west end of Red Lake; M-town decided to go home, sober up, and be with his wife and kids. Before he left, M-town told his dad to hide Poe's gun. Later, Poe called him, drunk—it was the last time they talked. The next call was from his cousin—Poe shot himself. M-town was in shock as he drove from east Red Lake to the party. He was met on the way by his friends and youngest brother. M-town was the general, his troops surrounded him, his cousin crying, "I am sorry." M-town went to the hospital, an FBI agent told him to leave. He walked into the forest, put his arm on a tree, head against his arm, and cried.

At the party, Poe had been menacing people with his gun. He removed the magazine from the handgun, cocked it, put the barrel to his head and pulled the trigger. There was a round in the chamber.

Poe, still alive, was transferred to the hospital in Grand Forks, North Dakota. M-town drove there with his wife and cousin. On the drive, a brilliant meteor shower lit the night sky. At the hospital, the nurse said, "your brother is not going to make it." M-town slipped into the room. Poe was sitting up, bandaged head, one eye all bloody from popping out of his head, tubes down his throat and attached to his arms. M-town laid his head on his chest listening to a faint heartbeat. "I love you." he said. Then he screamed, "get up!" He pounded on his chest again crying out, "Get up." He dropped to his knees crying. He rose, pushed his way through family and friends, and walked out the door.

Poe had a traditional funeral. For four cold days in December, a ceremonial fire burned outside the Red Lake community center. M-town was drinking, snorting coke and arguing with his dad. M-town said, "Why did you give him the gun? I told you to keep it hidden." He hit his father in the face. Realizing his mistake, he ran, but his father chased, tackled him, and held him on the ground breaking his little finger. The next day his dad, with one black eye, came to his M-town's house and apologized. M-town apologized in-turn. They smoked weed and buried Poe in his father's yard.

M-town was angry. Every relationship he valued turned against him. His life filled with betrayal, dishonesty, abuse, and disloyalty. He could not forgive or forget. He stopped loving and turned to hate. He was arrested and charged with possession of crack cocaine with intent to distribute. Convicted, he was sentenced to three years in Federal Prison in Sandstone, Minnesota. He was 21 years old.

While in prison, Pinkie's ex-girlfriend, now the mother of M-town's child, and one of his drug couriers, was found murdered; strung up in her home to look like a suicide. M-town was released from prison in 2004, but a parole violation sent him back. After four months, he was released, determined to change his life. He remarried, quit drinking, and took a job in marketing complete with suit, tie, and briefcase. He worked hard at building a business, but it did not last. He started drinking and fell back into his criminal ways.

By now, the U.S. government identified M-town as a drug king-pin. The FBI, ATF, and DEA went after him: raids, set-ups, informants wearing wires. They closed in drawing the noose tight.

During this time, M-town's mother reached out, inviting him to join her in a sweat lodge ceremony, an Ojibwa tradition of forgiveness and healing. M-town told her she was crazy, she pleaded with him, his wife said go. M-town relented, brought his wife and son, and met his mom and a medicine man at the sweat lodge. They reconciled; a new beginning.

In 2009, M-town was indicted by a grand jury, convicted of conspiracy to distribute illegal drugs and sentenced to 20 years in Federal Prison; a sentence later reduced to 14 years. He spent one last night, the day after Mother's Day, with his wife. She hugged him and cried. He said, "I promise I will be back for you." He said goodbye to his wife. He hasn't seen his kids in eleven years.

After the gang war in the Oxford Prison yard, M-town, his gang, and his cousin, were sent to the SHU, Special Housing Unit, AKA the "hole." In the hole, M-town had time to reflect. How did I end up here? Why did my two marriages fail? Why is my life filled with dishonesty and hatred? He met a Native American from Michigan who introduced him to a newsletter covering Native

American issues. Prior to this point in his life, M-town didn't identify with his Native American heritage, being more associated with
the criminal life and gang culture. He wanted something more;
he needed something to guide him, to help him from returning
to the criminal lifestyle. He turned to the Ojibwa Grandfather
Principles: wisdom, respect, courage, honesty, truth, humility, love.
Over the next 15 months in the SHU, M-town rebuilt his code
of behavior based on loving, forgiving, and accepting.

The Federal Bureau of Prisons decided to make an example
of M-town and his cousin sending them to the maximum security prison in Florence, Colorado. One step below a super-max
facility, The SMU, Specialty Management Unit, was a cell with
bed and toilet; meals handed through a slot in the door. In this
tiny space, he was confined for 23 hours per day. This was home
for the next 21 months.

His brother's death set in motion a series of events that
changed M-town's life. Perhaps the meteor shower was a sign
from the Great Spirit for a new beginning. He reconciled with his
father, then his mother. Sent to prison and held accountable for
his behavior, he awoke finding his culture and identity. He learned
to love those he hated, respect those he disrespected, forgave those
that betrayed him; and accept, rather than deny, what life has given
him. Most importantly, he learned to love and forgive himself.

From the SMU, M-town was transferred to the U.S. Peni-
tentiary at Florence. In 2014, he began the long journey home:
first to Pekin, Illinois, then McKeen, Pennsylvania. At McKeen,
the warrior spirit was tested. In the yard of the medium security prison, he met an old enemy from his gangster days. Both
Native Americans, their hatred ran so deep they wanted to kill
each other. Instead, they met on the track, talked it out, and
agreed to bury the hatchet; a watershed event. From McKean,
he made the long multi-day journey though fog shrouded

Oklahoma City, up through Chicago, and crossed the border into Minnesota, overjoyed to see the state license plates of home.

In October of 2017, M-town arrived at Sandstone Federal Prison, his first low security facility in ten years. He spent 18 months at Sandstone and then transferred to the minimum security Duluth Federal Prison Camp. I got to know M-town at the gym, and through Toastmasters International. M-town has completed The Toastmasters Competent Leader, Competent Communicator, and Leadership Excellence manuals within a year qualifying him as a Triple Crown recipient. I was able to attend his two most recent speeches where one of the group said, "M-town walks to the front of the room with a posture and stride that exudes confidence, poise, and command."

I said, "your speech is passionate, reflective, and clear in message." I often run into him in his office, which also serves as the dorm laundry, head bent, focused on writing.

M-town's dream is creating the Warrior Resurgence Project with the goal of teaching the Grandfather Principles and re-awaking the Ojibwa cultural identity. Through ongoing work-shops, he proposes to spread the message that his people's problems are self-imposed and to break the cycle requires living by the principles of our ancestors. M-town has credibility. He has held every informal political office in his twelve years in prison: chief, warrior, liaison, and representative. He grew up in difficult circumstances and transformed himself from self-centered gangster to noble warrior. He has earned the right to speak for his people. In late summer of 2020, less than nine months away, M-town will finally go home. His story could fill book. It will be his choice what is written in the final chapters.

We all belong to the Earth and we are all connected. We need to recognize our interconnectedness—to understand when we harm another or the Earth, we harm ourselves.

Julian

"Gloriousness and wretchedness need each other.
One inspires us, the other softens us.
They go together."

—Pema Chodron, The Pocket Pema Chodron

Julian sits across from me in a Spartan classroom in the education department of the Duluth Federal Prison Camp. A bundle of barely restrained kinetic energy, he is constantly in motion. Wiry frame, lined face, and blue eyes hard as marbles, reveal his age as mid-fifties. Julian and I are connected: we both worked for the same company and share a passion for helping people live healthier and happier lives. Julian is serving a sixty day sentence for passing on non-public, material information in an insider trading case. This, I discovered, is not the real story behind the man. The real story began 30 years earlier: risky behavior, addiction, descent into living hell, and ultimately redemption and success.

On a Friday evening in 2002, Julian pulled into a McDonald's parking lot, walked inside, and called his kids who were staying with their mom. His older son answered. Julian said, "Hi son, I will pick you guys up at 7:30 on Monday morning and bring you to school."

His son replied, "You promise?"

He said, "I promise."

His son said, "How do I know you will keep your promise?"

Julian pleaded with his son saying, "If I don't, I will give you $20." Silence.

His younger son got on the phone. "Daddy," he said, "what will you give me if you don't come?"

All Julian could think was to say, "I will buy you a new wrestler toy, The Undertaker!"

He hung up, walked into the restroom, rolled up his sleeve, filled a syringe with liquid cocaine, and injected it into his vein.

His kids waited on front lawn with lunchboxes in hand... no dad. Cars rounded the corner...not dad. The boys argued, the older saying, "He's not coming."

The younger said, "Yes he will, dad promised he would pick us up."

For two days he had not slept, a continuous binge of drinking and drugs. Monday morning at 7 am, red eyed and barely functioning, he climbed behind the wheel of his fancy Mercedes to pick up his kids and take them to school. He pulled on to the freeway—traffic jam. Twenty minutes later he fell asleep at the wheel. Seven people called 911. Julian awoke to a Highway Patrol officer knocking on his window.

Julian was driving on a suspended license from a prior DUI. He was arrested and charged with two felonies. He never made it to pick up his kids.

Defining Julian's behavior as "risky" is an understatement. In 1991 at age twenty eight, he was convicted of Driving under the Influence, on a suspended license from a prior DUI. Over the following ten years, he was arrested for driving on a suspended license twelve times. He never considered not driving. It was risky, but in his mind... not wrong, just don't get caught.

In 1998, he was arrested and charged with another DUI while driving with a suspended license which triggered a felony DUI due to his prior DUI conviction. He was offered a break: agree to enter treatment and the felony would be reduced to a gross misdemeanor. He agreed. A year later, he was leaving a party with a young woman. They has been drinking and snorting cocaine. She was pulled over by the police. They were searched. The cops found a half of a gram of cocaine in Julian's pocket. He was charged with felony possession. He had a good attorney who worked the system. The felony would be reduced to a gross misdemeanor upon successful completion of a drug treatment program and random drug testing. He completed the drug program, but failed the random drug test multiple times. His probation officer let it slide.

Julian, at the time, owned two fitness clubs and lived a double life. By day he ran his clubs, Mr. Success, king-of-the-hill. At night, he lived the party life: dance clubs, strip clubs, cocaine, ecstasy, and alcohol. By 2002, everybody knew he was burning the candle at both ends. He was on a runaway train on a one way track.

The Highway Patrol officer who pulled him over on the way to pick up his kids called him "Needles." Julian had taken to wearing long sleeve shirts even in the baking desert heat of summer to hide the hundreds of tracks on his arms. Taken to county jail, he was strapped into a chair. He desperately needed to go to the bathroom. The officer gave him a choice: urinate in his pants or in a cup for a urine sample. He talked to his attorney on the phone who told him not to give a urine sample. Stripped of his dignity, a complete loser for failing his kids, he choose to hold on to his humanity and pee in the cup for a drug test.

He spent that night in County Jail: full lockdown in a fifteen by thirty foot cell holding up to 30 prisoners at a time, one toilet with no sides, a bag of food thrown at him, and an orange for a pillow. He was woken at 3 am taken to a pen, twelve prisoners standing and shackled together. They boarded a bus to court and waited for six hours, still shackled. Those prisoners not called into court, were escorted back to jail. It was living hell.

After 30 days, and numerous trips to court, Julian's name was called. Shackled at the wrist and ankle, garbed in jailhouse orange, he was ordered to have no eye contact or communication with anyone in the gallery. Out of the corner of his eye, he spied his ex-wife and two kids. At first enraged, he thought how could she do this?" Julian paused to reflect: I put myself here, nobody else is to blame. I broke my promise to my kids, she has every right to bring them here. Head bent, tears rolled down his face.

Julian's attorney told him he was in a difficult place: multiple DUI's, thirteen tickets driving on a suspended license, and one drug possession charge. His attorney said I have a strategy to get you released and the charge reduced. It was the same old story. Julian said, "No. I want to plead guilty. I can't do this anymore." He addressed the court saying, "I will plead guilty if you sentence me today."

Julian pleaded guilty to two felony charges: a felony DUI and felony possession of cocaine. He was sentenced to one year in state prison for each count ordered to run concurrently. As he was led out, he mouthed, "I love you." to his kids.

In a voice loud enough to be broadly heard, his ex-wife said, "Aren't you proud of your daddy? He'll never change." Julian was glad she said it. He told me, "It was a stake in the ground." He made a commitment to himself. Her prediction would not come true, he would change.

Julian was one of five siblings. His older brother was a natural child, he and his three younger sisters, adopted. Julian was an overachiever: starring in school plays, straight "A" student, good in sports, and sold the most raffle tickets. Teachers recognized him as a great student, but noted he had difficulty keeping his hands to himself. He was diagnosed as suffering from both Attention Deficit Hyperactive Disorder and Attention Deficit Disorder.

Family life changed for Julian in eight grade: his mother was diagnosed with cancer. She fought it for eight years; it wore her down, changed her. Locking herself in her room on Mother's Day became an annual event. She laid a guilt trip on Julian saying, "When you become a doctor you will find a cure for me." Was she serious? He didn't know. Their relationship became strained. Meanwhile, Julian's dad boasted a smile broadcasting to the world everything is great—even when it wasn't. At the same time his wife became ill, he was laid-off from a long-term job. He worked odd jobs—everything was just great. To his son, he was superficial and disengaged.

After his mom succumbed to cancer, Julian's, the wonder kid, turned to drugs and alcohol. Partying all night, eyes puffy and red, he would occasionally stop by to see his dad on the way to pick up cocaine and ecstasy. His dad would great him with a big smile saying, "How is everything?"

"Just fine dad, just great." Julian replied. He looked like hell.

"Good to hear son, you look good." All lies, all around.

After eight years of living the lie, the day of reckoning arrived. For the first time, Julian's dad was giving Julian a ride to drug treatment—at the county jail. His dad said, "Are you okay?"

"Why do you ask?" said Julian.

"People who are okay don't have five car accidents in a year." Uncomfortable silence.

"Oh that." said Shane and paused, "No, I am not really okay." They pulled up to the jail, the ride over, but the door had opened—just a crack, but open.

Julian entered state prison in 2002. The first days were rough, only made worse by the physical and mental anguish of drug and alcohol withdrawal. Gradually, his hedonistic, narcissistic, self-destructive faded into the past. He switched trains and the new train was leaving the station behind.

His dad came to visit. As usual, all smiles and waving hello. They sat at a table facing each other separated by a six inch high barrier. His dad said, "How are you son, you look good."

Julian said, "Dad stop! I am not doing well. I am a drug addict. For nineteen years I hid it from you." Julian started to cry. "Look at my arms!" he said.

His dad said, "Look at what?"

Rotating his arms to reveal his forearms, Julian said, "See the tracks? I shoot liquid cocaine. Then I do it again because I can't stop. I hate myself. This isn't your fault it's mine; my own decision. I am sorry." The tears streamed down Julian's face. His dad started to cry.

His dad finally said, "I love you son. We will get through this. You are smart, this is stupid. I am sorry I didn't help."

"You are a good father." said Julian. "You have already helped me more than you realize by acknowledging who I am. You will never see me like this again. I promise you." When you hit bottom, that absolute nadir of wretchedness, there is no place to go but up.

When Julian was released from Prison, the first thing he did was take his two boys to the zoo. His ex-wife had fought for joint custody. She won, but had no desire to raise the kids and sent them to live with Julian. His relationship with his boys came back stronger than ever, they were the most important thing in his life. At age 37, starting over in life as a single parent, he began a new life, sober and drug free.

Julian knew he wanted to stay in the health and fitness business, it was all he knew. His two clubs had been sold while he was in prison; the assets used to pay off company debt. He visited a health club, new in town, but part of a national chain. The company was familiar to Julian; he worked for the founder in his predecessor company. By a quirk of fate, Julian ran into that man, now the CEO, at the club with his youngest son in tow. The CEO asked Julian if he was clean. Julian said, "Yes, clean and ready."

The club was the first in this new geographical market and consistently failed to meet its sales goals. "I want you to come work here" the CEO said. "Nobody has your drive. We need you to light a fire on this sales team. You have more thrust than anyone in this industry. But if you go back to drinking and drugging, I will fire you on the spot, and then break every bone in your body." In the first full month after he was hired, Julian was the number one national sales associate in the company. By the third month, he was promoted to sales manager, and then general manager of the club. His meteoric rise continued the next year when he was named vice president of national sales.

The job required that he move back to the Midwest with his two kids. His youngest, a basketball player in high school, convinced Julian to help start and coach an AAU club basketball team. Never having coached before, he reluctantly agreed. Together they formed a team of eight young men, teenagers from a tough part of the city, euphemistically labeled, "at risk." Julian spent hundreds of hours of his time, and thousands of dollars of his money on uniforms, shoes, tournament fees, food, lodging and airfare.

Their first season, they won six games and lost twenty seven. No parents ever came to see the games; in fact, not a single family member attended a game in their three year history. One time, one of the boys forgot his shoes. Julian drove him home to get his shoes. Julian broke the uncomfortable silence and the boy followed. He told Julian all he wanted was a mother. His own mom was a crack addict, his dad murdered in a drug deal gone bad. The kid picked up his shoes from a friend's house where he was sleeping in the living room. This was home.

In their third and final season playing in the Under 18 age division, they won 18 of 19 tournaments, and finished with a record of 67 wins and 4 losses. For their final game they flew to Las Vegas, Nevada to compete in the AAU National Basketball Championships. They made it to the finals—and won—a moment of gloriousness.

Julian, coach, mentor and father figure, is still close with these young men. All graduated from high school, three will graduate from college, and they all have good jobs contributing to society. What happened to the boy who wanted a mother? Julian's executive assistant adopted him. Today he is finishing an MBA program in social work, intending to help those who, who like him, grew up in challenging circumstances.

It is a beautiful day here in prison. Ten days from the winter solstice, the sun still radiates warmth with the air temperature of ten below zero. Julian left today at 8 am. With no probation, he leaves a free man. He has paid his dues. Julian learned from his mistakes. Today, he is a better father, friend, and leader; practicing patience, compassion and empathy. He knows what it is like to live in self-induced exile; living in hell, thinking it was heaven. He knows what it means to have a soul because he has experienced the absence of soul: utter and complete blackness devoid of feeling. I am grateful for the opportunity to share Julian's story. The next chapter remains to be written.

About the Author

Steve is a professional writer with articles published in national magazines and international literary journals, including Adelaide. He also enjoys public speaking on topics including commitment, motivation, creating healthy habits, and aging.

Steve is an expert rock and ice climber, backcountry skier, and paraglider pilot. He is a competitive cyclist winning multiple gold medals at the Minnesota Senior Olympics. He has turned that passion into a career helping others achieve their life goals as a personal trainer and nutrition coach.

Robert Kelsoe

One Night in Sarria

The darkness of night greeted me as I stepped off the train and onto the railway platform. The station was dark, except for a flickering sign overhead that bore the name of the town Sarria. This was to be the starting point for my trek along the Camino de Santiago.

The Camino is a medieval trail that meanders 500 miles through northern Spain. In English, it is known as the way of Saint James. For 1,000 years, believers have traveled this route on pilgrimage to Santiago de Compostela where legend says that the remains of Saint James the Apostle are buried. On this particular trip, I planned to walk the final 80 miles.

I made my way through the deserted train station and pondered my current situation. I didn't have anywhere to stay, and it was raining hard. I stopped for a moment and put a cover over my pack and pulled the hood of my jacket down tight over my forehead. Silently, I made my way out into the darkness.

For the first time, I was beginning to question the wisdom of my plan.

My plan was simple: Buy a plane ticket to Spain, and spend Christmas break hiking from Sarria to Santiago de Compostela. My only objective was to cover the distance in 5 days. I intentionally did not arrange any transfers or hotel reservations. Instead, I planned to stay in albuergues (hostiles) along the way, just like pilgrims have done for centuries. My goal was to force myself into a situation where I had to rely upon my wits and the kindness of strangers for survival.

"Which way do I go?" I asked myself. I turned left and made my way down a narrow street. Then it turned right and became a major thoroughfare. I just as easily could have picked right, but intuition guided me.

The town of Sarria was much larger than I anticipated. I expected a sleepy village with cobbled streets. Instead, I found myself in a suburban city with a population of 13,000. The boulevard was lined with a mix of ancient and modern buildings that were decorated for Christmas with brightly colored strands of lights. Each light post along the street was adorned with blue illuminated snowflakes. I spotted a 20 foot Christmas tree in the town square.

It continued to rain.

As I walked down the sidewalk, I tried to stay close to the buildings so that the roof overhangs would shelter me from the rain. Each time I passed someone on the street, I would stop and ask "Alburgue?" My poor Spanish skills made it hard to communicate so I tried speaking louder with a Spanish accent. "*Alburgue?*" Still no luck.

An Alburgue is basically a hostel that is situated along the Camino de Santiago. They provide cheap room and board for pilgrims in a community sleeping area. The cost is usually around 10 Euro per night.

Eventually, I came across a group of college kids that spoke a little bit of English. We were able to communicate using a combination of hand gestures, Spanish and English. We flailed our arms about for several minutes and pointed in various directions. Eventually, they directed me to Rua Maior Street in the historic center of town. There, they said, I would find an alburgue that could provide room and board for the night.

I turned right and headed up a hill to the highest point in town. At one point, the sidewalks ended and I was forced to walk in the middle of the street. I quickened my pace as I heard a dog barking in the distance. Fortunately, it was late and there wasn't any traffic.

When I reached the historic district, I was shocked to find that the place was deserted. All of the businesses were closed for the Christmas break except for a small tavern that was tucked away in an alley. Inside, I saw a few locals sitting at a dimly lit bar. None of them spoke any English. I tried to communicate with the bartender and asked if she could direct me to the nearest alburgue. She said something in Spanish that I didn't understand and pointed down the street. "South?" I asked.

"Si."

I headed south on Rua Maior Street in the pouring rain. My clothes had become soaked and I was chilled to the bone. I could feel the weight of my backpack becoming heavier. For the next hour, I walked up and down the street knocking on the door of each alburgue I came to. Despite my persistence, there were no answers.

My situation was becoming dire and it continued to rain.

For weeks leading up to this trip, I studied guidebooks and scoured Internet forums for information about the Camino. According to everything I had read, Alburgues and hotels were readily available during the winter season. It was also my understanding that there were villages and hamlets situated about every 5km along the route, so food and accommodations

SHORT STORIES ANTHOLOGY - VOLUME 1

would not be a problem. It was becoming painfully obvious that everything I read was wrong.

Having given up the hope of an alburgue, I began to wander the streets in search of a hotel. Now, I began to ask people on the street "*hotel?*" Even though I was using my very best Spanish accent, I was still having no luck. Occasionally, people would point up one street or down another, but when I arrived at each destination, the hotel was closed.

For the first time in a very long time, I was beginning to feel homesick. "What the hell am I doing here?" I said out loud, "what the hell am I looking for?" It all began with a romantic notion of going on an adventure, but now I just felt dumb. This was the first time I had traveled without my family and I was beginning to miss the security that it provided. On most vacations, my wife had everything planned down to the smallest detail; Nothing was overlooked. On my own, I was about to crash and burn.

I looked down at my watch to see that it was just past midnight. It was late and I had exhausted all of my options. I felt like a failure. My hope of a warm bed was gone, so I un-shouldered my pack and sat down in an abandoned doorway. "I guess this is where I'm going to sleep tonight," I thought. It was going to be a cold night, but at least I would be out of the rain.

Just as I had given up hope, I spotted an older gentleman who was walking in my direction. He was taking his dog for a late night stroll. He was slender with thick black hair and an unruly mustache. He wore a rumpled tweed blazer with a rain coat over it. "Are you a pilgrim?" he asked in a thick accent. I told him that I was and asked if he knew where I could find an open hotel.

"Are you walking as a tourist or for spiritual reasons?" he asked.

"Spiritual," I said.

"Vagando por el amor de dios."

"What does that mean?" I asked.

"Wandering for the love of God," he said in English.

"Something like that."

His face broke into a broad smile and he extended his hand. I pulled myself to my feet and met his grasp. "I'm going to help you," he said. He pulled out his phone and began to search through his contacts. Soon, he made a call and began to speak to someone in Spanish. I couldn't understand what he was saying, but it sounded like he was negotiating. "Is 50 euros for the night okay?" he asked.

"Yes, of course," I told him.

At that moment, He stepped out into the street and began to hale a taxi cab that was passing by. He hung up the phone and began to speak to the taxi driver. After a few minutes of what sounded like another negotiation, He informed me that the driver was off duty and heading home for the night. He agreed to take me to the hotel, but it would cost 10 euros. I told him that I would gladly pay the fee.

"Gracias," I said to my new friend as I collapsed into the back seat of the cab.

"Buen camino" he replied. "I hope you find what you are looking for, my friend." Then he closed the door and we drove off into the night.

About the Author

Robert Kelsoe is a freelance writer & photographer from Southern California. He has a passion for crafting non-fiction stories based on his adventures and real-life experiences. His work has been featured in many publications including Reminisce Magazine, Adelaide Literary Magazine, Roam Family Travel and others. You can find his travel photography on Instagram @Traveling_Strong.

Brandy McKay

Dont Drop the Egg

Patrick turned eleven years old the day Bruster, Grandma's prize Bantam rooster, tried to kill him.

Patrick begged Grandma to bake a cake for his birthday. She agreed and sent him out to the coop to gather six eggs.

"Be careful to stay out of Bruster's way," Grandma called out.

She had nine breeds of hens and branded them the "Bruster Girls." Patrick hated Bruster. From day one, Bruster took every chance possible to show off and prove his protective skills, which included pecking at Patrick's feet whenever possible.

Bruster had a favorite hen, Claudette, a beautiful Rhode Island Red. Her plumage must have mesmerized him because he followed her everywhere. She would waddle, and he would follow.

It took years before Patrick unloaded what happened that birthday day. Before he dared to enter the coop, Patrick made sure Bruster and Claudette were busy at the far end of the chicken run. He gathered four eggs with ease and looked for two more. Then without consent Mother Nature called, and Patrick caught the urge to let go of some internal water.

However, Grandma needed six eggs, and only four were in the basket. If he didn't come back with six eggs, Grandma might not bake his cake. He reached in a nesting box and found another egg, and the urge became intense, but he needed just one more egg.

The force became more than he could bear. Patrick didn't have time to run to the house, so he did what any kid would do; he found a corner in the coop and started to pee.

Old Charlie, Grandma's white-faced barn owl, delivered an overexcited hoot. Patrick saw Charlie atop the rafters. Charlie hooted several more hoots before Patrick realized what had happened. It seemed Charlie tried to warn him, but it was too late.

Patrick didn't see the cluster of little chicks right below him and didn't mean to pee on them. It was an accident. These chicks weren't just any chicks; they were Claudette's brood and only a few weeks old. The peeps did not like being sprayed, and their frightful trill almost shattered the barn door as the golden shower landed on soft baby feathers. Old Charlie flew away.

From the corner of his eye, Patrick saw Claudette enter the coop. Bruster followed. She caught Patrick right in the act. Claudette let out a squawk of anger so piercing that if a train chugged on the tracks nearby, the engineer would have heard her loud and clear.

Patrick panicked. He tried to stop the flow of nature and splashed again. Fear took control as he showered another chick and then another. Claudette went ballistic as her babies ran in circles like a Category Five hurricane, all crying for their mama. Mayhem hit the coop: Claudette squawked, chicks peeped, and Patrick wanted to cry.

Bruster saw his girl Claudette and his baby chicks in trouble and went on the warpath. Bruster took one look at Patrick and, sure as heck, if fire could emit from a rooster's nostrils—flames flared. Claws dug deep into the floor, and he propelled so fast a mountain lion couldn't catch him. In midair, Bruster shot Patrick the Evil Eye. Terrified, Patrick put his arms up to protect his face. But it was too late. Bruster took aim and went right for Patrick's private body part. Big daddy Bruster nipped Patrick smack on the ding-a-ling. The birthday boy let out a rip-roaring scream so loud the termites took a run for safety.

Bruster landed on both feet, his spurs projected. Like a raging bull, Bruster eye-balled Patrick as he scratched the ground as if to say, "This fight ain't over yet, kid."

Patrick knew the war had just begun. He reckoned he had a split second to run before Bruster killed him. He dashed out the coop and sprinted to the house faster than a shot from a Red Ryder BB gun.

"Help, help!"

Right behind him scurried a crazed rooster in deep combat mode. Rooster feathers puffed, and Bruster grew twice his standard size. Bruster drove forward with such a determination nothing, not even Superman, could stop.

"Open the door. Open the door." Patrick picked up speed.

The kitchen door flew open.

"Run, Patrick, run," Grandma yelled, "Don't drop the eggs."

Just a few feet from the porch, Patrick's foot slipped on some loose gravel. He fell forward, then rocked backward. He struggled to take hold. Patrick figured any minute he'd be dead.

But the unexpected happened. In that heightened moment of fear, Patrick decided then and there that no bully rooster would get the best of him. He was a man now, and time to act like a man. With a new sense of pride and grit, he rose courage to the challenge and pulled himself together.

"Not today, you little pecker. Not today."

With all his might, adrenaline kicked in, and Patrick propelled a giant leap for the kitchen door.

"Get inside," Grandma shouted.

Patrick slid across the linoleum floor and the basket of eggs sored through the air. Grandma caught the handle with one hand and gave the door a furious slam with the other.

Grandma peered out the window to find Bruster. He must have flown right into the kitchen door because he lay topsy-turvy on the porch planks', his wings flattened. Bruster tried to lift his little head, but like a fallen boxer with the referee at ten counts, he couldn't.

At the bottom of the porch, high-pitched tweets and clucks exploded from Claudette and her brood. Bruster started to stir. The peeps' chatter increased, and a flood of squawks filled the air. He struggled to get up, one leg at a time.

From the ground below, Claudette and her chicks watched as Buster, little by little, fought to stand. At last, like a noble warrior, he stood at the edge of the porch, pumped his chest, and jumped down the steps: one and then another. When he reached his brood, the chicks scurried around him. In silence, Claudette and Bruster walked back to the coop, and the baby chicks toddled behind.

"I bet if chickens had arms, Claudette would have hugged Bruster," Grandma said as she handed Patrick a Band-Aid.

About the Author

Author of numerous short stories published in newspapers and magazines. Received her degree in Journalism and holds a Masters in Educational Leadership. Brandy followed her passion and writes full-time in Morro Bay, Calif. In her spare time she is a gourd artist.

Leandro Almeida

Watching

Have you ever gotten the feeling someone is watching you? Those chills down your spine? That sense of unease, or the prickling on your neck? Objects no longer in the spots you left them in? If you have not, I envy you. I constantly live with these feelings, and let it be noted. I live alone. I do not blame this on the supernatural, on the contrary. I believe it to be a physical person, to be exact, my neighbor, Victoria. A short, round, blonde woman, who always finds a way to insert herself into my life and I into hers. Today, however, I plan to find out if my suspicions come with reason.

I sit by the window and watch as she gets in her car and leaves for work; as she always does. Six days a week. From nine in the morning till five in the afternoon. As soon as her car turns the street corner, I head out of my house and over to her front door. I reach into the flowerpot next to her door and grab the spare key she leaves there. I unlock the door and walk in, taking a moment to look around at my surroundings. I will give her one thing. Her house was as clean as it could get. Her vinyl floor was spotless. The painting and pictures on the wall were all centered and evenly spaced. Not a spec of dirt to be seen on her white couch. Everything in their proper places and in proper order, as all things should be.

I head up the stairs and down the hall, stopping at the second door on the right. I walk into her bedroom and look around. Her bed was pushed back against the back wall, facing the door. Two sliding doors leading to her closest, were on the left wall, and a small desk, with little knick knacks on it sat at the right corner of the room. Nothing had changed. I walk over to her closet, sliding open the door. I met with, as usual, neatly hung clothes, a few cardboard boxes on the ground, and some undergarments folded on the shelf above, but now there was a new addition. A shoe box labeled memories also sat on the shelf. I grab the box and place it beside me as I sit on her bed.

I open the box and find that inside contains a journal and multiple polaroids, each one with a label on the back. I pick up the one that said first date. I turn it over to find a picture of myself sitting at a restaurant with a woman, except her face was crossed out by a marker. The next picture was labeled third date with a smiley face after it. I turn it over. My heart skips a beat. My hand begins to shake, and I can no longer control my breathing. The picture was of me and Victoria lying in bed together, naked, as she clutches my lower half in one hand. I flip the box over, the pictures scattering on the ground. Each and every one was of me. In the shower, at work, even at my parent's house. My stomach began doing flips as I look towards the journal. I open the journal to a random page and begin reading.

Dear Diary, Today I decided to be a good little housewife and help my husband around his house. I washed his clothes, making sure to squirt some of my love juices on them so he can always have my sent. I washed each of his dishes today, licking off any leftover food and giving it a good old spit shine. I also...,

The list went on and on. I cover my mouth with my hand as tears begin to form in my eyes, " This. This is be-"

"Beautiful," interrupts a voice from behind me.

I let out a gasp as I turn around to meet the voice, but before I manage to see who it is; I feel a sharp pain against the side of my head. My vision goes dark and I lose consciousness.

My eyes flutter open and I find myself staring up at the ceiling. I attempt to move, but feel the sharp pinch of the rope around my wrists and ankles. I fight the throbbing pain in my head and look around noticing I was in my bedroom. The bedroom door opens and I see the familiar round siluet of Victoria walk in.

She walks over placing a hand on my chest. "Good morning, honey. How was your nap?"

I stare at her at a loss of words not knowing what to say.

She lets out a slight giggle and says, "Oh, you must still be shocked by all the photos and from what your read in my journal." She places her hand on the spot she hit me. "I hope I didn't hit you too hard, to ruin that brain of yours." She pulls away from me and walks over to my closet. "Well, I don't need you to say anything right now anyway, so just listen. You and me, we are going to leave this town and go somewhere they won't ever find us. To where I can have you all to myself. So let's make your bag." She opens my closet and begins to pull out some clothes, but stops when she sees a box labeled memories. She holds it in her hand. "Funny you have one of these too? Let's see what's inside." As she opens it and starts looking through each of the labeled polaroids and reads each of the journal entries about her, her eyes grow wide.

She snaps her head towards me, the look of surprise. written on her face"W-why are you smiling?"

A sinister grin spreads across my face. "I've been watching too. Darling."

Tropis' letter

To whom it may concern,

My first memory was of how the smoke clouded the sky, as it rose from the roofs of the huts we rode away from. My second memory was of how my sister wailed in the arms of the man who dragged her away. My third being that of metal bars that surrounded me, keeping me from my sister and the world.

The numbers 506 and 507 scared our necks and the only words we knew were yes master, yes mistress, yes, my lord, and yes ma'am. From master to master, from cell to cell, from under one body to another, the chains and collars never left us; the only things we truly could still call our own.

Another memory that came to mind is that of a man. The man was heavy set, had many tattoos and a long, well-kept beard. He gave our current master a small brown bag tied at the tip, before taking us by the chains and leading us out of the master's house. A new memory was made shortly after, that of the glean of the blood that trickled down the knife; the roar of the crowd, masking the sound of someone gasping for air in front of me. The smell of blood, sweat and dirt. The feeling of my hand raised above me and a word I had never heard before directed at me, Tropis. I watched my sister go through the same ordeal, as I sat beside the bearded man. She was also called a new word, Aura.

The collars grew too tight and we were given new ones. The scars of 506 and 507 were masked under black ink and we met Aslows. Aslows taught us what memories are, he taught me how to write this. He taught us many things how to speak, defend ourselves, what a family was. A new word was learned during this time. Happiness.

Loss and anger were learned soon after. One day the heavy-set man came to us offering a new word, freedom. One Aslows had yet to teach. Our eyes grew wide and smiles spread across our face as he explained what this word was. He said in exchange for having our eyes look upon glistening blood one last time we could attain it. Aura and I eagerly accepted and dreamt of the adventures our future held.

My feet left marks in the red stained sand as I walked to the center of the pit, blades in hand, waving to the crowd; not as a hello, but goodbye. I bowed to the bearded man and looked towards my opponent, emerging from a set of wooden doors. My blades dug into the sand, my eyes went wide, my breath caught in my throat. A similar reaction seemed to be happening in Aura, who now stood in front of me. My eyes trailed to the grinning face of the bearded man.

Beg and plead as we did, claiming there had to be a mistake, that it wasn't meant to be. He simply rose his hands and the guards aimed their weapons upon us. He stood and gestured to the crowd, "They demand blood." I turned to Aura, a smile sat upon her face and her blade sat in her hand. Before I could say anything, a sharp pain filled my chest. Not one cause by a blade, but one just as deadly. Glistening blood trickled from the corner of Aura's mouth; the tip of her blade embedded within her chest. Her limp body now lay in my hands, her blood painting my skin. She reached up placing a hand upon my cheek, the smile never leaving her lips, "Be free dear brother." Her smile is the only memory I wish to hold.

As I was dragged away from her body as the sound of barking and tearing of flesh could be heard over my screams. I was left on the side of a dirt road, knowing nothing of the world around me. Beside me sat my blades and a small bag tied at the tip.

I write this not for one to feel pity nor as a form of farewell. I write this for justice. I write this for whoever finds this note to turn it in to the guards, for them to know of the horrors that happen beneath the kingdom. As evidence, the head of the bearded man sits beside me as I write this. His body lays bleeding in a nearby tavern, for the they demanded blood. I'm running low on ink so I this is where I must end it, but I bid you good luck and pray that you complete this task. For I have finished mine and will now experience the dreams my sister and I dreamt of. For the both of us.

~ Sincerely, Tropis

I'm still here

Pop! He pulls the scissors out of the ball and lets it drop to the ground. My hand reaches down to the ball, but I let out a scream of pain as his fingers dig into my hair, pulling me away. $p(h) = 101,325(1 - 2.25577 \times 10\text{-}5h)$ ... The equation continues underneath my cheek.

"This. This is who you are. Not that damn ball." The weight of his hand disappears.

The familiar sound of the key in the lock fills my ears. I bite into my forearm, muffling my scream, the slight pain providing guilty relief.

My pencil dances across the paper as the whispers of the class float around me.

"It must be nice being him. Top grades, rich family, good looks, he has it all."

No, I don't.

"I wish I was him."

No, you don't.

"I envy him."

You shouldn't.

People think they know me and who I am, but I'm not who they see. Because I'm not here. I turn my head to the window, resting my cheek against my palm; staring at a group of students playing volleyball and I see myself amongst them. The harsh school bell rings, returning me to reality. As everyone leaves, I stay to...study. The teacher walks up behind me placing a hand on my shoulder. "Shall we begin your lessons?" His hand begins to trail down my back.

I lay on my stomach, in my room, unable to sit or lay in any other position and reach into my desk drawer and pull out my guilty pleasure. I begin to scrape and chip away. Deeper and deeper and deeper. I fall into rhythm. My guilty pleasure, as well as my fingers, gaining a new tint of color. Deep, shallow breaths escape me, as I wipe down my guilty pleasure, staring at the deep, wide, gaps of bliss, providing the only form of feeling I know.

I scoop a spoon of rice placing it on my plate, along with the beans and beef we had and join my, 'family', at the table and we fall into the tuneless rhythm of knives and forks. My father breaks the silence, looking over to my younger sister.

"So, honey, how was school?"

"It was Good," she replies.

"Still top of the class I presume?"

"Mhm."

He smiles at her. "That's great, if only your brother would forget about that stupid ball and focus on school, he'd be the top of his class as well."

The plates of the table clatter as I push myself up. "May I be excused?"

He stares at me, but before he could say anything my mother cut him off, "Go ahead, dear."

I drop my plate in the sink and rush through our apartment over to my room.

I'm tired. I'm tired of it all. The teacher, my father, the books, the chains, I want to be free. Someone please help me I'm still here.

My bedroom door slams shut behind me and I reach into my drawer for my guilty pleasure. It chips and scrapes away at my skin, but my eyes lock on to my ball sitting in the corner of the room. A large patch of duct tape lay where it had suffered its mortal wound. I walk over to it, dropping my guilty pleasure and pick up the ball and hold it in my hands. The feeling like a distant memory. A breeze from the open window pricks my neck. I turn and walk over to the window and stare out across the city.

Yes this is it.

I lean further out the window, the memory becoming clearer the further I went out.

Almost there. I can almost see it.

Till finally I remember. I remember the feeling of the wind as I ran up the court. The feeling of the air as I jumped and soared over the net, my eyes getting a glimpse of that beautiful summit. And finally, the feeling of my hand making contact with the ball, now coursing through my body, as I thought, *I'm still here.*

About the Author

Leandro is a 19 year old boy born in Kissimmee, Florida and Raised in Sacramento California. He enjoys gaming, mma, voleyball, and anime. He has a pet german Shepard named, Panther, and a hedgehog named, Dot. He hopes you will enjoy his stories.

Bil Johnson

A Piece of History?

Following the publication of Joe Hagen's authorized biography of Jann Wenner, *Sticky Fingers: The Life and Times of Jann Wenner and Rolling Stone Magazine* (2017) some "lost stories" from the magazine have been uncovered. One such story, written by journalist Carlton Terlizzi (a Hunter Thompson-like comet of a writer), was a profile of the early '70's band, *Stumble Bums.* Terlizzi's account is a piece of rock and roll history that had been lost 46 years ago and is finally available for the public. For those *Stumble Bums* fans who are still out there, Terlizzi's story evokes memories of a band that was revelatory, poetic, garish, and fun.

For those who don't remember Terlizzi, that's understandable. Even though he was a contemporary of Thompson and Joe Eszterhas in the early years of *Rolling Stone*, he never produced books (like Thompson's *Fear and Loathing*) or screenplays (like Eszterhas's *Basic Instinct, Showgirls*) but he certainly raised as much hell. In fact, not long after filing the story presented here, Terlizzi jumped on his motorcycle, after an evening "carousing" with Thompson and Eszterhas all over San Francisco and was never seen or heard from again. Did he fly off a Pacific Coast Highway cliff? Was he abducted by the Symbionese Liberation Army? Did he decide to "retire" to a quieter (and more sane) life somewhere else in the U.S., like a witness protection program client? We'll never know, but we *do* have his writing. His last piece is what we've uncovered for your reading pleasure and edification. Enjoy!

Getting the Band Together:

The Half-Life of *Stumble Bums*

Carlton Terlizzi

January 1973

Angus McPuffin, Waldo Gropingles, and Oslo Dunkleklass are an unlikely trio. Each has a singular, distractingly unattractive feature. Angus's nose is remarkably thin and, halfway down, makes a sharp right. Waldo's left eye seems to have a life of its own and evokes an aura of Quasimodo. Oslo has the teeth of an Englishman (though he isn't), only worse. A composite sketch of the three would probably resemble a child's drawing of a clown — or a "monster." Yet all three have voices that are so sweet and ethereal the term "celestial" often accompanies critical reviews of their band, *Stumble Bums*.

It was the late '60's when Angus, Waldo, and Oslo met in art school, as so many band mates did in those years. None was a particularly good artist — Angus sculpted, Waldo painted, and Oslo was a photographer — but they were extremely earnest students who hit it off well in a freshman year *Theories of Art* course (which each barely received a passing grade for). In the fall of 1969 they were 20 years old and discussing the recent Woodstock Festival over coffee at a diner along 12th Avenue on the Lower West Side overlooking Jersey City. Their studies, over the years, had not gone well, Waldo's had been classified "in abeyance," the school's odd parlance for "one foot out the door." The other two were spending more time at their jobs — Angus at a record store and Oslo as an elevator operator in an Upper East Side high rise — than on their studies. It was over those cups of coffee that the boys were deciding their future — even if they weren't aware of it at the time. As they describe it:

I'm not sure I really see much in sculpting, moving forward, you know?" Angus confessed.

Waldo nodded. *"Yeah, I'm startin' to feel the same way about the whole painting thing. I mean, where'm I goin', really."*

"I love taking pictures — but it's really competitive out there. But you never know, right?" the always upbeat Oslo offered, looking back and forth at his friends.

"I think we need to honestly look at where we're going, y'know, and maybe consider some other 'options?" Angus, leaning forward now, had furrowed his brow as he addressed his friends.

"Other 'options?" Waldo, as per, looked clueless.

Oslo stood up, framing his face with his hands, clutching at his watch cap, grinning broadly: *"Why don't we start a band!"*

Angus stared, hard, at Oslo. *"Get the fuck outta here,"* waving a dismissive hand.

"No, really," Oslo persisted, *"hear me out on this."*

Waldo's crazy eye rolled around, trying to focus on Oslo as he revealed his idea.

"Know how we always sing along with songs we like on the radio?" He didn't wait for a response. *"Have you actually listened to our voices together?"*

Waldo, focused for the moment, looked at Angus, who shrugged and sheepishly admitted: *"No."*

"Well," Oslo continued, *"we sound good — damn good. And we each play instruments, right?"*

Waldo chimed in: "*We'd have to practice — a lot. A lot a lot, you know?*"

It was true. All three had early musical training: Angus on classical guitar; Waldo on piano; and Oslo played drums, starting in Cub Scout marching bands. Each still "practiced" occasionally but they had never tried playing anything *together*. And there was the daunting challenge of writing *original* material.

Maybe it was because they were 20 and didn't know any better. Maybe they actually had "gifts" that had never been tapped. Maybe the stars were aligned *just right*. And *maybe* the addition of Josh Ben Soto to the "band" was a particular godsend.

Ben Soto's father was a highly regarded music producer in New York City. An Israeli émigré in the early '50's, Sol Ben Soturian was a multi-instrumentalist who started out as a session musician and a Tin Pin Alley stalwart. As the music business expanded in the early Sixties, Sol changed his last name to make it a little more "Latin/exotica," in his words, as he moved into the control room becoming a producer and turning out some doo-wop hits as well as girl-group ballads. After Beatlemania, he was "making a living" turning out albums and 45's, honing his skills and breaking even. His son, Josh, was a prodigy on the upright bass, starting to play it by 4th grade and making the natural shift to the electric bass, sometimes sitting in for sessions his Dad produced. Josh had befriended Waldo early on in art school and continued to help him stay in school. When Waldo pitched "the band" idea to Josh he basically said, "*Why not?*"

And that was the beginning.

Josh was the natural leader of the group but "the boys," as they became known, took to being a "band" naturally and their progress was rapid. With coaching from Josh and Sol, they turned out being better musicians than they imagined and their dormant skills emerged overnight. *And Oslo had been right on the money about their voices*! They naturally voiced harmonies and could mimic the latest *Crosby, Stills, and Nash* songs with startling accuracy. Each could not only "carry a tune" but could also sing lead on a song — and they began "matching" tunes to the "best" singer. Josh had a voice that was compared to Don Henley of the breaking new group, *Eagles,* adding another dimension to the group's sound.

In the early months of practice they naturally "covered" popular songs but quickly realized they would have to start writing their own material and, unlike their half-hearted efforts at art school, "the boys" threw themselves into the work. Here's where some classic characteristics of the band emerged. Oslo, who informed everyone he should be referred to as "Oslo Flintland" from this day forward, was a lover of rock music "on the fringe." He listened to Frank Zappa and Capt. Beefheart as well as Dr. John and a raft of old blues guys. Waldo, eye flying here and there, was a "Top 40" guy and loved listening to "Top 20 Singles" from groups like Tommy James and the Shondells (*Crimson & Clover, Crystal Blue Persuasion*) as well as Sly and the Family Stone (*Everyday People, Hot Fun in the Summertime*). He would sometimes break into "*Build Me Up Buttercup*" (The Foundations) at a least expected moment. Waldo also announced a new moniker: *Waco Montana*. "Pretty cool, eh?" eyebrow arched (while the eyeball rolled), Waldo clearly had put a lot of thought into his Stage Name.

Angus told them he was considering being called Angus McAngus, but never made the switch. His musical taste was a lot like Josh's and ran toward the popular albums and their artists, an eclectic sampling of rock and roll that included The Flying Burrito Brothers, The Stooges, Led Zeppelin, and Blind

Faith. They all loved the Beatles, Stones, and Motown, of course, so there were many "influences" pouring into their musical cauldron — and all kinds of songs came out.

By the spring of 1970, the band, calling itself *Poots and Ladders*, had Sol Ben Soto's agent pal, Mickey Zielinski, book them gigs at the Room Room, Vicarious Café, and What's On Second? nightclub. Not big venues, for sure, but places to learn how to publicly perform and perfect their chops. All the while they were writing songs furiously and testing them out on audiences. Through some happy accidents they actually opened for *The Velvet Underground* on the Lower East Side and *The Stooges* in New Brunswick, New Jersey. That was the gig where "Waco" (Waldo) first saw Iggy Pop "stage dive" into a crowd. Several weeks later "Waco" tried it himself, as he wrapped up his song, "Breathing Through My Mouth," and discovered the crowd had never seen a stage dive before. He broke two ribs and lost a tooth. At that point the group decided to call themselves *Stumble Bums.*

Stumble Bums were a meteor on the rock and roll scene from late 1970 through early 1972, flashing then crashing, leaving embers of their music here and there on the landscape of rock and roll history. They produced two albums over that time, with talk about a few "Live" discs produced posthumously (after the "band" died, not "the boys"). There's still hope that some "hidden tapes" will be discovered somewhere along the line.

Their first album, released in late 1970, was *You, Again?* and featured a startled young woman turning toward a doorway where several guys with gig bags were crashing in. What made *You, Again?* distinctive was that one side of the album was *blatantly* commercial — with most of the songs written by "Waco" (with help from Josh). Side Two, however, was an Angus and

Oslo production, with songs ranging over a gamut of styles, time signatures, and sounds. There was one single ("Hold the Mayo") released separately, to "Prime the pump," Sol and Mickey told "the boys."

"Waco's" commercial songs on Side One were:

1. That Fool at School
2. I'm Not Your Used Car
3. If I Can't Be Your Guy, I'd Rather Die
4. In My Gaze
5. What's It Worth?
6. Running in the Halls

Oslo's and Angus's Side Two was comprised of:

1. "Tripped on My Dick"
2. "All's Well That Ends"
3. "A Comet Made Me Vomit"
4. "Clarabelle Went to Hell"
5. "It's okay, Dad, I'm Only Bleeding Out"
6. "Fart Party"

Needless to say, people had some trouble figuring out what the band was about. That was only complicated by "Hold the Mayo,"

"Waco's" teen angst love song (with a dynamite *hook*!). Here are the first few verses, as well as the chorus with the catchy bass hook (courtesy of Josh Ben Soto):

I was workin' in the Deli, when she walked in . ../
Yeah, just right, not fat or thin,/
A BLT was on her mind/

I told her, "oh, yeah, that's fine ..../
And as I built up all three decks,/
I was thinkin', "Hey, what the heck,/
Maybe she would be my baby,/
If I asked the right way, maybe."/
Just before I turned around,/
That's when I could hear the sound..../
Her eyes were big, her hand was up/
"Hold the Mayo on my Stuff!"/
Hold the Mayo, that's what she said,/
Hold the Mayo, or I was dead,/
Hold the Mayo, before you slice,/
Hold that mayo, she was cold as ice!

Angus and Oslo were not thrilled that "Hold the Mayo" was the first "hit" for the band but thought that once people heard their Side Two, they'd expand their audience. And it did, even though they never got higher than #47 on the BillBoard charts. Still, not bad for a first album.

"The boys" went back into the studio with new resolve after a short tour of East Coast venues in the summer of 1971. The "tour" featured events like the extremely inebriated Oslo somehow missing the band's bus back to NYC from the Hamptons and *walking* (and hitchhiking) back to his Lower East Side apartment by late the next evening. They also learned that, in Washington, D.C., you *can be fined* for passing gas in a club *after curfew* — costing the club $500 after Angus directed a microphone at Waco's butt. After they got back home Oslo mentioned he was disappointed they hadn't stayed at any place with a swimming pool, telling the band he wanted to emulate the Rolling Stones, filling a kiddie pool with Cap'n Crunch and KY Jelly. Beyond that, the tour went swimmingly and "the boys" were ready to crank out their second studio album.

Angus and Waco wanted to call the new album "Number Two" and put a picture of a pile of dog shit on the cover — but that was quickly voted down (by everyone!). There were lots of stories about drug and alcohol abuse, as well as arguments between "the boys" and the final product — called *Sunset at the Carbdboard Factory* — was clearly *four* blocs of *three* songs, each written by a different member of the band.

"Waco's" contribution was:
Mellifluous Balloons
Simple Man, Simple Song
Walkin' Home

All of these were catchy, "Top 20" type songs and "Simple Man" was a hit single, reaching #22 on the "pop" charts.

Oslo's songs were:
Sizzlin' Summer
Barkin' for Dinner
Roundheels

These were hummable, if a bit sophomoric, tunes that the band's younger fans particularly loved and "Sizzlin' Summer" made it to #29 on the charts.

Angus's writing produced:
You Talkin' to Me?
What're You Lookin' At?
Stick Up the Butt

These songs were a radical departure from anything the band had done up to that point —- driving rhythms, bass leads on some songs, and vocals that "attacked" the audience, even more than Stage Diving.

Finally, Josh added the songs:

War Ain't Good

Contrary Mary

Lost My Job Again

These were "social issue" songs and became quite popular with the politically oriented fans the band engendered. There was a segment of the listening public that loved the anarchy "the boys" represented. While none of Josh's songs rocketed up the charts, they are probably the ones that will have the longest shelf life.

Stumble Bums never went on tour with *Sunset at the Cardboard Factory* and the band broke up shortly after the album was released. While Josh Ben Soto remained a notable presence on the New York music scene "the boys" disappeared from public view. Oslo went back to art school, "Waco" became Waldo again and took a job in the family construction firm and Angus moved to the West Coast to become a plumber in Berkeley. Despite their record label's attempt at coaxing them into touring, "the boys" had "turned the page."

So, *Stumble Bums* was like that flash of light in the night that sears our retina and explodes, shattering into shrapnel, spreading across the landscape of our memory. They were a moment in the early history of rock and roll and their final legacy is yet to be recorded. *Hold the Mayo*!

Post Script

Carlton Terlizzi was 27 when he disappeared in 1973. The same age as Jim Morrison, Janis Joplin, and Jimi Hendrix when they left us.. While he may not share a place on rock and roll's Mount

Rushmore, as those three would, he was a writer of considerable talent who captured the energy and vitality of a particular and special time in our cultural history. Who knows what else he may have accomplished with his writing? If you're out there, Carlton, and reading this — come back.

Ansel's Package

It moved in with the warmth of a baby's breath as it falls asleep. Watching the dark brown swath of blood backwash into the syringe, Ansel felt his muscles relax as his back met the tile wall, the coolness of it dappling his skin with gooseflesh. His eyelids went to half-mast and he wasn't sure if the tune he heard was his own voice humming or some Muzak from the fast food counter out front.

"C'mon, Mac, how long ya gonna be in there?!"

The open-hand slapping on the door jolted the bolt-lock enough to revive Ansel. He quickly removed the needle, scooped up his works (dispatching them to the large outer pocket of his fatigue jacket), ran the water and flushed the toilet almost simultaneously.

"All right, all right," he heard a voice croak annoyedly. Was it his?

He passed a burly man on his way to the exit. Two hams of forearms were crossed on the flannel-shirted chest and a cap with an NRA insignia glared at Ansel. He avoided eye contact and ignored the muttered "Asshole . . . ." as the man slammed the rest room door.

It was an early December chill that slapped his cheeks; a sleet-and-cold after-shave smack that Ansel didn't need. He was down to his last 15 bucks and his last nickel bag and neither would last too long. He needed to do something in a hurry.

While waiting for the Master Plan to dawn, he moved into an alley. Ruminating over garbage cans and Dempsey Dumpsters, searching for valuable castaways, or at least returnable bottles, a small canvas book-bag caught his eye. Had it moved?

Ansel knew the skag was wearing thin already — what might it be cut with? — was he hallucinating?

He peered at the bag, thrust his face down into the bin to eyeball it. It did move! A sound, too?

Ansel stood upright, bracing himself on the edge of the dumpster, hands gripping it tightly, elbows locked, he looked again, as if it were a wishing well he had just tossed a coin in.

Now the navy blue bag — darker even with the steady rain's constant coloring — fitfully emitted a squeal. Ansel remembered hearing cats make that sound, as a boy, when they went into heat. Had someone dumped a cat for winter? It wouldn't be the first time.

He reached tentatively, the way one moves toward a hot stove, and poked — a quick, sharp jab to make the cat jump. It didn't. It cried louder, a muffled gasp of a cry, a gulp for air.

Ansel lifted the bag at the top, where the drawstring closed it. Helluva a big cat. And it didn't shift its weight to compensate for the lift. Maybe it was a pup. A steady sobbing was now emanating from the sack. More a staccato clutching for breath now.

Ansel held the bag away from his face as he inched his fingers into the barely opened space at the top. He turned his head away as he moved his hands apart and opened the sack — he'd been scratched by leaping cats before — but the bag shifted only slightly. He lowered it now, arms-distance away, blinking in the chill mist that sprinkled his eyelids, and looked over the edge and into the sack.

"Well, I'll be damned," his face moved into an unfamiliar smile, muscles unused in months put to work. "Well, I'll be a junkie motherfucker . . . "

The cry from the bag was quite distinct now. Human and infant. Hunger. Steam rose from the sack, with the faint aroma of used Pampers. Ansel's nostrils flared involuntarily.

"Now what'm I gonna do with you, I wonder . . . ."

He picked up a stray newspaper and covered the opening of the bag as he sidled into a doorway, out of the rain. Clutching the little bundle to him, inside his coat now, he began rocking and humming, forgetting, for the moment, his last 15 dollars, his last nickel bag, and even the fact that Ansel Robbins could barely fend for himself.

It didn't matter if it was the cold, or the cry, or the smell that woke him. Ansel was bolt upright now, with a squealing child in his arms and the dark of night holding him as tightly as he gripped the baby. He was shivering and knew he needed a shot. The child was howling — for food and a change of diaper, for warmth. Ansel's mind was alternately a cauldron of ideas and a fused block of magma. In his strobe-light consciousness of addiction he leapt to the child's rescue and soothed his own ache for the needle momentarily. His forearms throbbed, he could feel the pulse behind his eyes pressuring his pupils. The baby's cry was constant now, an ambulance siren, multi-toned but always high-pitched. Ansel could feel the child's cry resonate his own throat, his lungs. He was freezing. He was sweating.

Leave the alley. Find a place to shoot. The rain finally stopped. The baby attained a new level of pitch. Standing now, Ansel thoughtlessly held the sack as if it were filled with books. It hung at the end of his arm, almost dragging along the ground, swinging with an arhythmic cadence, occasionally spinning off his leg. The cries continued.

The streets were shiny, newly waxed, it seemed, and the cold December night rose easily from the surface, straight up the pants leg, standing hair on end, bristling the scrotum.

Ansel's mouth was dry now, his palms soaked. The crying wouldn't stop. He need a bathroom to fix himself but couldn't bring the kid along. Once he shot, he'd be okay, he'd take good care of the baby. Once he shot.

The diner at 3rd and South would be open. He'd buy a coffee-to-go and use the john. He'd leave the kid somewhere behind the place, nestle it somewhere — no one would hear it or see it. Hell, it must be 3 a.m. or so.

The alley was dark, puddled. He felt cold water sponging his socks. Something angular and metallic cut his shin. Here it was, though, a Dumpster. The kid was only whimpering now. Maybe it was going to pass out. They can't cry forever, can they?

He reached into the Dumpster. Wet and slimy debris, rotted cardboard and diner remains sifted through his torn gloves. A corrugated box, waxed laminate, imperiously dry here, became the safe-haven, a manger in the corner for his sobbing package. He tucked it tenderly in its place, promising to return quickly with aid and comfort. Ansel understood the urgency in the baby's needy cries; he'd soon help this child of refuse.

It was powder blue and black tile. No mirror. A urinal and a stall with a door barely held by one hinge. He put some water in the spoon and moved carefully into the stall, balancing himself on the edge of the toilet seat while using his leg as a workbench, neatly aligning his tools. His concentration was pure (much more so than his heroin) and only broken by the occasional metal-on-metal banging behind him. Something in the kitchen? He heated the spoon as he tightened the belt around his bicep, steady as a rock. No matter how strung out he was, the anticipation of the shot calmed him. Even the intrusive rumbling of the motor behind him (a kitchen exhaust fan?) couldn't disturb his concentration. It only took a minute to bubble, to fill the syringe and feel that familiar, friendly puncture. As the needle penetrated, softly, easily, Ansel relaxed and thought of the baby in the cold, of how he would go to the all-night 24-hour store and get some disposable diapers and milk for the child. His eyes were closed, the muscles in his face relaxed, only the Clang-Clang-Clang behind him marred the moment. And that exhaust fan — so loud? Maybe he'd get a reward from some Social Service Agency for returning the child? Money for dope? Wouldn't that be right, though? Only fair?

The warmth of the stupor coated Ansel for countless minutes. A rumble, a vibration, and a final metal "THWANG!" rattled him back to consciousness and reminded him of the waiting child.

With renewed vigor, Ansel strode from the men's room and picked up his coffee-to-go with a sprightly lilt as he flipped a few coins on the counter. He braced himself for the cold as he pushed the glass door open, running through a checklist of all the things he had to do, had to get.

As the frigid air filled his lungs, he looked to his left, to the alley. The rumble and clanging sounds of the kitchen rang again, as an olive green city Sanitation truck *emerged from the alley*!

Ansel slumped to the steps of the diner and watched the truck disappear into the blackness of the city's darkest night. It's beady taillights mocked his simplest thoughts.

The chill rain had returned, slapping Ansel's face and reminding him he would have to shoot again soon to stay warm.

Snow Day

At 6:15 a.m., Wednesday, the phone shrieked:

Brriiinnnnggg!!

His pulse trip-hammered the ear drum, a rapid tattoo felt, not heard. He was sitting upright, short of breath in the dark, sweat from his pectorals greasing his biceps. Alan never wore a shirt to bed, not even in these coldest of early February nights.

Brriiinnnggg!!!

He started again, heart pirouetting behind his sternum. It wasn't night at all.

Briinnnggg!!!

Braced for this one, he picked it up. The plastic was chilly in his palm. The tips of his ears were too frigid to notice if the receiver was cold.

"Hello." His voiced croaked with night's gravel.

"Alan?" The dulcet maternalism of Marjorie's tone was all he needed to gain his bearings.

"Alan?"

"Yeah, . . . I mean, yes. Yes, it's me."

"We're cancelled, Alan. Snow day. Call Joan, she's next on your chain. Okay?"

"Yeah. Sure. Joan. Right."

As Marjorie's click settled in his ear Alan sat in near-dawn light, muted by snowfall and yellowed shades. He was never able to fall back asleep.

The soles of his feet met the bare wood with a soft slap and a tingle. He popped up and threw the burgundy bathrobe on.

This house holds the cold like a corpse. It moves from room to room with you, icy fingers rubbing your ankles, the tops of your feet, and hands become thermometers. This isn't discomfort, exactly.

But it's close.

Plaster walls somehow get colder than the air. If your bare skin rubs it, little epidermal mountain ranges rise in symmetrical ribs along your arm. Wet dogs don't dry off in a house like this. Their sneezes explode throughout the night and the tip of your nose seems as cold as theirs, just not as damp.

Moe and Larry, Alan's twin mongrels — large auburn and white shaggy-haired mutts — were padding around his legs, excited at the prospect of going out for a run.

"Okay, okay," Alan marched down the stairs precariously, as the dogs bumped past him, tails flailing his thighs as they bustled by.

Opening the door the first glare of snowfall pierced the house. Alan squinted, the lines around his eyes creating a contour map which revealed age on an otherwise youthful face. The dogs bounded out gleefully, spraying snow in lovely gossamer arcs as they ran.

Alan shut the door and walked woodenly into the kitchen, knees stiff, ankles occasionally cracking, reminding him that fifteen years of standing in front of English classes — particularly after an active, athletic youth — had taken a toll. His foundation was older than the 37 years his birth certificate claimed.

He had created the "breakfast nook" with mornings like this in mind. As the caffeine steam warmed his face and his legs snuggled the coils of an ancient hot-water radiator, he looked out the window. Moe and Larry were carousing in what looked to be five or six inches of accumulation; they rolled on their backs, making dog-angels. To his left, his bird feeder (a small table) was hosting a United Nations of avians. A blue-jay anchored one side of the table demanding, in no uncertain shrieks, the cardinal across from him stay on that side. Starlings and sparrows, juncos and swallows, darted on and off.

Joan! He had forgotten again!

This was their fourth snow day (they'd lose a Spring Vacation day now . . .) and it was third time Alan forgot to call Joan. He dashed for the phone.

"Hello." Her voice was cranky.

"Joan, it's Alan. . . "

"I know. We're cancelled. Marjorie called. Good-bye, Alan." Click, metallic hum.

"Shit." He replaced the receiver with force, but not a slam. "Shit." It echoed up the stairwell.

Their fourth snow day.

Alan let the dogs in.

It was six months since the papers for the divorce had come through — the final ones. Six months since he had seen the boys. That day seemed colder than this. Regina got custody and she cut him off through a simple move. Florida. Sure, he had visitation rights. But 1500 miles was a long commute. And Regina wasn't cooperative. And funds weren't abundant. The divorce started it, he guessed. The birds squabbled on the feeder, a flurry of wings, high-pitched accusations and helicopter forays at one another. Alan reflected on the last half year, on this fourth snow day.

He had already missed seven others. "Sick" days. "Mental health" days, he joked with his closest friends on the faculty. He got up for another cup of coffee.

Staring into the placid blackness of the liquid, stretched taut across the cup, he couldn't transform his dark reflection into their images. He was losing their memory just as he had lost them.

A single crop from his eye exploded in the center of the cup and hot droplets stung his hand.

★

Alan ambled into the living room and flicked on his ancient t.v. A 19-inch SONY. In its day it claimed to have "perfect resolution."

Quite a concept, really — *perfect resolution*. He imagined that if one could resolve things *perfectly* there was probably no need for "mental health" days.

Alan sipped his coffee slowly, burning the tip of his tongue (would it blister later?) and vacantly gazed at The Days of Our Lives. There was some kind of funeral going on — or a post-mortem, anyway — and the characters (what people have such *health-spa* tropical sheens in February?) were appropriately be-reft, yet somehow furtive. He rolled back in time to Michael's funeral. It was a short hop, really, only three years ago.

Michael would be forty now. An artist with more than slight talent — but driven by demons and a sense of failure. For a long time Alan couldn't understand it. Michael had it all: handsome, intelligent, successful in his profession. At the funeral, though, Alan began to see.

He always knew they shared a sense of madness — of some-thing larger than their lives *directing* them. Michael claimed it *made* him paint — and pointed to Alan's histrionic success in the classroom as simply another manifestation of it. Alan would grudgingly accede. But the funeral — amid the wailing of their mother and the rigid demeanor of their father — exposed the cause of Michael's death.

It wasn't simply meeting the business associates; the New York advertising slicker-than-a greased-slide group. It was observing the mania of his mother and the demented compulsiveness of his father. Certainly it was more than the sense of selling-out to corporate ad-men that led Michael to the end of his tether. No, there was the knowledge that even independent artistic success could never overcome genes and upbringing. There was no other way out.

In time he might gain artistic freedom and thumb his nose at the commercial life he detested. But no amount of time, Alan now knew, could overcome the bouts of hysteria or the 36 to 40 hour binges of activity, of compulsive talking, driving, drinking. The exhaustion from work which had no clear goal, of projects which, in morning's light, had no purpose and made no sense.

Serious madness, Alan thought. And he knew it now, too. So Michael simply stepped off the platform just as the train arrived. A gruesome and dramatic end. No note, no explanation. He had, shortly before it, told Alan that someday *he'd* understand the family better — and maybe Michael, in fact, could guide him to that knowledge.

And, indeed he did.

He awoke on the couch with the suddenness the phone call brought earlier. His heart was trying to force its way out of his chest. Soaked with sweat, he was conscious of spittle that had sneaked out the corner of his mouth and slid down the side of his face. He didn't know if was afternoon or night — the shades were pulled and it was dark.

The digital clock winked at him in green. 4:57 p.m.

Alan was a marvel with a class. A dynamo. Sweeping gestures and roller-coaster vocals highlighted each forty-minute performance. Sometimes he felt as though he was watching himself on t.v.

It was his fifteenth year in the district. He was an "institution." Originally a Young Turk, his flaming wit, his ingenuous smile — "Me? No-no-no, not me!" — had charmed the staff and students alike.

About ten years into it, though, kids began arriving to class expecting "routines."

"Do the carnival story!"

"Tell us about the Bronx Zoo. . . "

" . . . the airplane rides to Kansas . . . "

Alan always obliged.

And he eventually even covered the literature. But it's tough to make *Catcher in the Rye* vibrant the 13th, or 14th, or 15th time around.

It began to snow again around six o'clock and Alan realized he wanted a snow day tomorrow, too. He ran a hand through his wiry hair, noticing briefly the thin spot near the pate, where the part ended — his fingertips reconnoitered a moment among the follicles, as if more might arrive any moment. He wanted another snow day.

It was about five years ago, he figured, as he placed Moe's and Larry's dishes down, when the marriage began to sour. Right around the time the New Boys were hired

The New boys had all come out of grad school together and were the spit'n'image of Alan a decade earlier. Everyone thought so. Everyone said so. Alan magnanimously took them under his wing. But they didn't flock.

He could see why.

It wasn't that they didn't like him — god knows, the banter was hilarious, the repartee couldn't get wittier. But slowly, ever so slowly, the way the ocean somehow steals the beach, he lost them. Their idioms weren't shared. He was jazz, they were hip-hop. He was Rushdie, they were Franzen. He was movies, they were streaming. Alan didn't fall through a crack, he was pitched down a chasm.

Yet his reputation remained and, even though the New Boys respected him, it was obvious the mantle had passed.

So now, the job was empty. Painless, true, but hollow.

And only Moe and Larry met him at home. Regina was gone with the boys. She had drifted suddenly, he thought, though she said, "No."

It was a year ago August, on the Cape. A rare August day without humidity, with a blue sky cinematographers would kill for. Regina turned to him, her black bangs flat against her forehead, the single line of her eyebrow emphasizing the depth of her chocolate eyes — she turned and said, without inflection: "*I'm leaving. The boys and I are leaving.*"

Even as he sat in his nook now, peering out at the gauze of snowfall backlit by streetlamps, his stomach did a single, nauseous somersault again.

"*I'm leaving. The boys and I are leaving you.*"

Alan had walked down the beach and thrown up. Now he could only sit, 18 months later, and feel his stomach turn enough to push spittle into the back of his throat.

It was 10:30 p.m. Larry and Moe were on their sides, ribcages rising and falling alternately, the wheezing of their breathing the only sound in the room.

Snow continued to fall. Another day lost from Spring Vacation? It didn't matter now, though. Not to Alan. The days were all the same, all running together like water down a drain, swirling about a bit, but awash all the same.

He'd never see the boys again, or Regina. One day was like the next and the pain was a living pulse that coursed through him without compassion.

Today was like yesterday and tomorrow would be the same. It didn't matter if he was 37 or 73. It wouldn't matter if it was a snow day or a Spring Vacation day.

He used two belts. One strapped around the pipe that ran along the far kitchen wall. It was strong, solid. There was a time, when they first lived here, he'd jump up and use it as a chinning bar, flattening the top of his head against the ceiling. He knew it would hold.

The other belt, attached to the fist, was looped, and dangled innocently above the chair.

It was simple now. He had rehearsed it so many times in his mind. It was like watching himself on t.v. He saw it all through a lens, like a director.

The man entered the room and strode carefully to the chair and stepped up on it easily, athletically.

He slipped the belt over his head, like a turtleneck, adjusting it as you would a tie.

And now, with a quick, edited shift to the subjective POV, the camera's eye pans down to the feet, seeing them with the toes over the edge of the chair, as if it's a diving board.

The right one steps out, deliberately, and weight shifts to the left knee, which flexes and quivers in the close-up for a moment.

At 6:15 a.m., Thursday, the phone shrieked:

Brriinnnggg! Briiinnnggg!

Leaves

Darby Bainbridge was six years old and nothing special, just a kid. That's what folks always said. Not in a poor way. Darby was just a kid.

He had a Golden Retriever dog named Bullox who was the color October's fallen leaves. Darby and Bullox played together for endless hours. Darby liked to chase Bullox by driving his Big Wheels directly at the dog. You could hear him around a corner, the wheel rumbling along the ground like a midget tympani, the axle a clutch of baby birds at feeding time. Bullox was never caught unawares.

Mike Rollenfeld got a new Prius for his sixteenth birthday. Mike was on the soccer team (a second-string wing) and more than anything wanted to go to the Prom with Virginia Karlson.

It was a cool autumn day. Crisp. Snapped like a perfectly ripe apple when you bite it. The hint of Indian Summer lingered, tickled the hairs in your nostril, the ones that would stiffen with next week's frost.

The autumn sun is unfiltered. There's a clarity to the days no other season shares. Like a 3-D picture, you can reach into the depth of life around you.

At 3:30 or 4:00 it's perfect. One-sweater weather, no cold-cloud from your breath. If you're sixteen and a high school boy you can feel your hormones rushing past each other in your veins, trying to find a way out.

Bullox matches the leaves perfectly that day. Darby marveled at his hound. Only the snout and a small tuft of wagging tail protruded. A dog without a body. Golden Retriever head peering out, a body of yellow and browned leaves. Darby got an idea. He sneaked away from Bullox as the dog rolled like a turtle on its back, displacing leaves in all directions.

The Prius felt surprisingly responsive today. The windows were down and Mike was trying to find the street Virginia Karlson lived on. He felt a little speedy and very happy. His smile was wired from ear to ear, a Halloween Lincoln's beard you hook on. He didn't drive too fast, though, because he was looking for *her* house. His head bobbed left, then right, trying to catch glimpses of numbers on garage doors and mailboxes as he rolled by. What was *her* number again?

Bullox stopped scratching his back and lolled his head left, then right. Again. Where had Darby gone? With considerable effort the dog shifted his girth and grunted to a side. He struggled to stand. He scanned. Perked his ears. A giggle? Across the street? Piles of leaves. Seven or eight, each about four feet high, just in the street off the curb.

Finally, a place where Bullox wouldn't find him! He thought it would feel like ducking underwater but it didn't. There was plenty of air. Beads of perspiration formed along Darby's hairline. His hair was just brown enough to blend with the leaves. It was a matter of losing the scent, though. Maybe he could even surprise the dog — scare him with a shrieking attack from the leaf pile!

Mike would have six months to convince Virginia she wanted to go to the Prom with *him*. Was it this street? Such perfect skin. Autumn russet hair, surely silken to touch. The air slid under his shirt, between the buttons, the chill caress firming the flesh for a moment, his chest going taut with a short gasp of incipient winter. Sycamore Street? Was it on Sycamore

Street? Quick right turn, slight tire squeal. Have to remember to put air in those.

Bullox was pacing quickly, stopping here, then there, his nose attached to the pavement like a trolley hitch. Several steps forward and a quick zag right, ahead three paces and then a lateral half-turn. Too many scents. He was a good dog, from good stock, but the sliding leaf piles, their New England Sahara shifts, were perfect cover. He couldn't make sense of it.

Darby started to nestle down. It was like a tent, but a little moist. And it smelled. Smelled cold. When you breathed on a leaf there was smoke. Focusing on individual leaves he noticed rivulets of veins. Each leaf was a miniature map and Darby began inventing stories for each "place." He forgot about Bullox for the moment.

This was it! Down the street farther? Near the corner of Winged-Horse Drive? Mike focused far ahead, losing sight of the foreground. His chin was up as he peered over the bridge of his nose, trying to determine if the Karlson's house was on the left or right side of the street.

He found it! THIS was Darby! The dog stared a hole in the turf, looked up and then down again. Did it trail off this way or that? Nose down, nostrils flaring, he tried to suck in more air than there was space for. Head up again, cocking for sound, eyes trained slightly left. The leaf pile! Bullox galloped off after the boy.

It was a blur down to his left at first, a pile of leaves swept by a sudden gust of wind. Mike refocused in an instant, in that elastic moment of clarity disaster grants its victims. It was a dog! A goddamn big dog! Golden and running. Mike swerved right, hard. The grip on the steering wheel seared into his lifelines. Both feet tried to push the brake pedal through the floorboard as leaves washed up over the hood, covering the windshield in a tide of yellows, golds, and browns. Before the car stopped Mike could feel the dull thud of contact, a slight rock of bumper and front axle. His hands were shaking. He was sure the dog was dead. No control. The muscles that hold the mouth straight were twitching, pulling his bottom lip down at the corners with an insistent determination. Mike was afraid to get out of the car.

He pushed the door open. The Golden Retriever was sitting just outside the door with a small woolen mitten in his mouth, as if he had just swallowed a child, whole. Mike laughed in relief.

About the Author

Bil Johnson is the author of the memoir, Right Time, Right Places: One Teacher's School Reform Journey (Adelaide Books) and two other education texts.

Laura Dunn

Two Minutes Apart

Fair was leaning against Fame's Prius staring at the clinic in front of her. Fame plopped a suitcase down in front of her.

"It's not going to be easy; you know that. Right?" Fame was searching for something, anything in Fair's face that would tell him how she felt.

"Rarely anything worth doing is." Fair had said, smiling sheepishly. She looked so tired, she had to be. She had large bags around her small green eyes. Her long curly hair was tied in a messy bun that rested on top of her head, adding more height to her already tall frame.

"Jacob doesn't know where you are?" Fame asked crossing his muscular arms. If Jacob knew where Fair was, he would surely mess everything up.

"Jacob was arrested too Fame. I don't even know where he is." Fair said this, rubbing the back of her neck. It was a habit of hers when she was nervous.

Great, Fame thought to himself. She still cares about him; she wouldn't be this defensive if she didn't.

"I'll be here the second they allow visits Fair. You can do this, okay?" Fame hugged Fair a little too tightly, causing her to cough and let go. They smiled at each other, but neither smile reached their eyes.

Fame watched his twin sister willingly walk into the rehab clinic. Similar in size and looks, but they could not have been more opposite at that moment. Was that the difference in two minutes?

One Year Later

"Fair is fresh out of rehab and this happens! I don't know what's keeping her together." Fame was smoking his third cigarette of the day entirely too quickly pacing on the balcony outside his apartment. It was nine in the morning.

"Fame, you can't sit around worrying that every little thing is going to send Fair over the edge. Even if it does, it's not your fault. She's your sister, not your child. You have to let this go man." Kasey said, just lighting his first cigarette of the day.

Fame chuckled. "Let this go? How heartless can you be?" Dramatically flinging his cigarette over the balcony, still lit, he stormed back inside. Slamming the sliding door in Kasey's face.

"Ouch!" A neighbor walking beneath the balcony at that unfortunate moment cried out.

Kasey did not rush his cigarette, in fact he sat down in the patio chair, part of the set that he bought for Fame when they first moved in together. Taking slow drags, he figured he would wait out Fame's mood a good glass-door distance away.

About ten minutes later, the sliding door slowly opened. "Hey man, are you cool now?" Kasey asked, putting his butt in the ash tray.

"Am I cool? Kasey, my mother is dead, I cannot get in contact with Fair for the life of me and – "He was cut off.

His phone blared a pop song that drove Kasey crazy. "Oh my god, it's Fair!" Fame said excitedly pointing at his phone.

Kasey rolled his eyes and walked back outside. Guess I'll be needing to pick up more cigarettes today after all, he thought to himself, lighting another.

"Hello? Fair, where have you been? Did you hear about mom?" Fame spewed the questions into the receiver.

"Fame calm down. Yes, I heard about mom, you have called and texted me over a million times. I've been at work; I can't miss any days right now or I go to jail." Fair sounded slightly annoyed, but at least she was being responsible.

"So, how are you holding up?" Fame asked.

"I'm fine, mom was a piece of shit remember? How are you doing? Busily worrying about everyone else so you don't have to face your own feelings. Got it."

The receiver clicked.

"Hey, that's not ....Hello? Hello?" Fame set his phone down with force, the screen likely would have cracked had he not had a case on it. Slowly, he sank into a chair at their kitchen table and began crying.

A hand appeared on his shoulder, "Hey, hey what happened now?" Kasey asked, settling onto his knee beside Fame.

"It's just such a shock that my mom was murdered. Who would want to do that?" Fame barely got the words out between sobs.

"Fame, she was a drug dealer. She is the reason Fair was hooked on pills to begin with. Drug deals go wrong all the time, there are probably a lot of people in this town that want her dead."

"Yeah, but she quit when Fair went down. The police didn't find any drugs at the scene either."

"As far as I'm concerned, whoever offed your mom did the world a service. She could never accept you for who you are, and she put her own daughter on drugs." Kasey got back up and leaned against the wall.

Fame sighed. "She was still my mom Kasey."

Kasey leaned over and kissed the top of his head. "I know she was."

Three Days Later

Fair walked into the funeral hall wearing a bright red mini dress and sparkling pumps. She was more made up than Fame had seen her for any event, including their senior prom. Everyone turned to stare at her and whispering commenced.

"What in the hell are you doing, this is a funeral!" Fame said whispering loudly, grabbing her by the arm and rushing them to their seats.

"This is not a somber event for me Fame, it shouldn't be for you either." A smile danced across Fair's face. "Hey! Wait, I've got to sign the guest list."

"Everyone will remember you were here. Don't be stupid, mom's investigation is ongoing, making a scene like this could suggest you had something to do with it."

"Oh, what the hell Fame, you know I didn't have anything to do with this." There was a silence between them. "Well, I didn't." Fair stuck her nose in the air and folded her arms, making her look decidedly childish.

Fair pointed an obvious finger across the room, "See that man over there in the suit nobody from our family could afford? He's a detective, and he's already been around twice to see me." She held up two fingers. "I think I'm in the clear." Fair stood up and straightened the wrinkles out of her dress. "Now if you'll excuse me, I'm going to go pay my respects."

Fame rolled his eyes, but as he was going to say something more, Kasey had appeared beside him, hand on his arm, shaking his head.

Fair walked up to the casket, but it was closed. A picture of her from thirty years ago stood in front, it read 'Teresa Haymaker 1968 – 2020'. Her mother had been on her couch watching TV, the person that killed her had slit her throat from behind. "Jeez, she would have hated to have a closed casket." Fair muttered to herself.

"Her throat was cut, it was not in good taste to leave it open. If you'd like a peek – "

"Oh god no, ewe. I know her throat was cut. Who are you?" Fair had backed up a few steps.

"Oh, I beg your pardon. I'm Errol, the funeral director. I deal with the dead to make a living." He chuckled at his own joke until the chuckle turned into a cough. Revealing yellow teeth.

Fair didn't know what to say, so she simply walked back to her seat next to Fame.

"What is with the funeral director, he gives me the creeps." Fair said.

"I found him on groupon." Fame shrugged.

Fair gasped audibly in response.

"Oh please, at least I did that much. You were just going to light her up behind the dumpster at McDonalds and spread the ashes on the bottom of your shoes." Fame said defensively crossing his arms.

"The drama." Fair said, elongating the syllables.

"Uh guys, don't look now, but guess who just walked in." Kasey said, slowly rising.

"Jacob? What the actual fuck is he doing here?" Fair asked, flushing a deep red.

"Fair! Have you been seeing him again?" Fame looked as though the vein on his forehead would pop out.

"No! No, no, no. I swear to God. I haven't seen him in over a year. He has been trying that whole time to get in contact with me, but I never respond. Hell, I've changed my number twice and he somehow always finds me." Fair put her head in her hands.

Kasey walked over to Jacob where he was leaned over, signing the guest book.

"Hey, I don't want to make a scene here, but you have to leave. Now." Kasey said crossing his arms.

"Kasey! It's been forever dude, how have you been." Jacob extended a hand, but Kasey did not move to uncross his arms.

"I'm not here to start any trouble, I'm just here to pay my respects. It's horrible, what happened."

"The respectable thing to do would be to leave this family alone." Kasey made a step towards him.

"Alright, alright." Jacob said, raising his hands up, chuckling nervously. "I'll go, but I really think Teresa would have wanted me here." Spinning around on one heel, Jacob left as soon as he came.

Kasey returned to his seat next to Fame. Fair leaned across Fame and in a comically loud whisper asked, "Thank you. What did he say?"

"I handled it Fair, let's just pretend he was never here." Kasey raised a dismissive hand, that meant that was that.

Fair wrinkled her nose but new better than to pry.

The ceremony convened, people spoke, including their mom's boyfriend Eddie. Eddie gave Fair sideways glances throughout the entire funeral.

Afterwards Fair, Fame, and Kasey met in the parking lot for a cigarette break before the reception.

"Did you guys notice Eddie giving me the death glare, what was that about?" Fair asked.

"I don't know, probably because you're dressed like a clown for a funeral?" Kasey said. Prompting the three of them to giggle.

"Hey!" Eddie yelled across the parking lot, almost running towards them. "What the fuck is so funny that you can laugh at your own mother's funeral?" He was hovering over them. Eddie was a big man, six foot six, three hundred fifty pounds, known to be an angry drunk.

Kasey stepped in front of him with his hands up, "Hey man, no disrespect, we were just kidding around. We are truly sorry for your loss."

"If they were any kind of good children, it would be their loss too. If I found out either of you had something to do with this, I'm going to kill you both and make your Nancy boyfriend watch." He spit on the ground and walked away much slower than he came.

Kasey spun around on his heels. "Oh, come on, it's always the boyfriend. He'll be in jail before the end of the week."

"C'mon, let's get to the reception." Fame said nervously, obviously shaken, and began searching his pockets for his car keys.

"I've got to get back to the diner. I told them I was going to a NA meeting, if I'm gone for much longer my manager will be calling." Fair said this, throwing a work shirt on over her dress and swapping pumps for tennis shoes.

"You had that all in your purse?" Kasey asked, laughing. "Got any snacks?"

Fair held up her middle finger through a smile and ran to the curb, to wait at the bus stop.

"Yeah, we love you too." Fame said sarcastically, rolling his eyes. Then he and Kasey piled into Fame's Prius.

The Next Day

"Fame come get your cell phone it will not stop blasting that stupid fucking song and it's too early for this!" Kasey shouted from the kitchen. Fame's phone was charging on the kitchen counter, and the ringing was ruining an otherwise pleasant morning for Kasey.

Fame stumbled out of their bedroom, rubbing his eyes. His hair sticking up in all directions. "I'm coming, I'm coming."

After staring at the screen for about thirty seconds Fame said, "Oh, it's Fair. Better call her back."

"Jesus, it never ends with you two. Well, there will be omelets on the patio when you're finished." Kasey said, pecking Fame's cheek on the way out the door.

The phone rang only once before Fair picked up.

"Hello." Fair sounded uneasy.

"Fair hey, what's up? You're calling kind of early." Fame said, looking up at the clock.

"Yeah yeah, I know, I'm sorry. Listen, did anything weird happen at the reception yesterday?"

"That detective that was in the nice suit questioned Eddie, but he wasn't there for very long. He came and went. Why?"

"I kind of woke up to a death threat."

"Kind of? What are you talking about?"

"I almost didn't call you, but I didn't know what else to do. Okay? I got out of the shower this morning, and nothing was missing, but there was a note on my coffee table that was definitely not there pre-shower."

"On your coffee table!" Fame shouted. Prompting a glance from Kasey outside. "You mean the murderer was in your house? You have to call the cops, like yesterday!"

"I did, I did. They say they're on the way, I just thought you might want to know. Besides, it may not have been the same person that killed mom."

"Well, what did it say?" Fame asked.

"All it said was, "You're next bitch." And they used the wrong form of "your". Which narrows it down to, I don't know, any of the idiotic people in my life."

"It says you're next bitch, and you don't think it was the murderer? Are you insane? Wait a second, aren't you always complaining about how Eddie would text you shit with horrible grammar all the time?"

"Yeah, but you just said the detective let him go, and I don't know how a man that big could break into my apartment without making any noise."

"Look, just hang tight. I'll come by in just a minute." Fame hung up the phone before Fair had time to make any sarcastic remarks.

"Kasey!" Fame shouted grabbing the nearest shoes and collecting his keys. "Kasey!"

Kasey slid the glass door open. "Could you just once instead of shouting my name, maybe come find me?" Kasey asked.

"I don't have time for your sass. Fair got a death threat this morning, I have to go over there."

"Well did she call the police?" Kasey asked.

"Yes. But- "Fame was cut off.

"What is you going over there going to help?" Kasey was growing frustrated.

"Kasey, I don't fucking know, moral support." Fame threw his hands in the air.

"Alright, calm down." Kasey rubbed his jaw, and after a moment said, "Shit, Let's go."

Fair's Apartment

Kasey knocked on the door, and Fair practically opened it before he stopped.

"Oh, I'm so glad you guys are here." Fair said, sweeping them in.

"Where are the police?" Fame asked scanning the studio with his eyes.

"They're gone. They took the note and they're gonna scan for prints, they did a little looking around. They said there isn't much else they can do if the prints don't come up though." Fair hugged herself and was pacing around the apartment, her long strides made it a short trip.

"What, they didn't even leave a guy to patrol the place for the night?" Fame asked.

"Look at where I live, people like me are not important enough for patrol." Fair said, looking down.

"Do you want to come stay at our place until they can get you some answers?" Kasey asked, receiving a surprised look from Fame and Fair both.

"Oh, I wouldn't want to impose." Fair said, shaking her head. "Besides, I should really stick to my routine, the bus route doesn't even pick up for a few miles from you guys' apartment."

Kasey nodded his head. "Then, we can stay here." Kasey looked around and besides a futon, kitchen and bathroom, there wasn't much else. "On the floor here." He said, motioning directly below them.

Fair smiled sheepishly. "I'm making chicken nuggets." Fair hurriedly walked to the kitchen and pulled a bag of frozen chicken nuggets out.

"Um, that's okay. I'll order us in some Thai food. Can't wait out nerves on chicken nuggets." Kasey said and he stepped outside with his phone.

"Wow, Kasey must like you after all." Fame said, chuckling.

Fair started laughing too, "I thought I'd never win him over."

"I still don't think I have." Fame said.

This made them laugh harder and they fell into a clumsy embrace. That's what Kasey walked back into, them laughing and hugging. They motioned for him to join and he did. Not knowing why they were laughing in the first place made them laugh harder.

"Alright, you guys are getting too mushy. You get ESPN on this thing?" Kasey said grabbing the TV remote.

"I get your Netflix account, and that's it." Fair said.

Then they all began to laugh again.

That Night

Fair had done her best to make a pallet of sorts with extra blankets she had in the house for Fame and Kasey to sleep on.

"We're too old to be laying on the floor. I can't find one comfortable position, can you Kasey?" Fame asked.

Kasey was already snoring.

"He can sleep anywhere, it's annoying. Why must I suffer alone?" Fame said dramatically rolling over.

"I'm sorry Fame." Fair said from the futon above, but soon, she was snoring too.

Fame spent a long time staring at the ceiling piecing impossible theories together. Who would want his mother and sister dead? Was he next?

He heard every car door, every parking lot conversation. Geez, these walls were thin. The upstairs neighbors took forever to settle down, and since Fair lived directly in the city instead of the outskirts like he and Kasey, there were sirens all night.

"THUMP!" Fame jumped, but neither Fair nor Kasey stirred.

"What the hell was th- "

"THUMP!" Something was banging against Fair's door.

Fame scanned the dark room, his eyes seemed to take forever to adjust. All he could see to think to grab was a frying pan, apparently too large to store in any of the cabinets.

The banging kept on and finally the door gave way, there standing in the doorway was Eddie.

Fame swung the frying pan with all his might, and it hit Eddie in the chest, but it didn't seem to shake him.

"Fame, get out of the way before you piss me off this is between me and her." Eddie was slurring his speech and he smelled heavily of booze.

"Did you drive here? What are you doing?" Fame asked raising the frying pan again.

Eddie pushed him with one arm and despite his muscular build, it pushed Fame back into the wall behind him.

Kasey and Fair were both startled awake by this.

"I'm calling the cops!" Was all Fair could manage to scream out as Eddie tripped over Kasey trying to reach her.

Kasey thought quickly and pinned his arm behind him while he was on the ground.

"I know it was you Fair! I know it was you. You can fool that detective, but you can't fool me! You're a crazy bitch and you wanted to steal your own mother's drugs from her, you're such a dirty whore junkie you killed her because you thought you could get high!" Eddie was screaming and pushing against Kasey with all his might, Fame joined in and it was an effort for them both to keep him pinned down.

Fair was telling the cops through her tears, "It's my mom's ex-boyfriend, he's attacking me and my brother please help!"

Eddie put one final push and got free of Kasey and Fame's grip. Towering over her he said, "The truth will be known." He stormed out the door slamming it behind him, but it didn't stay closed because he'd broken it on the way in. Sirens were filling the air and lights were blinking outside the window. Illuminating everything inside.

Kasey and Fame were panting, Fair was still crying. They were looking back and forth to one another, but none of them could say a word.

The Next Day

"Are you sure you're okay to go to work today, I'm sure you could call in this once." Fame was saying as Fair rushed around the apartment getting ready for work.

She stopped in the doorway, her bag over her shoulder. "They arrested Eddie last night, as far as I'm concerned it's over. Plus, my boss is hot. You guys can go home, just lock up on your way out." The door bounced behind her.

"Or not." Fame said to himself.

"You ready to go home?" Kasey asked sleepily. It had been a rough night for all of them.

"Yeah, I'm just going to call her maintenance man to come up and fix this door while she's at work." Fame said signaling to the singular post it note on her fridge that read, 'maintenance'.

Kitty's Diner

"Hey Fair, can you stay for the night shift tonight please? Cheri called, her kid is puking his guts out or somebody is." James, her hot manager asked as he walked from the kitchen with two trays full, one in each hand.

Fair sighed, how could she say no to that. "Um, sure James. I got to get to a meeting sometime this week though."

"Oh shit, yeah. Take tomorrow off, just please stay tonight."

Fair nodded at him, "You keep hiring us felons James, what can you do?"

He just laughed and rolled his eyes, "We've all got a past."

She hurried back to her tables, the day went by so fast she barely had time to think or take a pee break for that matter. One by one the customers began to dwindle, the wait staff thinned as the night went on, until it was Fair doing the tables and James cooking.

At about 12:15 James piped up, "I think we can call it a night Fair. I'm going to go count down in the office." He locked them inside as he said it.

"Just wipe everything down once over and you can lock me in. Thanks for your hard work today." He said, patting her on the back his hand lingering a moment too long. He jerked it back and hurried to the back office.

Fair sighed, rubbing the back of her neck. She felt nervous, but why? Eddie was in jail; she could go home and move on with her life.

Fame and Kasey's Apartment

"Fame! Your stupid phone won't stop ringing!" Kasey shouted from their kitchen; Fame didn't hurry. He was finishing up a cigarette on their balcony, they were having such nice weather.

The glass door slid open a few minutes later. "Who was it?" Fame asked walking to his phone.

"What am I, clairvoyant. I'm slaving over the stove here." Kasey hated when Fame asked questions that he could answer himself, but he also loved it.

"Alright, alright. Sorry I asked." Fame said, reaching for his phone. "Hmm, I don't know the number, but they left a voicemail."

Fame clicked on it and put it on speaker phone. "Hello Fame, this is detective Coleman. We had to release Eddie today, he has an alibi for the night your mother was killed, and it stands up. There is no way Eddie murdered your mom, he was just drunk last night. I'm having trouble reaching Fair, but she is in danger. Please give me a call back at 512-..." Fame slammed the phone down and met Kasey's eyes.

"We've got to get to Fair's apartment!" He yelled grabbing his keys and running down the stairs.

"On Taco night!" Kasey said exasperated. He flipped all the burners off and rushed after Fame.

Fame was dialing Fair over and over, but she wasn't picking up.

Kitty's Diner

Fair looked at her phone to check the time, but her phone had died. "Oh well." She said to herself.

She walked back to the manager's office, "Hey James, everything is cleaned. I'm leaving, you sure you want me to lock you in?"

"Yeah, I'm behind here. I'll see you...not tomorrow."

"Friday." She said smiling.

"Friday." He repeated cheerily.

She walked to the front door unlocked it from the inside, let herself out and started to lock it again when she felt like someone was watching her.

Keys still in the door, she whipped around swiftly. "Is someone there? I have pepper spray!" She waited a moment, and when she didn't hear anything again, she giggled at herself for being silly.

She finished locking the door and began to walk to her car when she was suddenly grabbed from behind. She went to scream, but there was a hand over her mouth. Her mind went blank, she couldn't reach for her pepper spray, she couldn't think to do anything and then suddenly, darkness.

Kasey pulled the Prius into the uneven parking lot of Fair's apartment complex.

Fame jumped out of the vehicle before Kasey had stopped all the way and flew up the stairs to Fair's apartment. The door was still not fixed, so he eased it open.

"Fair?" He called out. He scanned the studio, and when realizing she wasn't there he came flying back down the stairs.

"She must still be at work, we gotta go!" Fame said, he was growing more and more nervous.

Kasey pulled the car back out and it scraped the pavement, but neither of them flinched, the diner was five minutes away. Five minutes Fair might not have to spare.

When Fair came to, she didn't remember what happened at first. She sat straight up and realized she was moving; her wrist was throbbing and couldn't support her weight. She looked down at it, and saw it was swollen. She held it close to her and backed herself up against the door. She was in the back of a van; a van she had been in many times before. It was Jacob's.

She started to panic, and her breathing was shallow.

Jacob was in the driver's seat, he looked like he was tweaking and like he had been crying or something he hadn't noticed her movement. No doubt, he was high.

"Jacob – "Fair began, but he cut her off.

"Shut up! If you make a sound, you're dead!" Jacob screamed, his voice cracking.

I'm dead either way, aren't I? Fair thought to herself.

"Jacob, where – where are you taking me?" Her voice was weak.

"I said just shut up! You've messed up enough as it is already." Jacob barked.

"Messed up what?"

"Everything! You've ruined my life. We were supposed to get married, but then you went to rehab and suddenly you're too good for me?" He was shaking his head violently. "I can get clean, I've been clean before, but you wouldn't even give me a chance. Your mom wasn't supposed to get involved in this. You guys, you look so much alike from the back." He said, beginning to cry. "Teresa was always really nice to me, like the mom I never had, and I just…" He trailed off.

"Oh my god. You thought it was me sitting on the couch. You slit my mom's couch thinking it was me?" Fair started to feel hysterical. She couldn't control her breathing.

"I said shut up! This time there will be no confusion. You and your stupid brother always ganging up on me, you didn't even have the decency to let me say goodbye to her at her funeral. You sicked Kasey on me like some kind of guard chihuahua."

Kasey could be much more intimidating than a chihuahua, it worked didn't it? She thought to herself, and then aloud she asked, "Why do you want me dead, Jacob?"

"Because. Because if I can't have you, nobody can. Now shut the fuck up already! You never did listen to me."

"Hold on!" Kasey said, they were speeding down the highway when he could have sworn, he saw Jacob's beater of a van. Kasey did a highly illegal U-Turn and sped after it.

"What are you doing? Fair is in trouble we don't have ti—" Fame started but was cut off.

"It's Jacob's van coming from the direction of the diner. He doesn't live over there, call the police. Now!"

Fame was fumbling to dial his hands were shaking so bad.

"Detective Coleman? Hi, get police to Jacob Schwartzman's house now. We have reason to believe he is with Fair and that he may be dangerous."

"What's the plan here Jake? You're going to take me back to your parent's house and kill me?" Fair asked staring at the ceiling of the van.

"Why shouldn't I?" Jacob asked, stepping harder on the gas. "My parents are out of town visiting my grandparents. It's now or never." He almost whispered, like he was still justifying it to himself.

"I don't know Jacob; I know I did you wrong. I'm sorry. You know that I was just trying to follow my parole and stay out of jail. If I associated with you, it was a violation."

"I'm not worth violating parole to you? Fair I would have died for you!" Jacob said, pounding a fist into the steering wheel. He accidentally honked the horn and they both jumped.

"I didn't mean it like that Jacob, I just…" She trailed off; she knew in order to calm him down she had to tell him what he wanted to hear.

"I love you Jacob, I always will. I'm not tough enough for prison, okay? I was scared."

"Bullshit. You're not scared of anything."

"I am though, I am scared of prison! You should be too; you've been in and out enough." She scanned the van, wishing there were windows she could kick out or be seen through.

Jacob then lifted a pistol seemingly out of nowhere and pointed it directly at her, no longer looking at the road. "You had your chance." He turned back around and wiped his nose with the back of his hand, never putting the pistol back down.

"Hail Mary full of grace the lord is with thee…" Fame was saying under his breath.

Kasey rolled his eyes at him and stepped on the gas, and all of a sudden, a siren went on behind him.

"Oh gosh, I cannot be getting pulled over right now. Damn it." He said, slowing the vehicle and veering to the right. As soon as he stopped, the cop car flew past him, and then a few more.

"They're going to get there before us, she is going to be okay Fame." Kasey said, pulling back on to the road.

"He could have killed her at the restaurant for all we know, I'm not resting until I know she is okay.

"What in the hell...no." Jacob said as he pulled onto his street. There were at least a dozen police cars parked outside.

"Oh shit, oh shit oh shit! I forgot to take your phone; did you seriously call the cops on me!" He yelled in disbelief. She hadn't been the one to do it, but he acted as if it had been very unfair if she had. He spun the van around, and it made a loud screeching sound. More police cars were arriving and boxed him in. He threw the car into park and put his head into his hands.

Detective Coleman's voice sounded on an intercom, "Jacob Schwartzman. Turn off the vehicle and come out with your hands up."

Jacob turned around and grabbed Fair by her hair, he tugged so hard he pulled her into the front seat. The pistol was still sitting in his lap.

"Jake, you can't shoot me, they will kill you." Fair said, rubbing the back of her neck rapidly.

"Stop fucking fidgeting, I never found that attractive!" He boomed and reached for the pistol.

"Jacob, step out of the vehicle with your hands up, this is your last warning." The voice on the intercom was loud, but it was calm and even too.

He picked up the pistol and as he raised it to her head, she shut her eyes tight and threw her hands up.

"BOOM!" There was a deafening sound, and her ears began to ring. She opened her eyes, blood and glass were covering her, but it was not her blood. Jacob lay dead beside her. His eyes still open, seemingly looking right at her. The anger behind them had faded though. She began to bawl.

Police, EMTS, all kinds of official people seemed to be swarming the vehicle. They pulled her out, and everything went blurry.

The Next Morning

"Did you guys really get me flowers?" Fair said, smiling from her hospital bed. Her body was sore, she had a fractured wrist and had been concussed, but she was going to be okay.

"You had us scared to death when you weren't at the apartment. I never thought we would make it in time. I just kept hoping you were still at work…" Fame was chattering on and on, but nobody was really listening.

Suddenly, James walked in with a balloon and teddy bear.

Fair sat up right and pushed her hair out of her face.

"James, what are you doing here?" She asked, flushing bright red as she realized she didn't have a stich of makeup on and hadn't showered since before yesterday's shift.

"Uh, I didn't know what to get a person that was almost murdered. A teddy bear and a get-well balloon sounded about right though." He said shrugging, awkwardly handing her the bear and balloon.

One arm in a brace and the other hand hooked up to IV, she tried to grab it from him, but could not get a grip.

"Here, I'll put these on the chair over here." Kasey said kneeing at Fame to stand up from where he was lounging.

"Ow! Your knee is so bony!" Fame said.

Kasey rolled his eyes over to James and back.

"Alright Fair, I guess we are going to have a smoke downstairs. You call us if you need anything!" Fame said as he and Kasey walked out of the room.

"I guess you won't be making it into work on Friday." James said.

"I'm getting released today James, I can be there by Friday."

"How are you going to wait tables with a broken wrist?"

"It's only fractured, I'm left-handed anyways."

"Alright, well maybe when your shift is over, we can grab some coffee. You can tell me your war story." Looking out the window as he said it.

"We're the only place in town open for coffee that late." Fair said matter-of-factly.

"I know a place. It's a little smaller, but way less roaches I promise." James said and they both started laughing.

One Year Later

"Thank God twins skip a generation." Fair said, resting a hand on her very pregnant belly.

"What? C'mon I don't know what you'd do without me." Fame said, starting to light a cigarette, then putting it back down.

"Ha ha very funny, you need me too, you just don't know it. This baby is finally going to give you someone to worry about other than me."

"I'll never stop worrying about you, but I know you're a lot tougher than you look." Fame said, lightly punching her on the arm.

"Did you and James decide on a name yet?" Fame asked.

"Yeah, Teresa." Fair said.

"What, really?" Fame asked.

"Fuck no!"

Fame shook his head and laughed, then decided to light the cigarette after all. "You've got a sick sense of humor." He said, exhaling downwind. "Good thing you're pretty or James would probably think there's something wrong with you!"

"Get inside, dinner is ready and I'm not waiting around for it to get cold!" Kasey called from inside. James was already seated at their table.

"And you're a drama king, but that's the difference in two minutes baby!" Fair cackled at her own joke and opened the screen door.

About the Author

Laura is a senior at University of Houston - Downtown. She spends her free time creating, reading and visiting local parks.

Joanna Kadish

Gathering Storm

Stephanie looked for a condo in Oakland to share with a
few likeminded people, would Micah be interested. The only
catch—she played down this part, knowing that guys did not
get it; she'd been ridiculed by male colleagues at her engineering
job for her role as animal rights activist. It did not go unnoticed that some afternoons and entire weekends were devoted
to this work. She had to check her enthusiasm; she did not tell
them about how often she went on marches and wrote to her
representatives in congress urging them to ban the eating of
meat and decrying the carnivorous lifestyle of many Americans.
But her obsession spilled into work nonetheless. On a business
trip to Japan, she took time off to join the protest of a frog-
hunting ceremony, a century old ritual that calls for the villagers
to hunt frogs with arrows, which are then offered to the gods
at the Suwa Grand Shrine, joining a dozen infuriated demon-
strators to disrupt the event as much as possible with chants of
"Cruel! Cruel!" She waded into the Mitarai River (forbidden
to nonbelievers) and physically attempted to stop parishioners
from catching frogs, grabbing their nets and wresting them

out of their hands, yelling "Stop that!" and "Don't kill frogs!" pushing people so hard she slipped and fell into the river. The religious regard this spot in the river as sacred, not even the head priest is permitted to enter, and people said going into the river during the ceremony was a huge offense to the shrine gods showing no sensitivity to the Japanese culture. Because of modern sensibilities, only two frogs are sacrificed, with the impaling ritual taking place in the shrine's inner sanctum and not in public, but it was not the number of frogs killed in this manner that mattered to Stephanie, what it represented was far worse. Stephanie failed to talk Micah into joining her, he could not get the time off, which was just as well, because the one time she mentioned it at work, a couple of the meat-eating male engineers offered a few choice derogatory remarks and that made her fuming mad, and said she was too pretty to be raging manic. Men tended to say nice things about her tall, lean physique topped by massive curls, but when they met the hidden side of her, they were less complementary.

In talking to Micah about moving into her condo, Stephanie downplayed animal rights, saying it was a small part of her life. She did not mention that she held weekly meeting on the subject at her place that often turned into raucous events. Instead, she talked up vegetarian as a way of life, and suggested he try her veggie burger, a special blend of beans, mushrooms, nuts, and brown rice and subsequently pan-fried to a golden perfection. He was wooed, even after hearing her repeat the caveat, "No cooking of meat of will be allowed in my condo." Being an accommodating sort, he said he was fine with that, and said he wanted to live with people who lived holistically and practiced yoga. He had been living in a sober living house with several men, and he didn't feel comfortable there. He welcomed a change, and refused to scrutinize Stephanie's offer closely.

He preferred to trust his instincts that anyone who respected Buddha would treat him well. A month later, he moved in.

Micah was still unpacking when Stephanie went to work the next morning. As she entered the hallowed entrance of Doodles offices, thinking that she had entered a playroom for toddlers, liking the inclusion of playground slides big enough for adults to fit into and in a room filled with bold cheerful colors, work being treated as play and versus, she wanted to cry for joy. The brand is famous for its staff perks – pool tables and bowling alleys, free food and gym memberships. There were math games and puzzles scribbled on walls making once again her mind feel it was expanding like the wing on a condor. Joining Doodles was more of a valuation; proved that graduate school was worth the effort and time expended. Her professors knew she was there because she wanted an opportunity to do something significant, though it was a matter of more of what came first, the chicken or egg conundrum? Feeling heady like she had created the search algorithms for link building as key ranking signals along with the two co-founders, her eyes caressed the custom green living wall—stuffed with moss and other bushy plants—before moving to one of her colleagues, the woman responsible for making her life a living hell lately, the engineering director for the team she was assigned, sitting across from her, full of crazy suggestions on how to simplify code on the mobile project for Cyborg they worked on together. Before that, they used to work on things like making web pages load more reliably on poor networks, and then building and maintaining software systems that had more complicated moving parts than a Swiss watch.

She sat at a long wooden table made out of repurposed oak that she shared with a few of the people on her team, big potted plants all around, the room filled with huge windows and sunshine. Meredith sat close by reading out loud in her whispery voice: "'Listen to this: "I want to wish Andy all the best with what's next," she continued, "Larry Miller, Doodle's chief executive at the time, said in a public statement distributed to all employees. 'With Cyborg he created something truly remarkable — a billion-plus happy users.' And of course the company gave $90 million to the creator of Cyborg mobile software, along with a hero's farewell. But $90 million?"

"They have deep pockets to come up with that kind of money," Meredith said. "In order for Larry and Sergey to show their appreciation."

"If it was a woman engineer that developed a phone and have an affair with male underling, would she get that kind of payout on her way out?" Stephanie said, flipping her long curly locks over her shoulders. "Not on your life."

Women at the top are too busy to have affairs."

"No man would want to take the job of being her wife," the other woman shot back, taking her long hair in her hands and coiling it on top of her head. "Men at the top have big egos and have to run the show."

"How many gay women get to the top, probably none," Meredith ran her fingers over her unruly curls, as if to smooth it down, but her corkscrew curls bounced right back, "I worked hard to get my PhD and I deserve to make as much as a guy with a PhD but that isn't the case."

"Didn't Sergey say that everyone would be treated as equals? Including women? And that we would have a say in everything that happens at Doodles?"

"You know when Sergey said that when his family visited Russia and saw how the Russians lived, he told his father he was thankful that his parents immigrated to America. As Jews, his parents were not allowed to get PhDs but they found some loopholes and did anyway. They found certain fields were closed to them, like astrometry, which is what his father wanted to do, so he got his PhD in mathematics, which turned out to the godsend, opening many avenues. But they were the lucky ones, blessed with great intellects. We learned that outside of Moscow, people are in survival mode, half their salaries go to rent. Infrastructure is slowly shutting down, and half of the hospital wards are not working. Remember how Sergey talked about that? And his passion for freedom."

Stephanie heard from Meredith what the company did not make public: an employee accused Andy of pressuring her after a company party to give him head. Later to friends she said she did it with gusto yet expressed a bitter aftertaste to her cohorts, others on Andy's team that she happened to be friendly with siting at her table the next morning over coffee, noting she did not read that clause in the job description but said she performed her task insanely well, despite his faulty guidance and she better get a really good bonus. Anyhow, that might have instrumental in why he left so suddenly, with Andy was at his peak performance and Sergey praising Andy's understanding about robotics to the skies. The woman, with whom Andy had been having an extramarital relationship, had pressured him leave his wife for her, and that lead their breakup. The jilted woman marched into Human Resources saying he coerced her into performing oral sex in a hotel room. Doodle investigated and concluded her claim was credible, said the people in the position to know. They spoke on the condition that they not be named to the media, citing confidentiality agreements. Andy was notified, they said, and Larry asked for his resignation. Doodle could have fired Andy and paid him little to nothing on the way out. Instead, the company handed him a $90 million exit package, paid in installments of about $2 million a month for four years, said two people with knowledge of the terms.

When Stephanie heard that, she hissed: "I'm pissed as hell."

"That's saying it mildly," said Meredith. "Why don't companies hold their owners, founders, and C level employees to the same standard? Why don't their employee contracts implement the same morality clauses? Why do these jerks get the golden handshake for perpetrating horrible offenses? Why do alleged "leaders" get to disappear quietly with a shipload of money?" Meredith was on her way to stardom as the founder of Doodle's Open Research group, which was spearheading some interesting research, and could talk like that, knowing she was heading into the elite club of managers. "Let's organize a walkout of all women at all the offices around the world to protest sexual harassment, get everyone to walk out for the afternoon," Meredith continued. "We have to expose the hypocrisy. How can they tell us that the Doodles culture will be inclusive and we'll have a voice and then deny us?"

"Walking out is the only thing the patriarchy will pay attention to," Stephanie said.

Meredith wanted to send out an email to women engineers and marketing people (marketing was staffed mostly by women) talking principally about how Doodle handles harassment, but Stephanie thought they should also address pay discrimination, they knew people, mostly women, hired for the same job with roughly equal qualifications and were often paid less than their male counterparts. Meredith agreed and said time was of the essence. They planned to march in the middle of that same week, hoping to stage the walk out to be as disruptive as possible.

That weekend Stephanie and Micah went hiking up Mount Tamalpais. They decided on a trail that meandered through groves of live evergreen oaks with their dark rounded leaves, famously eking out most of their moisture from the daily and plentiful fog that appeared mornings and evenings, alternating in shady patches and then bursting into sun, with the peak at Bare Knolls opening up a full blown view of the beautiful coastline. Once at the Pantoll the trail descended down to the Dipsea. Fern canyons and tall more mature trees lined the trail until it reached the lower trail and views of Stinson Beach. At the end there was a steep climb back up. Micah tackled steepness like an athlete, running the whole way. She loved watching his long strong legs moving swiftly in front of her, paving the way to lustful thoughts. That night they became lovers. Stephanic found a piano for him a few days later. Micah started composing music again. His musician friends liked one of his songs so much they wanted to include it on the album they were putting together and planned to call it "Micah's Dream."

A few days later, the march went off. Stephanie was thrilled to learn that more than 20,000 women attended throughout the world. Bits and pieces of the march around campus stayed with her, and the speeches bemoaning Andy's exit package. And the energy, so much positive energy people were encouraging to Stephanie and Meredith, and the few others who took up the bullhorn demanding equal rights. They felt empowered, giddy with strange lightheaded ether that flooded her brain. Something like $90 million was the figure repeated over and over, as if no one could comprehend this large of a payout to one man. She couldn't wrap her head around it either; the sum was staggering, her head spin that management could come up with that kind of money. But the truth that no one mentioned, Sergey was deeply involved with Andy in robotics and a personal friend as well. Stephanie saw them together a lot, at meals, strolling campus, playing Ultimate Frisbee games, sometimes alone, sometimes with others. They had a good old boys club happening.

"Not enough women engineers," Meredith said. "That's the problem."

"Most of the women who work here are in communications, it's true, and not all of them were throwing themselves at Andy. But a lot of them were."

"We have to educate them."

"You don't have 20,000 people in the streets planned in three days if there isn't something deeply, structurally wrong," Meredith said.

Becky came into the room and stopped to talk. She was tall and portly, with a helmet of close cropped hair.

"People like Andy is why I decided to become a woman," Becky said, "I didn't want to be a jerk. Most guys are you know."

"Yeah most of them are jerkoffs," Stephanie said.

They shared the workspace and often shared the same views, but Stephanie had trouble with Becky talking as if she knew what it was to be a woman, and tried to swallow her feelings on the matter as if her throat had been assaulted by an overabundance of phlegm, and bring it down to a place it would dissolve in the mishmash of all the stupid things she had to deal with on a daily basis. The problem in a nutshell, Becky used to be guy, not so long ago. A year into his/her hormone treatment and Stephanie sometimes messed up and called him/her by his old name, "James" although now Becky was growing itty bitty breasts and had developed a curvy butt. And while his face had softened, Becky still was a guy, technically at least, never having had the bottom surgery. Having a penis, Becky claimed, meant nothing because she couldn't get hard anymore. "What? This old thing?" she said one time, "It's a useless appendage now." Stephanie thought of Becky and the trans movement as a product of an out-of-control liberal mindset probably acquired in schools where males are taught to be ashamed of their sex. And Becky talked like a man, how much did a boatload of horse estrogen really change anything other than cosmetically?

"I love being part of the decision making, and I won't stop speaking my mind," Meredith said.

"It's empowering to have a voice," Stephanie agreed.

The old boys' club at Doodle were not into golfing like in the old corporate model where work and play were separate functions, but it was the same idea at Doodle, in this so-called new age business model that mixed work and pleasure. Guys played Ultimate Frisbee and skydived with Sergey, that's when they talked deals, and women were not part of it. At the top levels, the guys were insanely athletic, and pushed it hard, that's why sports figured prominently in the design of the offices: What woman that is not having an affair with one of the top executives would be able or willing to keep up?

Granted Andy was a swinging dick with lots of clout already before getting into robotics, it was obvious that he thought a lot of himself when you saw all the young women hanging off his arms and at meetings and parties plenty of ass kissers shoving cleavage in his face, but that was true about a lot of powerful men at a company like Doodle where top management fraternizing with line workers was encouraged.

"I went up a few times," Becky said. "Not with of Sergey, of course, I was never one of the elites, although I would have loved it."

"Was it fun?"

"I was soaring through the sky as a superhero, an all-powerful being that could accomplish anything…scary and yet so satisfying."

"My roommate Micah loves skydiving," Stephanie said. "He has repeatedly asked if I wanted to learn how. He tried to talk me into taking lessons with him. Apparently you have to pull the trigger at the right time, and then you have to know how to roll so you don't break your legs going down."

"That's why you take lessons," Becky said.

"I'm with you Steph, seems way too dangerous for me," Meredith said.

They went about their day solving algebraic functions, looking at the binary trees that make up sorting information into categories that can be manipulated to lean into whatever direction the company wanted to see happen. They all had their rituals to get through the day of intense reasoning. Whenever Stephanie was in the cafeteria where she was a frequent visitor to latte stand, and saw other women who had gone on the march, usually she went up to them and personally thanked them. It was always in the back of her mind, mulling over the injustice of it all, guys somehow always were in charge of most everything, making more money, and hogging the limelight. Later that day on the suggestion of Meredith, Stephanie pulled information from a labor organizing site on the mechanics of setting up a union and put it into a newsletter format to all the people who had attended the march. They would not allow opportunity to slip away, not when they had the buzz going; the women she bumped into at the latte stand sounded engaged.

At the next meeting with Meredith talked management into dropping out of the running for JEDI, the massive Defense Department cloud computing contract potentially worth $10 billion, saying she had the support of thousands of engineers. Doodle sent an email to employees that it decided not to participate in the bidding process thinking that the contract may not align with the company's principles for how artificial intelligence should be used. And then all over the news, they learned that another company –Cylops—had taken that government business to become the largest cloud service in the world. They also learned from third party sources that Sergey and Larry were pissed about it, thinking the other company was not as proficient at AI and less professional as coders, and did not deserve the title of best at anything.

They heard about these grumblings at the top as hearsay, but it rang true. Then they both noticed that almost immediately after the walkout, their workload changed, pretty quickly too, from too much to incredibly light, to the surprise of Meredith who kept saying "Wow. Unbelievable."

But what made Meredith's blood pound with fear and dread, when she discovered a curious email from her immediate supervisors that made her grab her desk and upon re-reading it throw a book at the wall, allowing her anger to flare anew. Without thinking it through, she followed that up with a hastily written message posted on many internal Doodle mailing lists, saying the company was at fault. This decision came on the heels of Meredith and others publically criticizing the inclusion of the president of a Foundation affiliated with Stanford University, one of the most influential think tanks of conservative thought in the US, and highly esteemed by scholars. It didn't matter how venerable the intellects of the people gathered under the think tank's umbrella, Meredith didn't like conservatives, she avoided them whenever she ran into them when getting her PhD at Cal or anywhere and thought of them as horned monsters; as a flaming liberal she would smite them down like the Pirate Queen, the legendary Queen Artemisia I of Caria who vanquished her enemies with great cunning, switching flags pretending to be the enemy in the Battle of Salamis and wreaking havoc when she had them in her crosshairs. But Meredith didn't want to engage with conservatives, read their books or listen to their talk, particularly if she didn't agree with them.

When Stephanie suggested that company might be better served by hearing from both sides, liberal and conservative, Meredith shut her down with her talk of "harm avoidance." She was certain she could get top management to sign on by marshaling the support of a frenzied mob of women.

"So no conservatives allowed," Stephanie said.

"That's right," Meredith said, objecting to the company's hidden policy of punishing those who resist discrimination, harassment, and unethical decision making. She made a point of saying that Doodle permits these behaviors. "This harms people inside the company, and communities outside who bear the brunt of Doodle's bad choices. If we want to stop discrimination, harassment, and unethical decision making, we need to end retaliation against the people who speak honestly about these problems."

"if I'm hearing you correctly, you're saying that the half of the world that thinks conscientiously has to be silenced and subjected to the liberal adventure-seeking mindset?"

"Yes."

"I don't know if you know this, but we inherit some part of how we process information—there have been numerous studies that show political beliefs may depend heavily on very basic processes in the brain that formed our ancient instincts to avoid danger and filth, which we experience as fear and disgust. Peter Hatemi, a genetic epidemiologist at the University of Sydney and his colleague Brad Verhulst, a political scientist at Pennsylvania State University, published a study in 2015 in PLOS ONE showing that changes in personality over a 10-year period do not predict changes in political attitudes. And psychologists at the University of Warwick in England recently proposed a theory along these lines in a January 2016 paper published in Topics in Cognitive Science. And others since have come out saying the same thing."

Meredith's scowl deepened, contracting her brows in a sullen, angry manner that brooked no dissent, intimidating Stephanie into frightened silence, pretending to be buried in her work. There would be no disagreement between them. Stephanie remembered something that Micah, a student of Buddhist thought, said to her, "In a controversy the instant we feel anger we have already ceased striving for the truth, and have begun striving for ourselves." But there was the added nut, there was no way she could contest her superior and keep her job.

Meredith was called to a meeting with her boss in his corner of the office—on the walk there she felt she faint and might have lost it but she soldiered on—and learned that her role at the company would be "changed dramatically." Furthermore, she was told that, in order to stay employed there, she would have to "abandon" her work on AI ethics and her role at a research center she cofounded at a university in New York. But she was not deterred, unwavering in her belief that conservatives need to be rubbed out from under the heel of her jackboot. She went back to the office area she shared with Stephanie sounding a defiant note to anyone she spoke with, including Stephanie after the post was made public: "I'm so grateful for your support, and I remain staunchly committed to my work at the council. Doodle's retaliation isn't about me. It's about silencing dissent and making us afraid to speak honestly about tech & power. NOT OK. Now more than ever, it's time to speak up."

Later in the cafeteria standing in line, waiting for her custom-made salad, Meredith vented: "I have worked on issues of AI ethics and bias for years. I'm one of the people who helped shape the field looking at these problems. I've also taken risks to push for a more ethical Doodle, even when this is less profitable or convenient. But it's hasn't been easy advocating for change. Doodle has a culture of retaliation, which too often works to silence women, people of color, and gender minorities. Retaliation isn't always obvious. It's often confusing and drawn out, consisting of icy conversations, gas lighting, project cancellations, transition rejections, or demotions. Behavior that tells someone the problem isn't that they stood up to the company, it's that they're not good enough and don't belong."

"Who gets to decide what is allowed, what kind of clients to keep?" Stephanie said.

"There has to be guidelines," someone behind them said in a voice that sounded like Becky's. Stephanie turned around and saw it was Becky and smiled with a wave.

"What if I told you I have conservative leanings?" Stephanie said.

"What do you mean?" Meredith said.

"I believe in upholding a strong social fabric and economic order that serves majority of people, and helps them get a decent education, provides a path to jobs and allows them raise their families without the heavy hand of authoritarianism," Stephanie said.

"That's what I believe, too," Meredith countered.

"Well, then, back up your claim of pluralistic thinking. When did it become okay to brand conservative thinkers as bad? These are the true revolutionaries, the ones that have studied the issues without bias, looking at both sides, but you have decided with no evidence that these people are not to be heard from. You only want to hear from the radical left. What you propose smacks of authoritarianism."

"Tough titty," Meredith said.

They took their salads to their table and dug in. A trolley with a display of superb chai and equally excellent rose or mango lassis—a blend of yoghurt, water, spices and sometimes fruit that tastes like a milkshake, originating from the Indian Sub-continent—came by the table, all free for the asking. Meredith selected the cardamom-laced chai, and said it was the best she had ever tasted. Stephanie asked to taste it and the two of them talked about the great food they were treated to, you couldn't get it better anywhere else, and all of it free to employees.

But Meredith was not interested in talking about food. Plainly that sort of talk bored her, she suggested that they plan a "town hall" meeting that Friday to discuss what was happening to them, did others also see instances of retaliation?

Back in their office area, an email in appeared in Meredith's inbox marked high priority: "We prohibit retaliation in the work-place, and investigate all allegations," a Doodle spokesperson said in a statement that was sent to all employee inboxes and given out to the media. "Employees and teams are regularly and commonly given new assignments, or reorganized, to keep pace with evolving business needs. There has been no retaliation here."

The atmosphere at the company became too tense to en-dure. Both of them decided to leave the company, telling people they were pushed out.

A few months passed and Stephanie went to a 'flash speak out' in the meat aisle of Ralphs Supermarket in support of a Direct Action Everywhere protest. She joined other protesters chanting and holding signs, and blocking people from accessing the packaged meat, texting Micah several photos of the twisted and angry faces of protesters juxtaposed with the faces of fright-ened shoppers, disturbing his equilibrium. He felt anxious, would have reached for palliative drugs if any had been on hand. He did what the rehab counselors had suggested, to find something to soothe his anxiety. He thought of his craving for chicken, which his mother cooked often when he was growing up, he especially liked it fried. Stephanie was not expected until late. He went to the grocery and picked up some chicken, and butter fried it in a pan. He planned to air out the place before she came home.

As he was sitting down to eat, Stephanie came into the room, her hands fisted, facial muscles twisted into a knot.

"You're early," he said.

She said "What are you eating?" and started screaming, "No, no, no," in a voice he had never heard before from her, sounding as if she was being beaten with a switch. Living with her these few months as lovers he had become increasingly turned off by her fixation on a meatless lifestyle, it wasn't enough that she didn't eat meat, no one in her condo could either; even her cat was forced to eat vegan. Stunned, he apologized, saying he was dying for a piece of meat, and just this one time, he would not do it again. But she was not to be appeased. Like a raving lunatic she tossed his plate with the chicken still on it against the wall.

He threw his stuff into boxes and called a few rooming houses and moved out of Stephanie's a few days later, his life totally upended, leaving all the furniture he had purchased behind; he thought it was too much of a hassle to get past the hydra-headed Medusa to claim his stuff. He went from opulence to living in a depilated house a few towns away, the front room cluttered with thrift store finds, a porch swing, a piano, a bed in the corner, clothing heaped on the floor. The landladies, a couple of middle aged Filipino immigrants charged an exorbitant fee, seeing that he had no other place to go. They took advantage, and he knew that, but felt powerless to do anything. He paid the rent including first and last, thinking he'd find a better place at his leisure. At least he had his own room.

About the Author

I've been published in Juked, Catamaran Literary Review, the Adelaide literary magazine, Potato Soup Journal, Literary Orphans, Cultured Vultures, Quail Bell Magazine, Citron Review, Urban Arts Magazine, Crack the Spine, and numerous others, as well having placed as finalist in many contests, such as Black Coffee & Vinyl Presents: Ice Cultures project, summer of 2018, Cutthroat 2016 Rick DeMarinis Short Fiction Contest, and in GlimmerTrain's Emerging Writers Contest for 2015 and 2016, as well receiving top award for essay writing at Adelaide Literary Magazine for 2019.

Tom Carter

Something Like an Oyster

One thing I have going for me is that a lot of poets and writers have gone mad and a lot of us have been temporarily delayed in hospital. So, I feel I haven't anything to be ashamed of. Not many have witnessed a murder though. I did. It was quick. It was messy. It landed me in the hospital where I nearly died. Six months and nearly 130,000 milligrams of Thorazine later, I was still trying to reconstruct the facts of the case. It was ten years later that I finally made a museum of the mind of that rollercoaster through outer space, just this past year. Since the start of that transformative moment, I graduated with a BA and MA, became a published author, obtained a Massachusetts's state driver's license, and learned how to fill-out a job application. I don't care what you might be thinking. I fought my way back from depths and deficits, and I don't mean to cede a centimeter. At any rate, I still maintain it was a killing. All the drugs, therapy, and coifing, badgering sisters won't change a thing. After all this time, who cares anyway?

I mean, besides my mother. She starts to cry every time I start explaining what happened that day, so I try never to bring up that dubious hour of infamy. But sometimes I just can't help myself because my mother if anyone deserves answers and truth. So sooner or later, something just ticks off at the margin of an innuendo, and I end up with a mother fanning her red, teary face, gathering gobs of tissues in her hands while I go darting in and out of doors to see if any sisters are anywhere in sight.

My mother's general intent loving as it may be is to shock me into sanity and silence by constantly reminding me of my "wordless, two-week staring" catatonia into space and, of course, "the drooling," for which the sterling staff at Park Lawn (sounds more like a graveyard) ingeniously tied a purple cup around my neck to catch the gauzy saliva that "made a spiderweb from his lips to his cup and all down the front of his shirt," a sweetly intoned metaphoric catastrophe penned by Sister #4, photographer par excellence for Vogue, no less, who receives endless kudos for her "photographic masterpiece," memorializing my demented state that, incidentally, ends up on Instagram "somehow." I know, it's pitiful and sad, I get that part. But what can be said of someone, moi, once touted as "so brilliant," "so up-and-coming," but now regarded as "so passé, so "like come and went" – that's right, the Hegelian, the Nietzschean, the f'ing Kantian. That's me, a regular Mr. Smarty at the After-Party.

Talk about smart? They don't even find the murder weapon for three days, finally getting around to checking my father's hand-me-down Alexander Julian blazer after an officer begins rummaging through all my things in the hospital room that smells like licorice, burnt metal, chicken cacciatore and White Diamonds. When the officer pulls the weapon out of my jacket pocket and looks at me, my mother's cheeks begin to slightly wobble with tears welling up in her eyes, then she 'admits'... she had felt "a sharp object" through my jacket when she hung it on the back of the door.

Then in marches Sister Boomerang-a-dangthang, an affluent defense attorney, first in line of a bunch of know-it-alls, which does not prevent her for being a glutton for punishment in the zinger-fling game and who, of course, has to show up first, dragging in tow her Stanford Law professor husband of the "always-bailing-your-ass-out" claim to fame who on his third breath in the room begins pontificating about how I need to take "personal responsibility for the mess you have once again created..." bla, bla Mr. Fancy Schmancy, which causes me impromptu-to to blurt out, "Ha! What a joke!" notoriously announcing I was "squarely placing the blame at the feet of Emanuel Kant, Esther Hicks, the Apostle John and Father Daniel!" A collective groan and a quick escape to the door for all in the room but me, I can tell, you was the apex of that moment.

Alright, I will spare you the pogo stick around the barn. What I witnessed was actually a suicide which at the time I thought was a murder which, though, suicide technically is. Logically speaking, if you kill yourself, isn't that murder? Physically succeeding was not my intention. In fact, I had no intention at all, that's the really beautiful thing about it. It makes perfect sense to me though maybe not to you which is why I must turn inside-out-from-within for you to understand.

Let me explain. There was a killing. As I pointed out earlier, the police even uncovered the murder weapon. That's right, two halves of an oyster shell.

All right, stay with me here because this is where I lose most people, like Homecoming Queen, third in line of a bunch of asinine bovines who begins fake-crying and shrieking at me not an hour after the police left who were like, "Oh my God, rolling their eyes!" at me... "Oyster shells my pretty ass," she belts out like an opera singer, "You should lose all dignity even to think we're that stupid to fall for one of your loony alibis. You did it to yourself," she snarks and sniffs, "We told you a hundred times, *each of us*, not to go back down there to that sleazy oyster shack where you just indulge your pathetic oyster fantasies because you can't get none." *Ooh*, double negative... and alibis? (Yea, you got it - drop dead gorgeous is drop dead dumb). The other sister, I forget which number, the one that looks like a frog that's had plastic surgery, the one Homecoming Queen adores hating but with whom she just loves getting her click on against me, approaches my bed looking like she has an unripe persimmon lodge up her nose and jets the oyster shells on the tray in front of me, baying, "So hotshot, notch those in your holy belt."

After several months, six to be exact, of Thorazine treatments, psychotherapy, Red Rover, meditation timeout (in the holy shrine of the padded cell), nonstop Daytime Soap ops, frankly, I'd opt for the Black ops, and "demonstrable improvements," "The Team," looking colorfully angelic in all white, deigns to allow me "some time on the agenda" to speak on my time at Ferndale, or whatever they call the place.

I promptly announce I am changing my story having come to some clarity due to their psychotropic assistances and proclaim what I really witnessed was a suicide, not a murder. The intelligent but sassy blond psychiatrist, a cross between Jody Foster, Marie Currie and Glen Close, and who is definitely having an affair with the handsome Director of Psychiatry, MD, explains that I nearly died because I had contracted food poison from eating a bad oyster, leaning forward very sensibly asserting, "Thus, the oyster is *not* a murder weapon," sitting back in her seat, crossing her arms, and casting her eyes around the room to all the other self-congratulatory sane people in the world who instantly adjust their faces with a self-satisfied reality check.

All stare at me with a curious admixture of amusement, annoyance, and ennui. But it does not escape the corner of my eye a seemingly sympathetic ear - that of the hot, young mental health technician, a student of psychology at the local university, whose blush meets mine whenever we come into too-close proximity to one another, but who now looks mildly interested in what I am about to say. I, on the other hand, am more than mildly interested in her bare, shapely ankles, one of which is connected to a crossed leg in tight white pants endlessly bouncing up and down... but I digress, I guess. The Thorazine has affected my mind but apparently not my body, but today I feel more finely attuned even if my head sometimes feels trapped in the stratosphere shot through with tails of stars. The Lead Psychiatrist looks at her watch, thumps the head of her pencil on her desk, and moans, "And....*yes...*"

I stand up. I begin with a clearer voice than I thought possible. –The kicker is an oyster isn't what it seems... it isn't really an oyster... what serious-minded person has not doubted the oysterness of oyster or the ness-ness of anything, for that matter? Whatever it is, we could only really know what it is by becoming what it is to finally say what it is. I mean, and how do you accomplish that feat unless your Orpheus who could tell us in a Protean minute? But then who wants to be torn body limb-from-limb? So, then old Kant comes along and does his own Maenads' demolition on the body, decreeing we can never know the *things-in-themselves*. Damnit, when we were having so much fun!

In a way it makes sense since what an oyster is is what everything else has become - a chicken brooding over a grip of eggs hatching the next generation of lies and illusions, all hanging out and incubating in five senses till a titration contorts another embryo of perception and all too soon, all the while wrecking the conceptional modalities of mind long-suckled on a purported independent reality or notorious noumenal prerogatives. Independent reality, what a fat farce! More like a first-order optical illusion that multiplies the divide of humanity's meaningless linguistic abyss, rife with the lost messages of Everyman, or better said, EveryWoMan. But everything is like this, making certain what it or anything else is is quite impossible. So, we sleep.

When I look down after staring northeast by 2:00 into space, I am not prepared to see that every mouth in that room hanging wide open. If a fly were present in my estimation it would have nine perfect options for a permanent home which I nearly say, but do not.

Besides, I quickly continue –What a ridiculous name is oyster, cutie little tasty morsel come masquerading out of the Void of the Unrepresented as *cloistered seclusion, inimitable loneliness, Luck of the Irish, tender inviolable world of the maiden, prize of perfect discretion*, but, Noooo... not that one, while I am sure, maliciously trolling me, like taking plenty advantage of me and my too-many Jack and cokes that I shared in plenty that night with Lola what's-her-name let's not forget.

So, you want accountability? Well, here it is – I willed and allowed that one poisonous oyster access to my body. Just ask Esther... she told me so in a dream. Of all the oysters that that shady Shack shook out in 34 years of being a venerable hole-in-the-wall, only one, according to my brother-in-lawyer, none other than beelined itself into my mouth, down my esophagus, into my stomach, and Bingo! adulterated my bloodstream enough to cause my heart to stop beating for 69 seconds. And if you do not believe it, read the blanking police report.

It is precisely this, something like an oyster comes along and yanks at the somnambulant heart of the human. If you're on time, you wake-up, apprentice yourself to its upward-pointing pathway, ascend the higher dimensions of Being and become an expanding idea in the mind of the Grand Source of it All, not to mention homecoming to the repository of the Universal Ideas that by faith alone descend from the kingdom as rightful heirlooms, paving under grace the royal road to our most excellent futures! I possess if nothing but faith alone which is why one day, I will shed this purple chalice, and have it all! That's right, and draw freely from the kingdom - of which Eden is but a Mini-Me - which is a lot easier entering into through the eye of a needle than it is through one of those delicately sauced membranes, speaking of which, I just love to t...."

Suddenly, just as I am winding into the peroration of the superior quality of the oyster beds from which many-a voracious oyster-eating moment of mine had been bade, I am forthwith manhandled like an irredeemable criminal and rudely high-tailed it from that esteemed room of health and wellbeing so fast I think the Rapture itself has descended and the White Angels of Heaven are there personally to escort me upwards. Instead, I am summarily pushed into a cold, dark room that stinks like hell's apothecary, hastily strapped into a chair, and within minutes that philosophically laden disquisition becomes a signed warrant for "an increase in the sweep of your medication regimen," I am told.

I'm like, *wtf* does that mean?

Well, it meant drool cup's back.

If I were to have a creed, it might go something like – for those who keep the polestar of wisdom in sight, sundry are the changes that season the banquet of life, infusing understanding and empathy into the years, the ultimate existential aim humans ideally seek. Which is exactly what I was trying to explain this past Christmas to my family and friends at our family's traditional Night Before Christmas celebration. However, some people just do not want to affirm another's personal journey or its attendant emergent effects of mind. Thus, once again, my views are insolently disabused and met with fierce denunciations by many in attendance, led by none other than, the Stitches of Eastwick practically caterwauling in chorus "What a pathetic, spoiled jackass you are," accompanied by my mother in a violin of tears.

But know, I stalwartly withstand these slings and arrows with Zen-like quietude of mind, and frankly enjoying it, maintaining that on the day of my death, while waiting for the ambulances to arrive (the first ambulance experienced mechanical failure while the second was involved in a little fender bender).... along with mon aide de camp, the Oyster, "I killed 'the old man' in me to make way for 'the new man,' as the Apostle John says in the New Testament," which I distinctly remember Father Daniel very clearly pointing out to us boys at altar boy camp. All this I joyfully relate to the confounded crowd of aghast onlookers dressed like Christmas packages, calmly explaining, "I now acknowledge these new, clear and abiding ideas molding me into an autopoiesis moment of bourgeoning soul, the seeds of which are strewn on the pathway before I lay foot into the future." Well, apparently, I nearly landed myself somewhere and it was not the future, or at least not the one I would be hoping for. Had I not cut a quick and clean get-away out the back door during the fruitcake, eggnog, and Hennessey hour, and shunted my situation into some hidden harbor out in Martha's Vineyard, one afforded by, no less than, the fat lawsuit money from both the oh-so accountable hospital and restaurant, which by the way, had collected beaucoup interest during those secluded years of my spiritual awakening - I probably would have a purple drool cup suspended from my neck indefinitely.

"Yes!" I announce excitedly, just last week at Le Cou Cou in Manhattan, telling Sis of manicured-fingernail infatuation, who seems to think admiring her French-embroidered red and white fingernails is more important than looking her flesh and blood brother in the eyes, "... *Yes*, I willed it! I attracted that single life-altering, delicious oyster that wonderfully upended my life in 69 seconds, instead of drawing into my soul the perfect pearl of my cloistered dreams, a practice I have managed to correct, learned to reverse the order of operations for making the most of my desires, forgiven everyone including myself, and letting it all go!" But even that last humble admission is not enough to squeeze out just one last drop of patient goodwill from my favorite sister who just grimaces and pushes her plate of Tartare de Boeuf into my water glass nearly toppling it over. After rummaging through her Gucci handbag for a near three minutes she commences to squirting enough White Diamonds all around to surely hustle me more than a few blushes from the precious love of my life when I return home this afternoon. After this unwelcomed display of undignified fumigation, she begins huffing and puffing her fake white mink on in gladsome ready departure, finally flipping her massive crimson mane back and rolling her real blue eyes all in one irritating motion, declaring, "You keep talking like that and you're going *back* to bedlam, bro, mucho moola, or not."

After Sis leaves, I pay the bill, tip the pretty winking waitress, walk out to the curb on Lafayette with its stupendous buildings towering in greatness not a block from my brownstone, and smile. She did not even seem to notice I had eaten a whole two dozen oysters for my lunch and was feeling fine. And probably does not know that I am going home to a woman who thinks I am the perfect idea in the Divine Mind, which is exactly what I feel about her.

Justin's Dénouement

from the novel, Justin Conté-McCoy

Serenity, something I have yet to realize, a solitary man come now two-thousand moons and more as occasional fisherman off-the-coast of some southern European country where I help bring in the local haul for many a hungry villager. On other days aficionado of the sea am I bending and hooking my sails off islands' jutting coastlines or running my rig up endless inlets pacifying my innisfree or upwards still more the ancient haunts of misty estuaries where looming waters wander gray and rich in the loam of earth's home, where speak tongues of seven seas, marrying my mind no more to bloodless, dusty tomes gaveling out right or wrong - but to the tree and acorn, the hummingbird and honeybee or nine bean poles of wattles made.

Thankfully, no longer do the villagers look at me as though I am spy or a thief in the night come to steal their last centime, but know I would gladly lend a hand to mend a broken hull or give to any the last straw hat off my head. Many a mother and father have offered me their precious daughter's hand. It is not that I am not fully grateful for their trust. I am. Sometimes I wonder what the villagers must think of me, a lone bachelor seemingly out to sea.

But try even as I may, I cannot command myself to traverse that deadly line of love or hazard to cross that bridge that burns return, for no amount of love or lust can lure me back to the mast-strapped, siren-rapt sinking-ship to-the-bottom with love. Except for an occasional scintillating night in sultry allegro-entangled impassionato with a certain lady friend, love, in its highest regard, is for me as much a forethought as an afterthought is to a murderous tiger.

Mistake it not, my mightiest hour has yet been blotted from the annals of time. In these whispered portentous moments, I pass not as the fool I was – or as self-deluded dupe who crucified himself to the tree of truth beneath which I yet lie bleeding, who leveraged the body of enduring love against the margin of deadly denial that so blindingly hijacked me down the highway to hell, enslaving me to a venture destructively wagered with personal liabilities and familial histories, when gambled against the unknown forces of love, did doom me like the last coffin nailed full of stones put out to sinking sea – *but* who stands before the almighty judge of the world as I do now and swear me damned and dead if ever I be such a fool again.

Still, there are days that catch me up like a mangling net with titan grip that wrings me out a hatred that roils with the bloody gusto lapped by the hounds of hell, till I implore the gods and the Lord on High to make the heinousness more humanly sufferable. Precisely speaking - of *her and them*, fiancée and loving family of my former days, who perforce in ensemble of viscid webs did ambush the full and satisfied hunger of my soul, shot hard to the heart of the matter and cut the destined bloodlines of my highest hopes, anchor of unquestionable faith to whom I tied my soul's ship of state but who so simply severed it like so many frail threads of the spider's web in so many fell breaths of lies.

To begin with, there is *she* whose blood flows and tolls the break of day within my very veins. This we know, in all its unfortunate historical and destructive denunciations. Despite my better judgment, I find my love for her still parts the waves of the sea for her to emerge more glorious flying ever victorious into my arms forever staying. Many undoubtedly would perceive unnatural these affections and affinities that would raise hackles of deepest antipathies in the minds of more.

It is not without deepest sorrow that profound voices still beg from the very bed of my soul that for, *yes*, just one last kiss of skin on skin, hers to mine, that sucks up and locks in sync each and every succulent cell that such combination would be impossible to break.

Yet contrariwise, another voice elbows in in barking denunciation, pointing to that particular leaf on the proverbial family tree that is hers no less swaying in eternal ancestral breezes which none can one iota alter, nor can I now shove this fact in the usual annulling confines of denial's annealing incubator, that is, when faced in full sight no more than a few branches away, *shielded* in leafy view, is mine that shakes in the self-same breeze and drinks from the self-same roots from womb to worms.

Secondly – are *they*, Familia Paternal, who so willingly and pitilessly with aforethought and malice in contemptible and manipulative coordination with *her* conspired to lethally pilfer the one and only heartbeat of my baby's body, for which each and every one will inescapably pay in ample and just accord, in and by whatever he or she most deliciously cherishes and treasures, have you money, pride, possessions, prestige, even limb or life – sing que sera, sera! Amen.

Suffice it to say, such meretricious retribution will be one point on which I shall never relent though it be of high and most damnable and perilous planks I walk though a downward pointing pathway to a most probable decisive end.

Only justice complied renders the ultimate sacrifice of one's life sweetest victory when pain of open wounds command long-suffering grimaced faces, for bitter are the risks that spin and toss the coins of fate – which in like turn demand that *they* – family famed in my heart long for love – pay for their complete and unalloyed villainy, for their plain old stupidity

and for their meddling and scheming forays in too many directions possible to keep reasonable and exact tabulations – that
is, for all they did to three generations of her family, to first,
her young and innocent grandmother, next, her unsuspecting
even younger mother, and later to my fiancée not so innocent
or unsuspecting but who long-labored under their tyrannical
smiling faces, I should say, before she entered into that clandestine, ignominious league with them against me; and then, not
least of all, how their menacing prowess extended to others as
subsidiaries of their ignorant, self-centered agencies, particularly
in the death of poor Rebecca Small and her pitiable parents,
dead, both of them, within six months of the aftermath of their
precious daughter's outrageous demise, and finally not to mention for their perfumed and calculated concealment of a dark
and squalid past that hand-tied, hogtied and hamstrung me
who was already a-run-amuck headless ostrich in a crazy, hazy
phase, all because the House of Conté-McCoy and its eminent
history was built of invisible stinking skeletons pawned from a
ghostly, ghastly yesteryear.

And I would be plum remiss not to mention their every
inhuman whim that like a silent deviant whirlwind that about
my fiancée's bubble of being went stabbing, axing and hack-
sawing until it finally burst calling forth Pandora and all the
fruitless clean-up crew. But what's the moral high ground, when
human topography in their minds' eye is mown to a plain old
straight-line, where any modicum of justice is flattened in its
highest regard for the most basic codes of human decency found
ever so sweetly in their preserving honesty and possibility of
goodness pickled in a jar of formaldehyde squirrelled away like
a fine aging wine in the fetid cellars of their hearts?

Such speechless treachery, devised by them and her and
crafted in the late hours of love, boasts an incredible traitorous

pact minted in mutual luciferin expediency, which can hardly be imagined even as a last resort in a clear line of desperate human choices, much less in necessary first moral principles famed by them all in warped a priori abandonment – Such that damns humanity, the blood and bone! damns the pulse in the hope and glory! damns the wholesome promise inherent in all they were! and worse, in all they harmed and destroyed, syllogistically spun and torqued to a necessary bloodless conclusion that no manner of heavy prayers, well wishes or good intentions could counteract or sweep them to the finish line before the contemptible crowning of all those undeserved-laurelled heads.

But nothing matches in regrettable intensity to my now obvious and oblivious inability to affect even a modest countervailing response against all they brought to bear against her and me, i.e., before she nailed me to the double-cross. As it were, their formidable political might and vast financial wherewithal was such that all the coordinated efforts amassed at my disposal, the cadre of my allies and total capital and portfolio outlays, being then of such relative meager measure compared to theirs that had I flinched, I would have been so smashed and flattened, ramrodded and thrusted so far beneath the ground in one fell swoop, you would have thought the possibility of my ever having existed a cold sweating mirage after a heavy night of drinking. So, I in self-exile set sail in disappearance of fitful moral outrage and abhorrence with plans like my cousin Malcolm to never materialize again. No doubt had I not imprinted a permanent departure to the scene, I am convinced that I or someone else would have been the next blotted out and all too soon.

So as they say, I vanished without a trace and downed the draught of redemptive advantage bestowed on me by the load of codes put at my disposal, granted this be not without repugnant reluctance to accept those blood-pocked hereditary links - more than millions given to me on my grandfather's deathbed, in what might be called his lapsed and degenerate estate of grace, putting at my disposal by a mere clandestine passing of one piece paper from his hands to mine, a whole page of codes unlocking the money bags of the world, as they say. I will not deny my suspicion not a little later that nonpareil are the seeds by which that poisonous honey pot of my luck was made, granted in scandalous admission, in an excrescent formulation of that beautiful love affair I so wretchedly cherished. You know the horrid account of which I speak, and all too well. The filthy dirty money, as they call it, yay, I accepted it, but have for more than half-a-decade horded and fostered its aggrandizement of power for the sole purpose to purchase a silent but violent coup d'état upon my paternal family's unsuspecting state of moral disgrace, hemorrhaging their blood-money wells within the veins of their very eyes, while desiccating so many balance sheets that will domino them all from the trapeze of family fate and fame.

It is also well-noting that despite an endless cache of cash for more than half-a-decade, my family has forestalled their futile search for me not a fortnight ago after fruitlessly pitch-forking out millions in a bonfire of inanities.... Despite this, they will never renounce their search for the stinking money trail over which I have obscured with such odiferous smells, buried it deeper than hell, and will one day if I am so compelled by the intel of my investigations may upward haul it buckets from the well, smash, disperse and dispel everything they find worthy or beautiful let alone meaningful. Look sharp, kinfolk, for you will soon find the true code and spell on which I smite the smithy's bell.

For the record, I am well-preparing in body, mind and soul, in angling intensity to return to that citadel of sinister repute and will one day propel their heinous histories of fraudulent worth and indubitable, unimpeachable honor to the court of judicial review, in which I plan to act in solemn solidarity as plaintiff, sheriff, prosecutor, judge, jury, witness, and if needs be, executioner, wrapped in one dynamic explosion after another, for the screaming yelp in me cannot otherwise be staunched for no amount of good graces.

But for what exactly am I well-preparing? Better ask which of the single-headed, two-faced beast shall conquer the higher ground in me - lust for revenge or justice for righteousness sake, or will, can, dare I, or so presume I splice the difference? These are the days I tremble beneath the growling roar of a troubled mind that it be not sacrilege to pray for the grace of God in gathering hope to see the air shot through with a burgeoning and imminent just reward.

....Well, anyway, until then, as I said before, you can sometimes find my sails hugging the shores near my home, where it lay straight up a narrow trail through a wide staircase of hills, dotted by hovels and houses alike, a-wash in a chalky cleanliness, splashed in a pastel of redolent rose to princely purple, interwoven with a mystery of wisteria that green colors the mauve of time, while a soulful music it seems these people everywhere play, all through which I daily ply upwards my way at end of day to my two sparsely furnished rooms, above the fray of the world, my sandals full of blond and abalone grains of sand and crunchy bits of shells.

...Still yet, there are those days, when first it comes upon me... when the finger of time draws back the curtains of the dead to play time out of mind, as if in a dream or in some scene stirring in a distant mist that, nevertheless, clocks a blow square between my eyes. Truly, it is in shuddering moments as these for which one truly lives, that break an opening, for it is through the fire that

one must force the flames to part or through neglect destroy the only way forward, one that defies that crushing prophetic diurnal decay....

... *so, when it comes upon me*, overlooking evening's endless sea, when the blood-red wands of the sun fall in blinding refractions, prism shot across the bow of heaven, it is then that I fall on my knees, slide back the wooden panel in the floor, draw out the leather pouch, remove each one by one and spread out the contents across the table beneath the western viewing window of my high and haute abode – my most precious possessions, the five lockets, that in many ways define, and refine, the grist of my life in a five-inch snapshot. Five lockets I gathered, except for one, unintentionally, two of them respectively bearing the likeness of her grandmother, one given to her by her grandmother, the other I stole from the safe of that man that sunk my heart for life, my grandfather, a third locket in which her mother appears in too-stark resemblance of my great-aunt when both just emerging from girlhood, the fourth containing the image of *her* on which I once endless drank as if she were the fountain of life itself, and then, the last and final locket, when opened is strangely blank of image, nameless of name, historically absent, the empty space of my child who never came to be, whose life was fruitlessly forestalled by plain unadulterated viciousness to deprive the innocent of life, and deprive life to bestow upon innocence the experience the contains the possibility of priceless beauty, and for some wisdom.

It is in these moments that I become more fully awakened into who I am while at the same time reaffirming something greater. On the table beneath my window, through which sometimes blows a distant breeze, I deal out the lockets in the same direction horizontally as the sea tumbles with the waves. Then, for a time I look upon each face, one after the other, sometimes shaking my head in lovely fascination, at other times, in agonizing disbelief.... *as time irresistibly draws me in* as the sundial absorbs the shade into a moment clear, distilling into shadow-less stillness, becoming a single drop of dew anointed upon a blade of grass, that, in peace pauses. Then drops.

And then it happens! Their faces and the faceless one all commingling in a tingling of soul-making moment *dissolve* into a solitary image that at once breaks down the walls of the world -and I am welcomed back into the family of things that alone truly brightens my heart.

Thus it is, in the closing hours of day's eventuating darkness that the only simple goodness I have ever known seeps deep into the plenum of my soul, a sustaining moment of unbridled contentment un-waning... until my head begins to droop.... and finally drops, with the nightfall, and the fading light.... on to the lone wooden table in my room.

About the Author

Tom Carter splits his time between the West coast of the United States and Europe, loves gardening, nature, and spending time with his family.

M.F. Robinson

Stone Table Paper Mill

It was built in the winter of 1939 right beside what would become the Leotie Military Cemetery, and appears at night as a house for the ghosts of the buried and it was built originally as a part of The New Deal to manufacture U.S. Army uniforms before being converted into a paper mill.

It's one of the oldest businesses in town still operating and will soon become forgotten. It's employed somewhere over 3000 hard-working and not so hard-working citizens over the years.

There's still three bathrooms on the plant floor from the days of segregation, and Sydney who's been working there since 1964 remembers those days. The third one which hardly anybody uses anymore is beside the junk machinery that hasn't been sold yet, where there's no ceiling lights, and covered in cobwebs and dust flurries, with a broken door lock and broken flush lever and where a few rats will die every year.

Through the cheap and plastic paned windows, you can look and see the world outside, the pine and oak trees and the endless roll of the Appalachian Mountains and the cutting waters of the wild streaming Leotie creek, all of it like an oil canvas.

Inside the plant is boiling hot. There's no air conditioning and the heat contained within the cement walls chokes out oxygen, picks up the dust and hurls it into the everybody's vision. On first shift there are forty-three employees.

Sydney cuts 16 x 16 sheeted stacks of paper and cardboard on the great steel knife, and he's been doing it for forty-four years. The blade is two feet long and when Sydney cranks down on the lever the blade bites down at the paper like a shark's jaw and every day he wipes down the surface with a tub of Pilgrim John's brand grease so it appears almost brand new even though it's as old as he is.

His father threatened to disown him when he was twenty because he almost told him he was in love and was fixing to ask for a black woman's hand in marriage and so he ended up never doing it because he loved his father and held a great respect for him too.

The woman's named Miss Loretta Flowers and she nearly saved Sydney all the way up from a pretty mean gambling problem and she married another man about four years after they had fallen in love, about a year before Sydney's father died.

Sydney spoke at his father's funeral and cried some when he spoke. Throughout his life he borrowed a good bit of money from him due to his betting habits and when he was growing up his father took him squirrel hunting which was mostly what they ate for their meals, and he'd lead his son through the woods of Southern Appalachia, and spoke to him about the blade of a knife, the old trees, the clay that is billions of years old upon which they walked, and about once a week since his father passed away, while sleeping at night he'll dream up this image of following his father through the wilderness as a child, and he still thinks about Loretta most days and his father and he loves him still and will never forgive him either, still loves betting on football games every Saturday and Sunday, and loses most of his savings with every wager he places, and on the other days of the week he cuts the cleanest paper anybody ever wrote on.

This morning Wohali Clifton comes in late. The sun in the sky emerges like a newborn's crown and he gets out of his wife's 1991 purple Buick while she hollers at him and he slams the door as she peels out the gravel lot, tires dragged and spurting up stone, and the door swings open and then closes rapidly as she turns down the road. Wohali says to himself, Goddamn woman, dumb bitch.

They met in high school and were married at eighteen. Her father held a pistol that he carried upon the beaches of Normandy pointed up at him when he came and requested for his daughter's hand in union.

Wohali walked with crutches and a limp and had a full braced cast wrapped around his left leg. "I'll marry her," he said.

"Well shit son I believe you'd best had." She was sitting beside her father, with Wohali's seed growing insider her womb.

The Autumn prior to their wedding, after setting records for scoring and assists, steals and rebounds over four years as a starting point guard and small forward, Wohali accepted a scholarship to play basketball at the University of Tennessee, and enjoyed the greatly the lifestyle that came with it. He promised his mother, at age fifteen, that he'll get her out of the trailer park and buy her a house with a pool, make sure she doesn't have to work another day in her life. He was certain as it was his own destiny that he'd be playing for the Boston Celtics in only just a few years.

His mother died, this past year, while working nearly sixty hours a week as she had done for fifty of her sixty-five years on earth.

While attending UT, Wohali met a cheerleader and she became pregnant a few months later. He gave her money for an abortion, which she kept and then kept the child too, and she told him about it four games into the season. He called up his hometown girlfriend and tried to break up with her over Christmas break, reckoning it the correct thing to do, when she told him she's pregnant too and that he's the father. In the first game of the new yew year, he broke his leg and they took his scholarship and he couldn't afford an education anymore and moved back in to his mama's trailer and took a job packing cartons at Stone Table.

This morning, thirty years later, he comes in a hundred pounds overweight and just about a minute late and it's the third time this year. He wears a Larry Bird jersey that his grandchildren got him for Christmas three years ago and basketball warm-up pants. He's balding and covers his head in a backwards orange UT hat and stands down by the shoot that spits out cartons of notebooks and packs them tight, and tapes them up and stacks them onto a pallet, knowing that the supervisor will keep him for ten of the thirty minutes given for lunch, to talk to him about being on time, about attitude. When the supervisor walks down the way past the machine, the LC-341, they nod at each other, each saying to themselves, ever so politely, Go sit on a fat one you bitch, and, Take it and shove up your ass lazy motherfucker.

The supervisor's name is Johnny Bledsoe and back before he became supervisor, back when everybody liked him, they called him J.B. He worked in the plant for twelve years, starting out as a container loader, stacking fifty-pound cartons in the dark hellish heat of the trucks, eventually becoming a very skilled mechanic and operator of each of the twelve machines in the mill, which if assessed together, accumulates for over forty million dollars in value. He handled each of them, in the image of a cowboy breaking a wild stallion. Back then, he wore faded blue jeans, a pair of Georgia boots, and old t-shirts with beer and tobacco logos, Marines and Olympics and eighties southern rock band prints on them, the same shirts he wore during high school wrestling practice, where he got second in the state championship three years in a row, always losing in the finals in the last seconds of the match, being cursed his father told him, cursed. He was probably the finest mechanic ever to come through Stone Table and it's how come he got promoted, and getting promoted is mostly the reason why nobody likes him anymore. He doesn't care for the new title or the paperwork it involves, or having to tell somebody else what to do, but the job pays a little bit better and that's the end of it. He misses coming in and keeping to his own and working with his hands and sweating out a hangover and drinking up the entirety of night with friends after the day being done. He won't miss being supervisor on the day, God willing, in about a quarter century from now, he retires. I've busted my ass my whole life, he says to himself sometimes, then, maybe to God'll say, "The hell does any of it even mean?"

Part of his job description is to take the flood-piss from the company's general manager, Mr. Renell Lonnie.

"Goddammit J.B.," Mr. Renell says, "we got three trucks coming in this afternoon and you don't have half enough product ready for what they're picking up." On his desk is a forest of paperwork, bills and order-forms and quarter reports and red ink bleeding all over. He shakes his head and looks up with led loaded eyes, veins pumping underneath the neck. "Do you like your job?"

It's a hard thing for a grown man to have to say Yessir all day long like a child, but J.B.'s mostly gotten used to it.

"You like the money that comes on your check every two weeks that's signed by me?"

"Yessir."

"Well I'm glad somebody here doesn't have any stake in the day's work, because I'm losing money faster than an orphan loses faith in God. Now are you gonna have this order ready by four o'clock today."

"Yessir."

"Cause by God it's your ass if you don't. Do you hear me?"

"Yessir."

Paper's a dying industry and Mr. Renell knows it. His own father suffered a heart attack, cutting paper on the knife beside Sydney, in the plant and the time of death was called before they got him on the stretcher, and he can still feel the presence of his spirit in there, the cardboard and the dust, the aroma of shredded wood chips, the heat, the tuition that paid for his four years at Georgia Tech made by honest labor and long hours and more sweat than can be weighed, the voice of his father. There's a great hurting involved in keeping the company from drowning. He loves it as though it were itself a part of his own blood.

He surveys the machinery down on the floor of the plant as a captain gazing upon the horizon, a storm of machine jam-ups and thunderous waves of 2500 pound paper rolls spinning through the ink cellars, perforation, knife and bands, wiring and cover slots, as though it were land ahead, the miracle that is the economics of productivity.

In the beginning of the process, before the rolls are delivered to Stone Table, there's a company that comes to the forest and cuts down the trees and nobody hates it more than Mr. Renell but it's how the paper is made.

Eventually the notebooks are shipped in forty-foot containers across the country and placed on shelves in dollar stores and purchased by millions where all those sentences will be written, the essays on Walt Whitman and Langston Hughes, American Presidents and entrepreneurs, and the inner thoughts of those who each day in existence, struggle and suffer and search for something, like a missing soul, and then write it down from pen to paper in their journal, their Stone Table notebook, all of it as though it were a collage of humanity across the country.

Mr. Renell hired Jorge when he was eating dinner at Tetas y Cervesas, during the fourth bachelor party in twenty years for one of his college buddies, and just watched Jorge in awe, who was working as a bus boy and janitor at a pace inhuman, then asked him what he made and then asked if he'd like to make twice that much. He says it's maybe the best damn hire he ever made. People'll turn still and watch him work and wonder at such effort, the grace he moves with while setting up the machine and turning it at a speed past rate, checking the paper and adjusting the parts on the fly, always moving, very much like an athlete.

"How come is it a Mexican loves this country more'n anybody else? I mean I swear he just works and works and works, and every single second a the day likes he's nothin' but just the luckiest sum'bitch to get to do so," Wohali says as Jeanie Fae walks past his machine on her way to take break. She is almost fifty and already in her life has lost all three of her husbands to a form of cancer and she wears cut-off blue jeans, and her hair long and in curled tips and permed and a softball jersey sponsored by Psychotic Stallion beer. When her mother was pregnant, she took mifepristone and misoprostol to get rid of the fetus inside her but the medicine didn't take and Jeannie Fae came into this world with irreversible delayed motor skills, a godly gaze and a pre-destined speech impediment that stumbles and stutters out of her vocal cords with each syllable.

She says, "I reckon it's just one a them ole conundrums."

"Bullshit."

She heads on outside to the benches to sit down for a few minutes and get some sunshine, and takes a seat next to another employee who works upstairs and they smoke Marlboro Reds, four of them each in the fifteen minutes allotted. There're people all the time tell her those things will kill you and she says, "Maybe so, but I'll likely kill you first, I tell ya, you keep on minding my business that way."

She usually says when her smoke buddy asks how she's doing that she's alright, she just still misses all the time the men that she loved and lost. "It's hard working," she says, "but there's nothing else you really can do."

Usually on her third cigarette, she says, "but I'm really quite fortunate to be here, when it comes right down to it. I don't wanna brag or nothin', I don't, really, I mean that, but I'm a miracle made by God and that ain't even braggin' neither, I'm just saying what's fact. My mama done all she could to keep from havin' me in this world but here I am."

She's working today at the end of the shoot for the machine that Jorge operates, next to Big Walt who they say doesn't even know what soap is.

After a few hours and they start really sweating and it stains the body like a curse from God, she hollers out, Wheew-ah-mitey. "Big Walt, you stink boy. You need to go home and scrub all over once you get offa work. Don't be 'fraid a no soapy water neither. I take a bath each night, Big Walt and I clean myself up so I start to smelling nice. Every night, Big Walt, don't take none off. Now when I get in the bath watur, I wursh everywhere, toes'n all. Need to wursh your ass too. Have the whole durn plant smellin' like you down there 'nless you wursh your ass boy."

Mr. Renell comes down and cranks up the machine and then stands in as an extra packer beside them and he'll stay there that night until midnight probably, running the math in how to keep the company staying in business, these walls where his father earned the paycheck that made him who he is, this place where his father finally up-and-died.

He decides to shut down production on the LC-341 and the mechanic shifts its gears and parts to run also the order due at the end of the day. Mr. Renell will have to bring a quarter of the workers back in on a Saturday to make up for this. He thinks about the money he'll lose. He's down there, this day, with them and packing notebooks up into cartons and stacking them down on pallets.

J.B. cleans one of the old junk machines and operates it at a condensed rate so that it doesn't overheat and break down, and he has to place the covers, cardboard back slots and do all the wiring manually, to produce the product they're about two days behind on for shipment this evening. He'll stay over tonight five or six hours to finish the paperwork but his salary won't allow for the overtime pay.

Over the course of eight hours, they make almost half a million notebooks as though their labor, their sweat, their lives and heartbeat were written down and laid upon the plates of earth.

About the Author

M.F. Robinson was born in Georgia where he currently washes dishes for a BBQ joint. He has a novella published in The Write Launch.

Michael Warren

Rhumb Line

Jeremy swung his legs over the side of the bed at 0630. He awoke thirty minutes earlier, when the hot water began snickering through the iron radiator in the bedroom and the Chelsea ship's clock in the hallway chimed two pairs of two—four bells, six o'clock, the beginning of the starboard watch. If it were summer, the sun would be shining through the open window. But this was not summer and it was dark inside and out.

After awakening, Jeremy lay in bed to await the ritual Greeting of the Cat. The cat also heard the radiator and knew that Jeremy was awake. It jumped from the floor onto the chair, then onto the foot of the bed. It crept forward, careful not to step on the ridge formed by Jeremy's legs under the blankets, purring loudly. Jeremy's hand lay on top of the covers. The cat lowered his head as he approached the hand, and sniffed at it. The sniff passed muster (it always did) and it gave kitty-kisses until Jeremy raised the hand and gently cuffed the old cat's head in his palm, stroking over the cat's boney shoulder and back.

When the cat was younger it jumped directly from the floor onto the foot of the bed, but now it made two shorter jumps from floor to chair, chair to bed. Jeremy wondered if some day he would need to follow a similar course in reverse to get out of bed. Some days his hip was so painful that he rolled on his side, rose on one elbow and dropped his feet over the edge before he cautiously pivoted into a sitting position.

"Do you hurt as much as I do?" he whispered to the cat. But it had already left the bed, on its way to the food dish downstairs.

Jeremy stood and walked to the bathroom. As his leg muscles became re-acquainted with his weight they contracted unevenly, and he staggered. He stopped at the foot of the bed. Holding the footboard, he straightened and stretched his legs, then his arms and back. Now he moved with more certainty, still as an eighty-year-old, but one with some memory of a younger body.

As always, he courteously closed the bathroom door to contain the noises of his morning routine. After voiding his bladder, being careful not to splash, he brushed his teeth, applied soap to his chin, neck and cheeks with a moistened brush, shaved, and showered. He dressed in his usual uniform of black cotton mock-turtleneck shirt, blue jeans and a light sweater, the blue one that he took to the cleaners once a year. After returning to the bedroom he strapped on his watch. He slipped a pair of blue wool socks, wrapped in a tight bundle, into the toes of his shoes and quietly carried them down the stairs to the kitchen.

In his bare feet he was careful to not make a disturbance as he left the bedroom, but the old stairs made loud crackling noises that echoed in the morning quiet as he descended. The stairs had been making these noises for at least thirty years, since he and Rebecca moved into the house, and likely much longer. Some nights the stairs crackled when no one was on them. When Jeremy heard this, he stopped whatever he was doing and waited to see if Rebecca was there, or perhaps see the cat coming around the corner. But the cat was not heavy enough to make the stairs crackle. Other forces were at play. Maybe the house was stretching, preparing to carry its wooden weight into another day.

In the kitchen he sat on a chair and pulled on his socks and shoes. The bedroom chair was unavailable for this exercise as it was covered with stacks of laundry. Rebecca insisted he put it away, until she finally gave up. Now he left his laundered and folded clothes on the chair, drawing from the pile as needed until it was time to do laundry again. It was not untidy. But he saw no difference between placing it in a drawer to be taken out when needed, and leaving it out, so long as the pile was organized and neat.

He folded everything, as soon as it came out of the clothes dryer. He did not like the disorder of unfolded underwear. Jeremy took Rebecca's clothes to the basement along with his and washed them. He folded everything precisely the way she wanted – insisted – it be done. He carefully laid pants on the table, smoothing one leg, then laying the other leg over the first. Shirts and blouses were arranged to nicely fit on the closet shelves, even though his would not end there. Everything must be smooth, dry and warm. He stacked the clothes, then carried them to the bedroom and put them where they belonged, awaiting the next laundry day.

After retirement, Jeremy fell into a morning routine that seldom varied. The order might change based on the weather, or the timing to accommodate an early appointment, but the routine was comfortable and made sense. It was the natural order, the most efficient way to do what needed to be done. Even though retired, Jeremy felt an obligation on weekdays to adhere to a disciplined schedule. Today was Sunday, however, so his pace was more relaxed.

After pulling on his socks and shoes he made coffee, six cups in the drip coffee maker. He set their two mugs on the counter with a little milk in each. It was safe to leave them sitting on the counter as the cat could no longer jump that high and would not disturb them.

As the coffee maker chugged like a small, slow locomotive, Jeremy unlocked the back door, bending to grasp the key kept on the small nail just above the floor. Stepping outside, he walked in the cold morning air to the front of the house where the morning paper was hidden. The deliverer seemed to be uncertain about the most inconvenient place to toss the paper. They alternated between the middle of the lawn, the end of the driveway, the bottom of the front steps, or some secret place among the bushes. Jeremy complained to himself that they should know he never opened the front door, ants crawled from the lawn and bushes into the folds of the paper, and during winter storms the north wind blew the paper from the driveway across the street and into the neighbor's yard. He would not admit that there were no convenient options, instead gently cursing the insensitive nature of the unseen carrier.

Both the local paper and the Sunday New York Times were resting in the grass next to the end of the driveway.

He returned to the kitchen, removed the plastic wrapper from the papers, then stepped into the downstairs bathroom to relieve himself again. By the time he washed his hands the coffee maker no longer fumed and puffed. He filled one mug with coffee and carried the papers into the living room.

Crouching before the fireplace, Jeremy prepared to start a fire, a Sunday ritual when the outside air was chilled. His knees popped as he knelt on the flagstone and began the meticulous steps of building a fire: paper under the grate, three sticks of fatwood under twigs and small kindling, larger sticks and one small log balanced on the top. The pile of logs stacked in the corner was nearly depleted, but there was enough to get him through the morning.

Jeremy's fires always started on the first try, after first lighting three twisted newsprint pages and holding them, burning brightly, near the flue to prime the chimney. A strong updraft was essential, and nothing less than three flambeaux would do. If a puff of smoke escaped into the room, Rebecca would chastise his carelessness. She was very sensitive to smoke, and could smell it even if still in bed.

When the fire was roaring, he replaced the screen and sat in the stuffed chair to read the first section of the paper and sip his coffee. The local paper was small, even on Sundays, so it did not take him long to finish. Back into the kitchen, he poured a second mug of coffee and made his breakfast. Rebecca was a late sleeper so he was in the habit of working quietly to not disturb her. He sliced one Thomas's English muffin with a knife and toasted it lightly, one cycle in the toaster oven, so it was firm and crisp but not hard and black. Then he pasted it with peanut butter. Rebecca called it warm bread, and would toast her sourdough slices a second time to form a deep brown, almost black, crust.

Over the years so much of what they did converged, like the amount of milk in their coffee, or the way they brushed their teeth, or their views on social issues. Their tastes had become homogenized. But not breakfast. He liked his warm muffins, Rebecca her burnt sourdough.

While the toaster oven heated his muffin, Jeremy fed the cat. When ready, he carried coffee and toast into the living room, sitting once again on the stuffed chair. The cat ate half its dry food, then disappeared to some dark corner of the house for a nap.

By noon the papers were scattered across the floor. The fire was dead behind the fireplace screen. He was not supposed to make fires anymore because he set off the alarm too many times despite his meticulous care. The last time the fire department came to stop the noisy smoke detector, they charged him one hundred dollars for a false alarm. His doctor said no more fires and no driving. He sold the car, but still lit fires when Sunday mornings were cool.

The ritual on Sunday was to read The New York Times, listen to the fire and quiet classical music, and nap. This sufficed as church services, the "Church of the Holy Fire and Sacred Times". Jeremy and Rebecca did not subscribe to church dogma. Contrary to what they were taught as children, they created a catechism that conformed with their beliefs. Rebecca's family were Baptists and Jeremy's Mennonite, but neither of them were. They believed in the holy trinity of logic, science, and rationality. The unreliable stories of two-thousand-year-old un-enlightened men about the existence and form of God were fictions, irrational attempts to explain what was then un-explainable and teach children how to be moral adults. They believed in morality, and though they saw no objective evidence of God, logic allowed for the possibility of God. But they knew the form of any possible god was unlikely to be as told in the stories. Though containing truth, they were not likely true.

Jeremy suspected Rebecca still hoped there is a God. She found the memories of the church and her family comforting. This was one of the subjects they savored in silence on Sunday mornings. It would be nice if Rebecca was right.

At noon each Sunday Jeremy walked to the hospital where he bought an inexpensive and solitary lunch in the cafeteria. The walk took less than thirty minutes, a few more than 3,700 steps from the bottom of the back porch to the cafeteria door.

Last week it was 3,723 steps. He was confident he could do better today as his hip was not angry. He would attempt longer strides.

Jeremy slipped on his sunglasses, his fleece jacket, and his Red Sox hat. He walked out the back door, locking it behind him. The air was chilled but not cold, the sky a light but very bright blue with high fall clouds. The glowing leaves on the trees hung silently.

At the bottom of the back stairs he clicked the pedometer on his belt and stepped into the driveway. His focus snapped onto the next few steps, seeking the most direct route for the walk.

He took a deep breath and turned right at the end of the driveway, staying close to the edge of the pavement. Another right turn onto Wilbur Street. He stayed on Wilbur for one block, walking an oblique angle across the street, taking a direct route from the right-hand corner by the house to the left-hand corner at the end of the block. There was no traffic on Wilbur. It was a quiet street that ran along the side of their house lot, next to the tall hedge that grew from the front of the house to the back of the lot. He sometimes found beer cans or toys under the hedge, which he would put in his coat pocket and dispose at the hospital.

It took Jeremy years to perfect the hedge, and now it looked magnificent. It was eight feet tall by the front yard, dropping to four feet at the back of the sloping lot, the top of the hedge perfectly flat and level. Thirty years before, when they moved into the house, the hedge was clogged with weeds: bittersweet, wild rose and maple tree shoots. It had not been trimmed in years. Clearing the invasive weeds by hand, on his knees, crawling under the branches, took five years. It was hard work, but the privet filled in where the trash plants had been removed. By the sixth year, the hedge was a solid wall of green each spring, with only a few new bittersweet shoots to remove each year.

The neighbor's hedge across the street was as bad as theirs had once been, with more trash than privet. Though they never met, he often rehearsed the conversation he wanted to have with them, instructing them on how to get rid of the trash weeds and plants; how to kill them at the roots without damaging the roots of the privet; how to trim the privet so that in time, in another five years, their hedge would look as good as his. "If you want, I would be happy to show you how." He had this imaginary conversation with them every spring, but nothing ever changed.

At the next corner he turned left onto Watson Street, following the rhumb line from waypoint to waypoint. Jeremy took satisfaction in a course well walked. He was careful to follow the shortest route to the hospital. He tried alternate paths, but none of them were as efficient as the one he followed now. The only variation was traffic, parked vehicles he encountered, and piles of snow at the ends of driveways in winter. Overcoming these variations made the walk interesting.

He made a short detour on Watson Street where someone parked a pickup truck next to the small house on the corner. A construction dumpster was behind the truck. Once he stepped to the side to avoid the truck, he set a new course to the next corner, Bond Street. The dumpster was an irrelevant obstruction outside the new channel.

The familiar piloting continued: one block on Bond to Stairwell Place; one block on Stairwell Place to Stairwell Street; across Stairwell Street to the break in the hedge that lead into the church parking lot; across the parking lot, finding the shortest course through the scattered cars; through the walkway between the parking lot and Broadway. A car on Broadway stopped to let him cross.

The sidewalk along Broadway was old, broken and patched. Jeremy noted one patch shaped like Florida. They had been to Florida just a few years ago, and again a long time before that when they anchored in No-Name Harbor. And when they came back through Canaveral Inlet, that was an interesting experience. "Remember when we anchored that time in Breeze," he imagined saying to Rebecca. "Dan and Stef were there too, we talked to them on the radio. The Stream was rough. They broke their jib sheet and motored the last four hours. Their engine overheated. Broke a motor mount." He repeated the conversation, remembering each line. "Breeze, Breeze, Arlo. When we make St. Augustine, I'll need some help lifting the engine. You guys make out okay? Over." Yes, we were okay, he thought.

As he replayed the conversation Jeremy stepped over another curb and crossed another street, holding both the course and the conversation in mind, remembering what they had done and what they had said.

We made it just fine. Put a second reef in the main and motor-sailed. Is that what I said, Jeremy wondered, or is this just how I tell the story now? I've told these stories so many times that the story is what I remember, not what really happened. Rebecca will correct me. Remember how terrified you were that first crossing? But later, it was just something to deal with. I crawled to the mast, tethered on, reefed, crawled back and we moved on.

This started another remembered snippet. Honey, be careful, be careful, use your tether, OK?

Don't worry, I'll hang on. Just keep us into the wind until I give you the sign, then bear off. This won't take long. Then after, back in the cockpit: OK. Are you OK? Do you want some hot chocolate? It's a good thing we put hot water in the thermos before it got stinky.

You take the tiller. I'll get us something. I'd rather you sail. Can you do that? Are you OK?

I'm fine. I'm not queasy at all. I'd rather go below and you take the tiller.

Remember six months earlier when you cried because there were jelly fish in the water. We sold our home and could not see land. Now we're having hot chocolate in a northerly in the Gulf Stream.

Jeremy walked with his head down except when assessing the next change of course, or watching the range of landmarks ahead to ensure he walked a straight line. It was important to walk the best course. There was no satisfaction in meandering. A course well sailed, a job well done, gave him pleasure, even when no one else noticed. His career depended on attention to detail, on getting things done and right. He was not a perfectionist like Rebecca, but he was careful and thoughtful. Sometimes his patience with detail would drive his bosses crazy. Until he mastered the details, he could not assess the larger picture. Even now, as he measured the time and angle and distance necessary to walk the best course, he did not keep to the dogma of the straight line. Sometimes data would indicate a straight line was not best.

At the next corner Jeremy saw a penny to his left, outside the crosswalk. To pick it up would cost him four steps. The price of a penny, but it was worth it. It would add a tack to the course. He invested four steps, then adjusted to a new course. By the time he reached the landing on the other side of the street he gained back some of the investment. Inches mattered: an elegant recovery from a necessary detour.

He reached for the penny and noticed it was "tails up". It was supposed to be lucky to find a coin "heads up". Maybe a little luckier, he thought, but it was still lucky to find any money on the street. Found money was found money, even an upside-down penny, and that was lucky. He picked up the penny and put it in his left pocket, conscious of the hole in his right pocket.

Jeremy left Broadway and crossed the parking lot to the automatic door of the hospital emergency room. He walked past the desk and smiled at the nurse, worried that if he did not smile and acknowledge her, she would ask him where he was going or if he needed help, or tell him he should not be coming in this door if he was not sick or injured. However, this was not likely. He passed this desk every Sunday. The nurses recognized him.

It's a pretty good hospital, he thought in another conversation with himself. The nurses are all very nice. Some of them are pretty. That time I woke Rebecca and asked her to take me to the ER while our friends were sleeping... That time....

The thought trailed off as Jeremy walked down the hallway past the first bank of elevators, around the corner and on to the second bank. Taking the first elevator might be a shorter route, but he had never measured the steps between the two elevators and some common waypoint. It was too late now. He could not go back. That would be the wrong direction for an efficient course.

He rode the second elevator to the basement and turned right after the door opened. No one was in the corridor. The door of the cafeteria was on the right. He could smell the hot food behind the glass partitions. Not as good as that place up island, what was its name? Not like in the City where we used to go. But it would be good and not cost much.

Oh, click it. 3,725 steps. "How does it know, Hon?" he asked Rebecca. "How does it know when I take a step?"

About the Author

Michael Warren is a writer and sailor living in Newport, RI. The experiences of growing up in a small Kansas town infuse much of his work. Previous works have appeared in Adelaide and High Shelf Press, and he writes a blog on aging without the support of children.

Read Trammel

A Van Called Vengeance

Here comes the vengeance

Everybody knows who Drew Bryant means when he says they're coming in the morning. He goes up and down the sidewalk in front of Stockman's telling about a whole caravan coming for vengeance. To burn and loot. Patti smoking a cigarette by the door says he's full of shit.

"I talked to a friend who seen them," he sneers as he takes hold of his too big belt buckle.

"You don't got friends," Patti says and snubs out her cigarette so she can go inside with that punctuation. She'd rather be up on her family's farm instead of pouring drinks for fake cowboys with their polished buckles and narrow boots that only get scuffed on cement, so full of testosterone they bellow like bull elk in rut and take out their blue balls on each other, but she needs the money. People keep dumping off cats at her mailbox and the barn's mice are staring down extinction. Lot of mouths to feed.

Drew Bryant gives her a couple of choice words that are lost in the din of Saturday night in Stockman's. His face is red in the neon of the Budweiser sign. He gestures with an ash-tipped cigarette and goes on.

"Anyway, they're coming," he says. "There'll be nothing left standing if we don't organize."

The typical skid mark of leaners and wobblers on the sidewalk is easily convinced and word spreads past the video poker to pool tables and booths. Enthusiasm gathers steam in loud talk punctuated by cue on ball, *crack*, and call your shot. There'll be no fights tonight because there's serious business in the morning. Boisterous bravado bolstered by beer buzz. Patti says they'll be too hungover to fight as she lines up shots of well whiskey.

Last call and Patti and Jane and Robbie, the bouncer with biceps like briskets, are shooing them into the street, the staggering sentries of Stockman's, where there's pushing and giving shit, but no fighting, boys, no fighting. There'll be plenty in the morning. Drew Bryant is around but this is bigger than him now and he looks lost in the milling mob of drunk dicks.

Sunrise—mid-morning—finds them posted up on Miller's Road waiting for the vengeance. Some are still wearing the blue jeans and boots of last night's shenanigans. A few look like they robbed a thrift shop of all its old sports equipment with mismatched pads and even a football helmet perched on a Neanderthal head. All eyes are red.

Drew Bryant is getting sick in the bushes down the ditch, though he said he's taking a shit. He got a few rounds bought and chipped in a few of his own. Eggs from The English aren't sitting too well in all that booze. He soon reaches the stage where it's just a retch and stars in his eyes while his skull splits. His belt buckle is speckled with chunder.

"Drew," one of the sentries calls. "I see dust."

Drew Bryant heaves himself upright and wipes at his mouth. He pushes through the bushes and up the slope to where they've parked their pickups. The man who spoke points to yon horizon and sure enough, there is a cloud of dust approaching. From over the field. The sentries straighten and point binoculars. Drew Bryant reaches into the bed of a pickup and picks up an assault rifle. He takes the binoculars handed to him.

Off grid roading

How do you avoid plastic, Slim asks himself as he bumps along in a van you can sleep in, but it's not built out for a hashtag. It just has towel curtains and an air bed with duct tape repairs. But plastic. It's everywhere. It's all over the van—buttons and buckles—it's the packaging for so much that he needs to eat, to live, it's even in him according to an article he half-read about how humans are now ingesting plastic from uncountable sources without even meaning to. He knows that it's bad for the Earth and there's that island of it in the ocean and it's changing the chemistry of the ocean so that everything, all the fish and coral, will die someday in the not too distant future. Slim could be alive to see it.

That's why he's mad when they put more plastic than they need in the packaging. Why does his allergy medicine need to come in a box twice the size of the bottle with a big plastic insert to keep the bottle in place? What does it matter if the pills get jostled a bit? Why does the bottle need a package at all? The box is mostly air and plastic anyway. It would probably cost them less to make without the package and then maybe it wouldn't cost so god damn much.

The van jolts as it drags through another fence. He lost the road a long time ago. Can't see through the bug-splattered window and all the dust billowing off the body of the automobile. It's coated and leaving a plume of powder behind it. Slim drove up Burnt Fork Road and camped for a few weeks while he tried to figure out how to get off grid and leave all plastic behind for good. But it rained like a sumbitch and then he tried to leave and then he got stuck, van got coated in mud which dried into a powdery dust that seems to have no end.

Slim rubs his eyes and pats the steering wheel. This van is a survivor. It's been through worse than that mud. He's taken it down a winding road of packed ice and felled branches, hugging one side and skidding toward the precipice on the other, white water below. Then there was that time when the edible kicked in and he followed the lake road which was transformed into a ribbon of gold by the setting summer sun and they flew along it, him and the van, like a plane following a path that led to treasure, even though at the end of that road was a young woman who was mad at him for driving high and parking in her rose bushes.

So what that if it has plastic and isn't decked out with cabinets and a real mattress and a shower like all these van lifers suddenly in vogue and taking his camping spots? So what if right now you can't tell that it's an eighties blue and indeed has windows? This van takes him where he wants to go and he goes there like a bat out of hell.

Because Slim wants to escape. His mind is tired of puzzling over the great waste of plastic and how to avoid it. He's tired of trying to scrape something together only to hand it all over in rent to a property management company that buys all the shitholes in town and prices them like there aren't mushrooms growing out of the walls and the hot water works only sometimes, just not when he wants it. No matter how hard he tries, though, he keeps coming back, snap, like some bungee cord is around his waist and he needs the plastic, he's caught in its net. Like he is now, speeding through some field and feeling like shit.

Acid washed jeans

Amber Greene wears acid washed jeans. The same pair with all the rips up and down the legs she wore last night. Some bro asked her what happened to them and she said she cut em shaving her legs. It sounded better in the dimness of midnight at The Badlander. She lies spread out on the bucket seat of Johnny's pickup. She's pretty sure they fucked in it last night.

It started with drinks with Lauren and Cheyenne and Meegan at The Union. That old dive still has the Labor Temple sign, though the temple's bare and labor is bent at the bar with brews like piss. Her aunt Marge is in charge of the bar and doles out twenty-five cent fines for dropped pool cues, fifty cents for balls that leave the table, accidental or otherwise. Marge sleeps upstairs sometimes with a random customer she sometimes has to carry right up on her shoulders. Her bartender Bill tells her she can do better and she tells him she knows. It's a chill place to start off and Marge gives Amber discounts on the already cheap drinks.

They were giggling at one end of the bar when Dalton and them showed up, then it was flirting and fixing hair in the one stall bathroom. She didn't ask Dalton about Johnny and tried to be interested in the dude who was clearly interested, but he had a lazy eye and too tight jeans. Dalton stacked quarters on a table and the boys were playing pool while Amber got bored and got Marge to pour them shots even though last time she told Marge no more shots and made her promise. Dalton had words with a weedy kid and his poser friend who pointed his shots and mostly made them.

Then there was pushing and Marge said not in here and Bill widened his chest. Amber was bored, Cheyenne was bored, Lauren was already drunk and feeling lazy eye's bicep. Meegan suggested The Badlander, which has club night on Saturdays and that sounded fine. But first, hipster poser and the weed were out smoking cigarettes and they said something to Dalton and then there was a fight, more like a grab and wrestle and throw a punch until poser was sitting on the ground, just sitting, with blood all over his face and bubbling out his nose and he just laughed and laughed as weed ran off into the night.

The Badlander was packed, colored lights spinning, and Dalton was wanting more punches, just got to punch some-body. Cheyenne pulled him on the dance floor by his belt and channeled that big dick energy into bump and grind. More drinks and it was hot, but fun to dance, even with lazy eye there and Lauren getting pissed and Meegan finding something interesting in the bathroom over and over again.

Amber can't remember when she left them. For sure there was a text and Johnny at Stockman's and she didn't want to go to Stockman's but ended up there anyway. All the usual douchebags were there, excited about something, and even Johnny seemed like he had more on his mind than a booty call. She can't remember much except Patti asking if she was all right and Johnny's hand in her back pocket and Johnny's truck starting rough in the darkness.

Now the truck is parked blocking Miller's Road with others and Johnny is leaning against the front bumper talking to his bros. She can see the muscles of his back through his tight, white, t-shirt. Can imagine her hands on them. Johnny is kind of a dick, but she keeps coming when he texts. Keeps coming to his truck.

Amber stretches sore. Her head hurts and she digs in her purse for sunglasses now that it's bright. There's a rumpled blanket on the seat, the extent of Johnny being a gentleman, though it's a rough blanket like what you'd put under a saddle. Amber grew up around horses on her granddaddy's ranch and misses the feel of her hands sliding on their muzzles, the pat-pat on brushed hair.

"Johnny, I'm bored," she calls out the window. And hungry. Cheyenne and Meegan and the others went to The English for late-night breakfast, her phone tells her. The truck is getting hot in the rising sun. Jesus, she keeps ending up here.

"What are we doing anyway?" she says, but not loud enough for Johnny to hear.

She sees the guy next to him tap Johnny's shoulder and all the guys are tensing up. She sits up, hands on steering wheel, and tries to see through the bug-splattered glass. Nothing down the road. But dust, coming fast from over the fields. She sees a man pull a gun from his truck. Another.

"Johnny?" she yells out the window.

The shooting starts

The sun has grown hot and all the sentries who'd been slouching are tensed up now, sweat sticking the shirts to their backs. Drew Bryant has his gun out and others with AR-15s pointed skyward, as if in a pose to repel any invaders. But some, like Matt, hold shaky handguns out in front and point at the growing shape tearing across the fields.

"Is that them?" he shouts to Drew Bryant. "Is that a caravan?"

"Well it's a van," someone answers.

Drew Bryant is speechless with a speeding van billowing dust coming toward him. He holds his rifle slack and keeps looking through his binoculars so that he won't have to show them his eyes. He doesn't know. He's in over his dick.

Slim sees the trucks on the road and sees he's on an angle for them. He's glad he found the road. Wonders what happened. You lose all track of the news up in the woods, which is good, which is how he likes it. Still, you never know what kind of shit could happen in what, a week? He remembers all the predictions about what could happen, the likely scenarios that never came to pass just like you'd think because you never saw it coming. Somewhere he saw someone say that all the fireworks incessantly being set up off in cities were a government conspiracy to get people desensitized to loud noise. For when the shooting starts.

Jesus, he needs to just stay up there, away, but he can't. He isn't equipped and cannot afford to equip himself. So back he comes to resupply, to crash on friends' couches and maybe in the van on some backstreet. Until he can scratch up some cash and think about buying a stove and installing cabinets.

Amber is gripping onto Johnny's steering wheel and watching the boys raise rifles as the van speeds closer. Their certainty that their barricade will cause it to stop wains as the van rumbles over dry fields, dirt flying from its tires and dust smoking from its body. The unseen driver is crazy, driven by a brutal vengeance. He will not stop.

Drew Bryant fires first, though he will later deny it. The difference is seconds as gun after gun fires toward the charging vehicle. Some kneel in tactical positions, some stand steady with legs wide, erections tight against their jeans. This is different than shooting targets on the range or speed limit signs. This is easier.

Slim sees the gun fire and glances in the rear-view mirror, expecting to see a stampede of bison sweeping behind him. Then bullets are hitting the windshield and he's hit and he's dead, tossed roughly as the van speeds on, his foot heavy on the accelerator.

Amber is screaming at the shots with hands on her ears. She kicks at the pedals and knocks off the parking break. As she dives down and forward, she knocks the truck into gear and it rolls forward. It bumps into Johnny's butt and he wheels around. It gives the neighboring truck a love tap and the owner starts shooting the creeping truck. Johnny's yelling to stop, but it's all gunfire, and the lurching van that comes crashing into him, the others, missing most of Johnny's truck where Amber trembles on the floor boards with the blanket thrown over her to protect from glass shards.

Clean up and pizza

Four cop cars show up and find a mess. The ruined van is down in the ditch rolled over and steaming. A smashed pickup is splattered with blood and there's an arm. Amber is covered in blood, little cuts, and shouting. Drew Bryant is sitting on the road, puke down his front. Other boys are high-fiving, blood on their goalie pads, still with hard-ons from shooting so much. They did it. They stopped them.

"Who?" one of the cops wants to know and his colleagues down in the ditch shout back it's a hippie.

Ambulances show up and add to the chaos. An EMT tries to attend to Amber, but she keeps pulling away. What are the cops doing? Aren't they going to arrest them? They just straight up murdered someone. Johnny's dead. The van smashed Johnny. They were shooting the van.

The cops are rounding up the hockey pads and belt buckles. They're telling them they need to come down to answer some questions. They can't fit them all in their cruisers, so maybe they could come in their own vehicles. Sure, they'll order some pizza.

"What. The. Fuck," Amber shouts at a cop. "Why is everybody so calm."

"Ma'am," he says. "There's no reason to be distraught."

About the Author

I have a MFA in Creative Writing from the University of Montana. My work has been published in Potomac Review, Bright Bones: An Anthology of Contemporary Montana Writing, Adelaide Literary Magazine, Driftwood Press, Yale Angler's Journal, Solstice Literary Magazine, and Foothills Literary Journal.

Kipp Van Camp

The Doctor

It was during a late-night practice phlebotomy session that I first met Mr. Jefferson. The lab tech called around 9:00 p.m. and asked if I'd like to draw some blood.

"Sure," I replied.

"Meet me in the ICU in 15 minutes," she stated.

I headed directly to the hospital. The student apartments were located directly across the street. They could always find student assistance for anything that occurred throughout the night. The system was beneficial for all involved.

The critical care department greeted me with the usual sounds I've found to be universal in all ICUs: continual beeping of heart monitors, persistent inhaling and exhaling of ventilators, and constant low pitch humming of fans cooling the patients. This ICU was no exception.

While I sat down at the nurse's station, the lab tech entered the room. She had called me on one other occasion. I recognized her. "Hi Tammy, what lab are we drawing tonight?"

"There is an older gentleman in ICU 5 who needs a cardiac profile completed," she informed me.

I asked, "Is this the first set?"

"No, this is the second set."

Back in 1988, when a patient was being evaluated for a possible heart attack it was necessary to study the cardiac enzymes every eight hours for a twenty-four-hour period. If the heart was not receiving enough oxygen, and some of the heart muscle was affected, the muscle cells in the heart would release an enzyme called creatinine kinase or CK. This CK might change significantly in an eight hour period.

"Do you want me to give it a shot?" I questioned.

"Sure, go ahead," Tammy said. "Draw a purple and two red-top tubes."

Long before electronic medical records (EMR's), I went to the chart rack and picked up ICU room #5's chart. The patient's name was Henry Jefferson. Before going into his room, I briefly skimmed his chart. Henry was 84 years old and came to the emergency room that afternoon with a complaint of chest pain. Apparently, he was on the beach when he developed heaviness in his chest and severe left arm pain. According to the emergency room physician's note, he came directly to the hospital for evaluation. I perused the doctor's orders and found that Henry had been admitted for angina, rule out MI (myocardial infarction), and bradycardia with syncopal episodes. Bradycardia meant Mr. Jefferson had a slow heart beat and syncopal episodes referred to blacking out.

After skimming the chart, I walked over to Mr. Jefferson's bedside where I found a small round-faced man with tufts of white hair on top and on the sides of his head. He was wearing a pair of large brown glasses and was staring out the window. One of the prized benefits of any patient placed in the ICU at Peninsula Medical Center was the beautiful view of the beach front and the Atlantic shoreline. In the daylight you could see the ocean waves and an occasional ship in the distance. It was 9:00 p.m. The sunlit view of the daytime horizon had been replaced with a more glib view of the nighttime ocean and beach. The sky was clear and along the shoreline were several lighted structures; a hotel, a few beach-front properties, and a lighthouse. Far into the distance was a vast darkness that extended forever with an awesome, eerie appeal.

Mr. Jefferson was staring into the blackness as I entered his room. "How are you doing Mr. Jefferson? My name is Kipp VanCamp."

"I'm a third year medical student. You can call me student Dr. Kipp. I've come to draw your blood."

"Oh, another vampire," Henry responded in a meek, but clear voice.

"From the sound of your reply, you must have been stuck a time or two since coming to the hospital." I said.

"Yes, I have. And I only came in this afternoon. I'm afraid you better put some blood back in before I run out completely," Mr. Jefferson said half-heartedly.

While I set up the phlebotomy tray I engaged in light conversation. Mr. Jefferson told me he was from Chicago and had come to Florida for a vacation. He'd never been to Florida before. He then shared he'd never been hospitalized until now, either. He'd always been very healthy and admitted he couldn't get used to the idea he might be sick.

After a couple of minutes of conversation, I informed Henry I was now ready to draw his blood. He nodded his approval as I inserted a 20-gauge needle into his antecubital fossa. I breathed a heavy sigh, as did Henry, as I inserted the vacuum tube onto the back end of the needle and out came dark red blood. I collected three tubes, then informed Henry I was finished. He acknowledged my one stick and I bid him farewell.

The night went by quickly and by early a.m. I was back in the hospital. Dr. Tim was already starting to round on his patients when I came to the floor. "Hello doctor," Tim said. I glanced around the nurses' station before realizing that he was talking to me. I had yet to get used to being called doctor.

After exchanging greetings Dr. Tim said he had a new patient for me. "He's an ICU patient who needs an H and P (history and physical) examination. His name is Jefferson." As Tim said his name, I recalled my phlebotomy patient from last night. Sure enough, it was the same man I had "tortured" the night before.

I entered the ICU and found Mr. Jefferson in the same position I'd left him only eight hours earlier. The room looked much brighter this morning as the sun peeked its face from behind the sea-lined covers.

"Hello Mr. Jefferson, remember me?" I broke the silence.

'He glanced above his glasses and a faint smile crossed his face. "You're the young medical student who's training to be a vampire."

"That's right Mr. Jefferson. But I'm not here to drraw your blud." I said in my best Dracula impersonation.

"Good. Some other blood-sucker already beat you to the punch an hour ago." Henry stated while raising his arm to show off his battle wound.

"Actually, I'm here to examine you and discuss your medical condition." I stated.

Henry was a retired school teacher from Chicago. He'd been retired for 24 years. He had two sons; one who lived in Chicago and one who lived in Maine. He restated that he had never been sick a day in his life, until yesterday. At the suggestion of his children he came to Florida a week ago with a group of senior citizens. His wife had died three months ago. Apparently, she had developed a bad case of pneumonia and her physical state declined rapidly over the weeks before her death. She was hospitalized for two weeks and intubated and placed on a ventilator the last few days before she died. While Henry recalled these painful memories, he began to cry. He related he had married at the young age of 18 and they had recently celebrated their 65th wedding anniversary a few months before his wife became ill. Henry described the past three months as lonely. He didn't think he could go on much longer. He expounded how he purposely planned this ten-day trip to Daytona, Florida with a group of senior citizens as a means of occupying his time.

Yesterday he was out on the beach with an older couple from Chicago whom he'd met on the tour. They were all feeding the seagulls when he blacked out.

"One minute I was tossing bread crumbs in the air, the next minute I was lying flat on my back in the sand," Henry said.

The woman stayed with Henry while the man sought help. He awakened upon the paramedics' arrival. He didn't recall any chest pain or any other symptoms but stated he hadn't been himself the past three months since his wife died.

I sat on the edge of Mr. Jefferson's bed listening to him, pondering Henry's life. What kind of a teacher was he? What was his family like? Had his 65 years of marriage been happy? He spoke of his recently departed wife with such emotion; he must have loved her very much. While listening I glanced up at the heart monitor just as several skipped heart beats occurred.

"Are you having any chest pain, Mr. Jefferson?" I questioned.

He sat expressionlessly and responded. "You mean those skipped beats? Yeah, I feel them. I've been having those for the last few weeks."

I continued to talk with Henry while performing his physical exam. While I listened to his chest, Henry's heart skipped an excessive number of beats. Kathy, the critical care nurse apparently noticed the same changes on the monitor. She entered the room. I persisted with Henry's exam. He repeatedly denied having any symptoms, but his voice became more faint with each word.

The telemetry heart monitor showed a heart rate of 48 beats per minute. "Do you think we should get an EKG?" I asked the nurse.

"That's a good idea doctor." At the precise moment she spoke these words, a cardio-pulmonary tech wheeled the EKG cart into the room.

"Boy that was quick," I stated.

"That's because I ordered it a few minutes ago," the nurse succinctly stated.

Over the past few weeks I'd been humbled numerous times and was getting used to the idea that I wasn't quite as smart as I thought. Here was another example of my lack of confidence at this early stage of my career. The nurse had already ordered the EKG minutes before the thought had even crossed my mind.

"Do you think we should call the cardiologist?" I asked, hesitantly.

"Yes, I have already called him and he's on his way to the hospital." Kathy remained a step ahead of me.

I consoled myself; at least I was asking the right questions, even if I was several minutes behind.

Henry had closed his eyes and was on the verge of un-consciousness. "Are you still with us Mr. Jefferson?" I paused momentarily for his response. "Henry?" I said more firmly.

"What?" he mumbled, and then went back to sleep.

"Should we give him some atropine?" I asked. My mind was firing on all cylinders.

The nurse abruptly stopped what she was doing, looked directly at me for a second, then said, "Well there is some hope for you. How long have you been a doctor, doctor?"

"I'm a third-year medical student," I said cautiously.

"I agree," the nurse responded.

With what, I wondered to myself; my suggestion to give the atropine, or that I was a third-year medical student?

"Let's give some atropine, 1 mg." I qualified the dose.

"I'll get it." Kathy stated.

At this point in my medical career I was relieved that Nurse Kathy was a pleasant lady. I had begun to realize many other nurses could have chewed me up and spit me out in this setting, and in fact, many would.

While she gave the atropine, in walked a short, stocky, middle-aged man. "What've you got, Kathy? Who's he?" He pointed my way.

"Dr. Benson, I've got an 80-year-old white male who was admitted with chest pain to Dr. Jasenowski's service." Kathy began a brief, but detailed synopsis of Henry Jefferson's condition. "He's having occasional PVC's and actually blacked out prior to you walking in. Minutes ago, just before I called you, he had a seven-second pause, then became bradycardic with a heartbeat of 48 beats per minute. Here is his EKG. I gave him 1 mg of atropine a minute ago. And this is Mr. Van Camp. He's a third-year medical student." She stated as she pointed my way.

Over the past few weeks I realized that protocol was everything in a hospital. In this setting I was Mr. Van Camp. I had not earned the title of doctor, or even student doctor, yet. The recorder in my mind replayed the recent conversation between me and Kathy. When Nurse Kathy was answering my medical questions, she had distinctly addressed me as doctor. In looking back, I was now certain that this was her point, I was the doctor, yet she knew more about the situation than I.

"So, what do you think, Mr. Van Camp?" the cardiologist directed his question to me.

I stood dumb-founded. My mind raced for some type of intelligent response. "Well, Mr. Jefferson has bradycardia and his slow heartbeat is causing him episodes of syncope."

"OK, Mr. Van Camp, so, what do you think is the cause?" Dr. Benson, a board-certified cardiologist, for a brief moment, focused all of his attention on quizzing me, Mr. Van Camp, the 3rd year medical student.

Without a hint of composure or intelligence, I impulsively blurted out the first thought that came to my mind. "His heart!" I said emphatically.

A look of irritation crossed Dr. Benson's face. He looked at Kathy and rolled his eyes. Then stated: "Where do you find these guys, Kathy? Is it me or has the quality of student gone down over the past few years." After a deafening pause, Dr. Benson continued: "Nurse, why don't you help Mr. Van Camp?"

Kathy jumped into the conversation with the same vigor of a cat pouncing on its pray. "It appears Mr. Jefferson is experiencing bradycardia secondary to a third degree or a complete heart block which may be due to a sick sinus syndrome."

My mind raced to try and keep up.

"More than likely," she continued, "he's experiencing a conduction defect in his septum, somewhere between the AV and SA node." Kathy's rapid response and comprehension of Henry's cardiac illness was impressive.

"And what do you think we should do for him?" Dr. Benson inquired, further.

"He needs a temporary pacemaker placed now to stabilize his heart rate and then he should have a permanent pacemaker inserted in the near future," Kathy continued her impromptu cardiology lecture. "He may also need some diagnostic studies such as an echocardiogram and possibly even a cardiac catheterization to determine if he has suffered some type of a myocardial injury that may have started this problem."

"Very good, Nurse Kathy! So, Mr. Van Camp, is there anything else you'd like to add to Kathy's excellent assessment and accurate diagnosis.? Or do you want to stick with your original answer, 'his heart!'" The cardiologist emphasized the two words in a derisive fashion.

I responded with a couple possible causes like thyroid disease or electrolyte imbalance, and then kept my mouth shut for the rest of the teaching session.

The external pacemaker was hooked up and as we continued our teaching session with Dr. Benson, Henry began to stir.

"Hello, I'm Dr. Benson. How are you?" Dr. Benson said.

"OK," Henry responded.

"Are you having any discomfort?" the cardiologist asked.

"No, " Henry responded.

"I'm a cardiologist, a heart doctor," Dr. Benson continued. "What you have, Mr. Jefferson, is a sick heart. Your heart isn't beating regularly and we need to fix it by placing a pacemaker inside your chest. I'll place a small electronic device under your skin, with electrodes attached to your heart. This device will then regulate your heartbeat."

"When?" Henry asked.

"I believe we should do this tomorrow morning. I'd still like to perform several tests on you today and if they come back normal, then we'll proceed tomorrow." Dr Benson responded.

"I'd like to call my sons first," Henry said.

"That's fine," Dr. Benson stated. "But we want to get right on this, ASAP. So, no delays!"

"Do I have any other choices?" Henry pressed.

"Not really," Dr. Benson stated, then left the room, abruptly.

It appeared Henry was worried about what he'd heard.

"Do you have any other questions Henry," I asked. "Sure, but I need to think about this a bit."

"That's fine," I said. "I'll be back this afternoon. Get some rest."

As I left the ICU, thoughts were racing through my mind. I felt so stupid when Nurse Kathy answered all the questions correctly. I, also, felt inadequate because I hadn't really known the correct answers.

The rest of the day was hectic. Rounds with Dr. Tim took most of the day as we had 16 people to see. Ironically, we had a noon conference given by the chief of cardiology, Dr. Benson, and his topic was bradycardia. I couldn't decide if this was co-incidental, or if he had decided I needed to learn a few things. I suspected the latter. We performed two procedures in the late afternoon. By the time I thought about Henry again, it was already 7:00 pm.

After a brief dinner I headed back to the ICU to finish my H&P and to see how Henry was doing. I found him sitting in his bed, his familiar stare as he gazed out the window.

"Hi Henry," I interrupted his contemplative state.

He glanced up at me and a faint smile came over his face.

"Hello student doctor. Have those egotistical doctors and nurses been picking on you, again?" Henry asked his question in a playful manner.

"Did you hear all of that this morning?" I questioned. "I thought you were unconscious," I tried to down play my em-barrassment.

"'I must have caught some of it, anyway. I remember the cardiologist asking you a question and then that know-it-all nurse, Kathy, interrupted you and gave her two cents."

I liked his version better than the one I had lived through.

"Are you ready for your pacemaker surgery tomorrow?" I voiced my concern for Henry.

"I suppose so," Henry said. "Is this called open heart surgery?" Henry's question gave me insight into Henry's real understanding of the pacemaker procedure and insight into his fears and concerns.

"No, Henry. This is considered minor surgery. The cardiologist will put a small wire in your neck and pass it through the vein to your heart. He will do this under x-ray guidance. When the wire is in the right place, he attaches it to the heart muscle. He'll then place a small battery and pacemaker device under your skin up here by your collarbone." I gave him a technical description of what the cardiologist would do.

"Will I survive the surgery?" Henry asked, pointedly.

I wasn't too sure how to handle this question. On one hand, Henry needed reassurance. On the other hand, strange things can happen in medicine.

"I don't see any reason why you wouldn't." I offered encouragement.

"Well I'm not sure it really matters," Henry said. "I don't know that I have much to live for, now that my wife is gone." While Henry spoke of his departed wife, he again became tearful.

"Now don't talk like that Henry. I'm sure your sons and their families want you around; and, aren't there still some things you'd like to do?" I asked.

"I do like to paint. I'm just finishing a picture of the Lake Michigan shore front. My wife and I had a favorite spot where we spent our free time feeding the birds. When she died, I couldn't make myself finish it. My son recently asked me if I could finish it for him." Henry's voice trailed off. After a few moments of silence, he asked me: "What kind of pictures do you like? Do you like water colors?"

"Sure, Henry. Why?" I asked.

"Well, I'd like to paint a picture for you, if I ever get out of here," he said.

"You mean when you get out of here," I gently reprimanded him.

"I'll paint the sunrise view of the ocean from this old hospital room," he stated assuredly.

"I'd like that Henry, but for now, let's get you well," I refocused his attention on the task at hand.

The next morning Henry had his pacemaker placed. He made it through surgery without any trouble. His sons flew in to be by his side before the surgery and to help him get back home when he was strong enough to travel. I had a few other conversations with Henry over the next couple of days, but they were limited.

The morning of Henry's discharge I stopped by his hospital room to bid him farewell. He appeared to be doing well. His spirits improved, greatly, since his sons arrival. By all account he was feeling better, too. His color had returned, and his strength had improved. He appeared strong enough for the flight home to Chicago. I was confident he'd do well.

I stood near the edge of Henry's bed conversing with him and his boys, when Henry gently took my arm and pulled me closer to him. "I need to tell you something," he said seriously. "I want to thank you for your kindness. I know it's early in your training, but I'll tell you something, you're already a fine doctor. And trust me, I know something about this. Not only am I a patient, I'm a teacher."

For a moment frozen in time, Henry and I sat silently connected by a unique bond, the bond of the patient and his doctor. After a minute, the conversation resumed. Like an educator teaching his student, Henry instructed me not to change my bedside manner. He then informed me that the cardiologist was a smart and talented man and surgeon who had the experience and abilities to fix his heartbeat. But Henry also pointed out that he knew his heart was still sick. I reassured him that his pacemaker would take care of his irregular and slow heartbeat. He acknowledged my words but didn't seem to hear them as he finished the remainder of his thoughts. After I bid him farewell, I headed towards the door to leave his room.

The last words Henry said were: "Doctor, thank you."

Weeks passed by and I occasionally found myself thinking about Henry. Ironically, I had learned a great deal from him. He'd kindly allowed me to practice my blood draws. He'd gently confirmed my instincts on how people should be treated with humanity and respect. He'd unknowingly taught me to be careful what I said in front of a supposedly unconscious patient. Most importantly, his tender statements and heartfelt emotions about his wife renewed my faith in love and marriage.

It must have been about 12 weeks or so when I received a letter from Henry's son. He stated Henry had done well, initially, when he arrived home in Chicago. At first, he had quite a bit of energy. He'd even finished the painting of his favorite spot along Lake Michigan, keeping his promise to his son. However, shortly after he finished his painting, he began to weaken. After a couple of weeks, he finally saw a cardiologist in Chicago. The doctor ran a myriad of cardiovascular tests and diagnostic studies that were inconclusive. He couldn't find anything wrong medically with Henry' heart. Three weeks ago, Henry peacefully died in his sleep. His sons felt he had died of loneliness from his wife's death.

His son wrote that Henry wanted me to know he hadn't had the strength to finish the picture he promised. Henry also wanted me to know that he appreciated all I had done for him in Florida and wished me the best in my medical career.

While I read the letter, my mind wandered back to those days I'd known Mr. Henry Jefferson. He'd made a lasting impression on me. Pondering the news of his dying, I too, felt his sons were right, he must have died of loneliness. I recalled the cardiologist's discussion with me and Nurse Kathy that morning in his ICU room; how Dr. Benson had dismissed my impulsive answer to what ailed Mr. Henry Jefferson. I couldn't help thinking, my answer, though simplistic, was actually more right than any of us had realized at the time. His problem was indeed his heart. It was broken.

About the Author

Dr. Kipp Van Camp, a physician and medical researcher with numerous papers and articles published in the medical journals and online, is also the author of dozens of short stories and two creative nonfiction books Always Allie (2011), and Misdiagnosis: A Practicing Physician's Case Study on Healthcare Reform (2012). The Secret of Rocks Hyraxes is his first published novel and the first book in the series of thrillers featuring the adventures of the same main characters.

Roger McKnight

The Higher the Hotter

From his place in the postal line, Rob Manley glimpsed a ponytailed young woman holding a couple of Christmas packages. He looked closer as she stepped to the window. A tight jacket and square shoulders accentuated her nimble movement. "They're for Mom and Dad, on the farm," she told the clerk. Self-consciously she checked the customers behind her.

"Sorry for taking so long," she added with a smile. As she paid the clerk and swept back some unruly bangs, Rob saw her catch caught his glance. A penetrating gaze, he thought. Unattainably attractive, too, he felt. She wasn't, though. Unattainable, that is. They met later at a New Year's party and talked about waiting in the post office line two weeks earlier. Not much to say about that wait, and he couldn't find words to describe her probing look, which rendered him speechless for a spell. Still, they hit it off and met again.

Her name was Bonnie, so he called her Bon.

"That means good in French," he explained on their first date.

"Me, I'm no softie, not a bonbon," she joked.

That was okay by Rob. Behind her gaze he discovered a woman of few words, but tons of spirit. They hiked in the woods or worked in coffee shops. She did sketches while he wrote. Other times they listened to tunes. She liked old-timers, ABBA or John Denver, and hummed their melodies. Schmaltzy, he thought, but entertaining. When they became intimate, he kissed her lightly behind the ear and said, "*C'est si bon.*"

"*Lovers say that in France,*" she whispered with a smile. "I know that oldie."

During the week, she stayed with him in St. Paul, but they preferred her rented bungalow outside the city. On weekends they spread a futon on her floor and talked by candlelight to the wee hours. Her frequent silences soothed his restless spirit and her even temperament gave relief from the hurly-burly of the busy world he loathed. When they made love, her deep look aroused him, so he imagined she peered into his soul, and her trim body excited him beyond the speaking of it. His visceral drive felt endless, and her thin, unshaven legs, with nearly invisible blond hair, added to the enticement.

"You're so strong, you excite me, over and over," she said and rested her head on his chest until the sun rose. "*When they thrill to romance,*" she hummed so the tune hung in the air, and he dreamed of their future together. Her, the calm unassuming artist, 25. Him, the dreamer and aspiring writer, 28.

Life changed after she finished her MFA and Rob found a job teaching Drama & Film in Wisconsin. They divided time between his Metomenie Tech and her place near St. Paul. She worked in assisted living and looked for a better job, but her Art degree brought no offers. After a year, she took a course in land surveying and carried a measuring tape, level, and rod.

"Surveying's not Picasso, but there're lines and perspective," she told Rob. "I'm practical. I need my work."

Not long and she started reading about Alaska and wanting to move. Time was ripe. "Maybe, but why not gradually?" he argued.

No fanfare. Her mind was made up. She wrinkled her brow and studied him long and hard. "I'm going. You know I must."

Rob remembered her by candle light, humming melodies. His body by hers. Their look of shared desire. Her determination to leave. Unable to sleep after she went, he walked the early morning streets. Hours creeping by. In time he received letters from Anchorage. She eschewed email and wrote by hand.

"I lick the stamp," she explained, "even draw pictures on the envelope."

At first she sounded homesick for the cornfields and prairies. Later she wrote about working on a survey crew near the Alaskan Capitol.

In August Rob flew to Anchorage. Bon showed him the harbor, the hills. Rednecks and city folk. On the weekend they took a train to Denali and glimpsed the peak. They discussed how strange and distant a place Alaska was.

"Feel funny, seeing Russia from your backyard?" Rob joked.

"They say Alaska gets in your blood," she winked. "I'm adjusting. Learning to deal with work crews, no-nonsense studs."

She acted friendly but distant. Rob tried breaking through the barrier, but failed. Bon mentioned setting up house and home with him only once, on the day he left and that in passing.

"Coming back?" Rob asked at the airport. "I miss you."

"I love my job," Bon replied.

Past the security gate, he looked back.

She waved. He turned and went.

In the fall they called. Or texted. Reticence became her hallmark. *I don't feel any more I can express my self-awareness by writing. It only comes through my scribble drawings*, she stated. She described how when they talked on the phone there were urgent messages she needed to give him, but words wouldn't come. By the time she sat down to write, she couldn't remember what they were. Instead she drew pictures and sent them. By snail mail. Attachments sometimes. They showed her co-workers bundled against the chill, homesteads abandoned to the elements, railroad tracks disappearing into the bush. Alaska seemed a hard place, but its emptiness inspired her, even if it hadn't yet filled her soul.

In November she came to see Rob. "Downtime for surveying." That was her explanation. He didn't ask for more, but kept track of the days.

Friday the 12ᵗʰ. They met at the airport and went to a pancake house for breakfast. Later they moseyed over to see their friend Connie, an older artist who'd taught Bon painting and showed her the ropes. The three had tea.

"You've grown up," Connie told Bon.

As Rob drove them to his place later, Bon spoke up.

"I feel real healthy. Really strong," she said. "But nervous. I got acne, about coming here. He, I mean I, should be too old for that nonsense."

Saturday the 13ᵗʰ. They drove to the Art Museum and saw a Scandinavian landscape photo exhibit. The museum called it *Northern Light.*

"I love these pictures," she said. "Reminds me of Alaska's woods."

"Deep and silent?"

She nodded yes. "With light peeking in among the trees."

They bumped into friends from her Art school days, including Bon's ex-roommate Andrea. Then they drove back to his place, stopping at Ebba's Café for dinner. In the evening he read her one of his short stories. She listened but didn't comment. His sister Shirl called from California and they said the usual stuff. Bon chatted with her, too, but couldn't say when they'd ever visit LA. "Be a while," she concluded.

Sunday the 14ᵗʰ. On another drive, they passed a country house they'd considered buying together. It'd been a lovely May day a couple years earlier when they discussed the purchase. Spring and rebirth. She loved the new lambs, so she'd gone home and sketched them in India ink. She showed Rob her sketches.

"Nice," he said.

She folded the papers.

"Sorry," he'd added later that day, "for not saying more about them. Don't know art so much."

Back in town, her glance fixed on him so it felt like a gaze, as it did in the post office the first time they met. She spoke in her straightforward way. "I have doubts about living with you any more. I don't want to stay in Alaska forever, but suburbia's restricting. It might not work for me. Jobwise."

Rob studied her. She looked the same mild and mellow Bonnie Benson. He wondered where the old feelings had gone.

"My job's the most important thing for me," she said.

They argued. About their past. The future. What they wanted.

"You alone," Rob protested. "No one else."

She shook her head.

"It's you," he repeated. There's always a way. I'll commute. Wherever you are."

Monday the 15ᵗʰ. Feeling depressed, Rob taught his morning classes. That evening he gave a lecture at the local

Lutheran Church on early silent film. They had coffee at the Pioneer House restaurant. They joked and teased as of old.

Tuesday the 16th. Bon borrowed Rob's car and drove to her parents'. Left alone, he wondered how to convince her to stay. By mistake he called one of his students by her name.

He went to bed early that evening, but woke with a start. What the hell? he wondered. We think alike, so why not get along? He lay staring at the ceiling. Time's a'wasting, try harder, he thought.

Dawn was approaching when he fell asleep.

Wednesday the 17th. Rob awoke feeling determined to win her back. She returned earlier than expected, disgusted with her mother for criticizing others.

"Meaning who? Me?"

"No, she was talking about a neighbor girl, who married 'a Jew boy.' Those were her words. My sis and I tried telling her you can't talk like that these days."

A family squabble had followed. Her father calmed them down.

"This is a new age," Bon continued. "I told her a woman can marry who she wants. Do as she wishes."

Thursday the 18th. Rob invited Bon to see Ingmar Bergman's old film *Scenes from a Marriage* in his film class. The students tried to discuss it in groups, but no one understood Bergman's meaning. Subtitles were distracting, they complained. Rob wondered. Were they too young?

That evening he and Bon yawned their way through a lecture at the local community center on nuclear weaponry and shuttle diplomacy.

Friday the 19th. They saw Ibsen's *Peer Gynt* at Cherry Creek, a local theater. They left expecting a fall chill, but the temperature had risen to sixty. Letting the mist evnvelope them, thcy walked back to his place and talked about why Solveig waited past childbearing age for a wanderer like Peer Gynt and whether she was right to take him back when he finally returned. What was in it for her?

"Imagine, waiting all that time he was gone, why was she so patient?" Rob wondered.

"The shoe was on the other foot there," Bon said and peered at him so her gaze reached him through the mist. "In *their* case, I mean."

He nodded. "In *our* case then?"

"Who's waiting for who? And for what? What's up between us?"

"Remember that European film we saw together once. *Last Year at Marienbad*?"

"Yeah, at the Film Society," she answered. "Rickety seats. Bad acoustics. The audience coughing and rattling popcorn sacks. Annoying."

"And the characters barely speaking. Or even gesturing."

She paused and thought back. Rob watched her shift weight so she merged in and out of the shifting fog, only the clear whites of her eyes showing through it steadily.

"The characters tried to talk," she continued, only to stop mid-sentence.

"But nothing much came out," Rob added. "That's my old friend Jerry's favorite movie. I always wanted to know what he saw in it. Two people struggling to find something, each other probably. Getting nowhere in the process."

"Were they even trying?"

"They fumbled."

"It was between *them*, I guess, not the world. The two of them."

"Us, too? Is it between us?"

"That's everybody's problem maybe."

"Universal?" Rob asked, looking at her out of the corner of his eye. "I wonder."

They walked the rest of the way in silence as the fog lay an ever thicker cover in the still air. Rob longed for her old playfulness and the ABBA songs she remembered but no longer sang. Or hummed.

Saturday the 20th. Rob drove to the city on back roads, just for the heck of it, and Bon looked longingly at the farms. In town he stopped at Jerry's, who offered them his place, he'd be gone all week. Bon's sister showed up. Connie, too. Bon's face brightened when she told them about the great outdoors beyond Anchorage and the mountain trails and rough roads she surveyed.

"In October I started watching from my window as snow crept down the hills to where we live," she explained. "Slow but sure."

Sunday the 21st. Bon stayed at her sister's till Tuesday. Even though her bus got back to Rob's on time, she was troubled, no explanation why, and hugged Rob long and tenderly.

Wednesday the 24th. They strolled downtown for lunch. It was a glorious sunny day, above freezing. He asked if she remembered a Sunday evening in December a year past when they walked from her bungalow to the Pioneer House for supper.

"We hurried home by the same route later, in an arctic blast," he added.

"Yes," she replied. "I wore clogs but no socks. My feet were freezing."

That evening Rob suggested a beer. They ended up at a 3.2 joint and ran into Phil, a colleague of Rob's, and his wife Jen. Later they went home with them for coffee. The four sat in the dim light of the kitchen, holding their mugs for warmth, while Jen vented her frustration at not finding a suitable job. "The only positions in these raw towns are for school teachers or tradesmen," she complained.

Rob looked knowingly at Bon, but she was wholly in shadow, her cat-like eyes uncharacteristically blotted to his view.

"There's no use for Art majors like us," Jen said to Bon with a wink.

"That's why they give Metominee the nickname Monotony," Phil joked.

It turned bitter cold that night.

Thanksgiving the 25ᵗʰ. They drove north for dinner with Bon's family at a mom 'n pop restaurant, followed by coffee and relaxed chatter, during which her mother left off her talk of Jewish boys. The first Christmas decorations lit up the fading daylight.

Heading back to the city, they were astounded, even at a distance, by a towering blaze over the downtown skyline. It reflected off skyscrapers turning them brilliant colors in the lonely holiday night. By the time they reached Jerry's apartment building, the flames were rising from an abandoned high-rise. The fire soared in terrifying fury from the top floor into the darkness above. Smaller nearby buildings blazed red and melted in the heat.

Speechless, Rob and Bon watched among excited bystanders as flames slowly died away when the high-rise imploded. The crowd screamed in fright then retreated as tons of massive litter crashed and smoke rose up.

Among the smoldering ruins, Bon watched and her eyes glittered. Rob squeezed her hand, kissed her neck, and ran his other hand through her hair. Without a word, they dashed towards Jerry's building, clasping hands as they burst into the apartment and made love on the carpeted floor, struggling to remove their clothes before climax. Afterward the passion flared up time and again, driving them back into each other's arms, ever more fervently with each embrace. After repeated lovemaking they lay back, bathed in nakedness while their sweat dried in the languid air.

At last Rob got up and poured each a glass of Bordeaux, while Bon reached for her clothes, scattered out across the floor. She rose up and dressed quickly, obeying a visceral need that drove her out to the street again.

"No, no wine!" she explained hurriedly.

Rob looked at her in surprise.

"Too restless," she protested.

"It'll calm you."

"I want the fire."

They returned to street level but saw only stray firemen picking among rubble. Rob walked through the debris kicking at lukewarm embers until the property was cordoned off.

"Maybe *Last Year at Marienbad* got it right," he said, once back inside. "Words fail us?"

"Or something."

"What about tonight? You felt something?"

Her eyes shone intently in the dark. She smiled.

Friday the 26th. From Jerry's they followed the skyway downtown and looked out at the rubble from the night before. Bon stood in thought.

"You know," she said, "they measure a blaze by its flames. The higher the hotter. On dry days they can soar and reach

150 feet. If hot and humid, only three or four, less energy to fan the flames."

"And you learned this surveying?"

"Yes, Materials and Measurements class. A Forestry guy told us."

Rob felt she wanted to say more, but instead they poked around in a few shops until a travel bureau caught his eye.

"That's where I found a good ticket price to visit you in Anchorage," he said.

Bon turned his way and nodded, without speaking. Instead she found a buckskin store and lingered. "I need real leather," she said.

Rob went back to the apartment and prepared dinner. Later they ate baked cod and broke out a bottle of Bordeaux.

After a glass, Bon sat down to the television, but he asked her to turn it off. "What happened? What were you thinking last year?" he insisted.

She rested on the carpet before the silent TV. He sat across from her and waited.

"I'm at a point, I can't get the feeling back," she half-whispered, crossing and re-crossing her legs. "I made the break and don't feel as attracted to you."

"What about our lovemaking? Was that nothing?"

She remarked how the winter previous they started having less to say to each other.

"I helped you with your interests, but you did little to encourage mine," he lamented.

"You'll do a lot of creative things in the next few years," she replied. "I feel it."

In deep thought or distracted for the moment, she nervously plucked at the carpet and traced an abstract pattern in it while crossing her legs again.

"I've never been much to talk," she continued without looking up, so he missed her piercing visage. "I do what I feel. Plumbing the depths doesn't interest me. I say things but they aren't really what I mean."

"You acted so different when we met."

"I was trying hard to be self-assured. I wanted to make a home for us, but you weren't interested. I got tired of being responsible when you were off writing. In your own world."

"I wanted love, not domesticity, but I drove you to work, came and got you after your shift. It was share and share alike."

"Yes, working in assisted living, like then. My patients. Their memories. But I wanted to make other things. Pictures."

"And the money you're saving? What happens next?"

"Dunno. Buy some land maybe. Come back here? I have my sister."

"What were you thinking last spring?"

"I don't want to talk about it," she said, choking back a sob.

Rob smiled faintly, with a sinking feeling. "Who's *he*?"

"Don't know. Just somebody. Nobody."

"Nobody who?"

"Somebody I work with. We're friends."

"Friends?"

She avoided his glance and then looked down again. "No more, no less."

After picking distractedly at lint in the rug, she stretched out on the floor.

"I can't make what isn't," she moaned, beseeching him to stop. "I'm much younger than that now. Know that song?"

"How can we be like one if we can't talk? If I don't know you, who *he* is, or *if* he is. We can work it out."

"What do you want from me?" she said. She looked down at the floor again, but then glanced up in frustration.

"A word. Any good one. A mystery what got into your head, but I won't give up. Not on either of us. One good word. I'll chase you to the ends of the earth."

"Feels like you already have," she joked for the first time since arriving back home, only to lift her head and peer ahead with an air of doomed finality or immense fatigue. Rob wondered which, or was it both?

"One word," he repeated.

Bon didn't answer but quickly checked the time on her iPhone. "It's getting late," she announced. "Time to move on."

Rob sat still. What goes on in your head, he wanted to scream in frustration, do all beautiful women act like this? Playing hard to get?

Yelling, he realized, would only increase the stress.

Later they drove to her friend Andrea's, who asked Bon about Alaska while Rob chatted with Andrea's mother, who dropped by for a visit. They discussed life in Europe, where Andrea's mom had been on vacation. After a while the two of them chimed in on Bon and Andrea's conversation. Eventually they all stretched out with glasses of dry white claret. Rob felt himself drifting into a mellow séance as the minutes floated by and then seemed to stop.

"Ah, this is the life, we belong here," Andrea sighed. "So good you're back," she said to Bon.

"Do we? Belong?" her mother wondered. "I could imagine somewhere else."

"Where?" Andrea asked.

"Oh, Berlin. The South of France."

"Could we afford it?"

As mother and daughter talked on, Rob felt Bon tuning out. She gazed his way so her eyes did the talking. Like flames rising and falling the night before, her burning desire for him conflicted with an angry chafing at his neglect of her needs. Of a sudden he imagined how her theodolites' and 3D scanners' tactile measurements, as well as the contours and shadows she put in her penciled sketches, pinpointed the linear meanings and closed contours he himself so purposefully approached but then circumvented in fictionalizing life and its ambiguities. He wondered how to bridge the gap between her perceptions and his.

Rob gazed at her across the abyss till Andrea waved a hand in Bon's face.

"Hey, Lovebirds," she said. Their evening ebbed away as the wine mellowed them even more.

Back at the apartment, Bon stood close to Rob and they kissed.

"You took charge," she said with a smile.

"Charge of what?" he asked, bewildered.

It was midnight when they went to the whirlpool. She massaged his forehead and showed him her temples where the acne had cleared up. He told her how great she looked, while she gently kissed him. Back in Jerry's apartmennt, she undressed and he spread out the futon. As she walked to it, he studied the soft, supple outline of her hips and the loveliness of her skin. Her nipples aroused him. Lying down, he kissed her and gently fondled her breasts. As they made love, he abandoned himself to the passion, like a flame rising higher and hotter. He covered her as they tumbled from wall to wall, emptying their passion.

Later they gazed into the dark. "I love you," he said and asked what she was thinking.

"How nice it is to lie here next to you and gradually fall asleep."

He guessed he'd carry with him the memory of them spread out in sumptuous repose, with legs overlapping across the futon, and him wondering if their chimerical flame burned high and hot enough.

Saturday the 27ᵗʰ. The alarm rang at seven.

"Time to get up," Bon announced.

Rob drove her to the airport. She bought them coffee.

"I'll come see you next year," she promised.

"Next year at Metomonie?" he tried to jest, but wondered at that uncertain expanse of time.

She looked up to find her gate. "I'm on Air Canada," she remarked. Nearing the ticket kiosk, she whispered, "I get so nervous. Such a long flight."

"It's out of your hands. Just get on and sit."

They hugged. She took her boarding pass and left for Security. After a few steps, she looked back and waved.

Rob waited.

She showed the attendant her boarding pass. He glanced at it.

"Bonnie?"

"Yes, he says *bon*. One word's enough." She gestured toward Rob.

The attendant fingered his moustache till a smile lit his face. "*Bon dit,*" he said with a chuckle. Near the hall entrance, Bon looked Rob's way. At the corner she glanced back yet again, then turned and was gone. The Security attendant watched. "*Cherchez la femme,*" he said with a sly Gallic smile, but Rob was already on his way and barely heard. He imagined another day, another place, in whatever future there might be.

About the Author

Roger McKnight is from Illinois, but now lives in Minnesota. He has degrees from Southern Illinois University and the University of Minnesota. Roger has also lived and worked in Chicago, Sweden, and Puerto Rico. He's published one novel, a book of creative non-fiction, and short fiction. Hopeful Monsters, his collection of short stories set in the Midwest and Scandinavia, appeared in 2019.

Julian Darragjati

Ecstasy

Amy's favorite pub in Florence was a windowless basement, with coarse-grained yellow walls that brought to mind caves and a ceiling low enough to trouble the tall girls dancing on the round tables, stooping as they bounced to avoid bumping their heads. On the bright side, it had a fine bar, live music, and something of the allure of the one-night stand. The local girls didn't care for that last part, but the American girls were far from home and had a reputation here – which Amy, I have to say, did her best to live up to. We'd come here often, she and I, and then leave separately, she with some guy and me by myself.

Amy never cared for Americans much, though. It had to be Italians and these she took to her place by Santa Croce, while I'd wonder the streets with only my skeletal key for company, which I'd grip like a knife, ready to use it should some mugger try to mug me. And in the morning, I'd knock on her door, holding a bag of pastries I'd buy at this secret *dolceria* I had discovered on one of those nights. The shop only opened once a week, in the way-wee hours. To avoid paying taxes, so

I assumed. There was something frantic and jittery about the way the stout men in the back rolled the dough, or the way the fat woman at the counter took your order. They wore the usual chef's white coats, and never looked you in the eye, or if they did, their gaze was brief and brimmed with fright that you might tell on them. Their powdered pastry puffs with sweet creamy filling was their specialty—what I brought Amy. Nobody knew about this place, not even Amy's Italian lovers. It intrigued her Amy the more intrigued. She valued mystery in men, and I wasn't about to give

Anyway, I left Amy dancing by herself and squeezed through the crowd to the bar for another round of bourbon. I'd lost track of how many. But I made it back before my spot was taken and I gave Amy a glass. She drank and went on dancing, holding the glass high, moving to the beat. Black sweat-glazed bangs dangled over her dark eyes. Dancing, she sometimes stared at the floor, sometime at me, grabbing my shirt from its neckline, now pulling me to her and now pushing me away, and ultimately giving me a thorough spin-about. There was something retro about the black skirt she had on that she'd made herself, and her armpits rife with hair. It was fitting, I guess, seeing how the pub throbbed with classic rock; four young guys were covering the Beatles. Amy loved the Beatles and could have danced all night.

Luckily, the music stopped. We returned to our table, just as a girl, straightening her skirt, stepped down from it. Amy slumped in her chair while I cleaned dirt from the table with a napkin that had come with our glasses of bourbon. She smoothed her hair back in quick strokes, then fanned her face with her hand. Her chest rose and fell as she breathed.

"I love it here," she said. "It's so quaint. And that band. Don't you love it?"

"I love it when you use the word *quaint*," I said, and finished my drink.

Her smashed, sweat-glazed eyes glowed at me in the low yellow light.

"As for the pub," I continued. "I think it's too damn crowded. And that band there, they resemble the Beatles more in looks than in sound. Did you see them shaking their heads?"

I shot upright and bobbed my head sideways, like the young Beatles, meanwhile playing drums on the table with my hands. Amy broke into laughter, slapping the table so hard it made heads turn. It felt so good to make her laugh. Behind her, the drummer was dismantling his drum set. He looked grimly at my direction, and I ducked low and leaned closer to Amy, hiding from the drummer's line of sight.

"Let's get out of here," I muttered. "Ringo there just gave me the meanest look."

Amy turned to him. "He's not mean. He's a hottie."

"Is he quaint too?"

"Oh, yes, very. Quaint and sexy. I wish they weren't leaving so soon, though. It's hardly two o'clock, isn't it." She lifted her glass at the man. "Hey, Ringo. Come have a drink with us."

"Oh, let it be, let it be," I said. "It's been a hard day's night and he's been working like a dog."

Amy giggled and waved her finger in my face and mumbled what a dork I was.

"He sang out of tune then," I said. "Let's stand up and walk out on him. There's never been a better time." I stood up and grabbed my coat that hung on the back of my chair. Then I moved over to Amy's chair for her coat. I took it and held it open for her as she stood up to put it on.

People were on their feet, getting their coats, too, ready to hop to the next pub.

"Where are we going?" Amy asked, slipping an arm into her coat sleeve.

"The secret sweet shop," I said. "This dork might finally show you where it is."

I winked at grim Ringo as we walked past the band and up the narrow steps that led outside. The chill of the early November morning slapped me in the face when we stepped onto the street. Amy shivered and I flung my arm around her. With the drums and the guitar still thundering in our ears, we moseyed toward the *Duomo*, cheerful as children. Amy's heels tapped on the cobblestones, blending with the rhythmic tapping all around us.

"So what's the deal with this place?" Amy asked, after a while.

"What place?"

"A secret pastry shop that only opens past midnight. Sounds like some fairytale."

It occurred to me then that the shop only opened once a week and tonight wasn't the night, but I kept this to myself, deciding instead to playthings by ear once we found the shop door closed. "*Boh*," I shrugged—*boh*, being sort of Italian for, *beats me*. "All I know is, it costs triple the price of what you'd pay normally, and they only take cash, so I'm pretty sure it's illegal. Maybe they lost their license, or maybe they never had one in the first place."

"Maybe they use illegal ingredients," she fancied. "Like ecstasy."

"Why, do you feel *deranged* after you eat them?"

"No. I just feel like I love everybody."

"You always feel like that," I hazarded.

Amy ignored that. "Must be the quaintest place on Earth," she said.

"Oh, you just wait and see," I said. "It's magical."

Talking like this, we weaved through maze-like streets and arrived at the *Duomo,* looming before us like a giant billboard silhouetted against the night sky. At least, that's how it appeared to me. Like it wasn't made of solid mass, but was a hologram projected there. The inlaid white and green marble of the low parts of the wall was sooty from all the carbon pollution.

Amy looked up. "Isn't it quaint?" she said. "All that detail."

"Oh, how, come on. Everything can't be quaint."

She shrugged. "I just say *quaint* when I don't know what else to say about something. Where have you been? I thought you knew the secret to sounding smart."

"Yeah, but in your case, you make a word look good, not the other way around."

"You're so sweet," she said, then added, with open arms, "Henceforth I shall be known as Amy, The Beautifier of Words."

All the shops were closed at this hour and there wasn't a car in the street, except for the parked ones, so we crossed without looking and came around to the front of the *Duomo.* To our right stood the octagonal baptistery with its large bronze doors and inlaid marble slightly less grimy. Facing the baptistery, on those wide cathedral steps, several young men sat with enough spaces apart to show that they were all friendless there. They smoked solemnly, and their eyes, as we stood there, slavered over Amy, undressing her, no doubt. Behind them, against the cathedral door, a young couple was making out with a kind of dry-humping passion that flouted public decency laws. I looked at them with deep admiration.

Amy elbowed me in the ribs.

"Ouch," I said.

She elbowed me again and flicked her chin at this skeletal kid in a ragged maroon shirt who had just emerged from around the baptistery and was climbing up the cathedral steps.

He held a bouquet of dry roses in one hand and a single rose in the other, pointed toward the kissing couple. The kid said something to the couple, but they went on making out as if he weren't there. The man had his back to the kid and the kid begun tugging at his jacket. Like the old cathedral he kid, too, appeared like some part of a hologram, like an image you could walk through. He wasn't there and nothing was, and nothing had any consequences.

Amy must have had the same impression as me, considering that we started off again, laughing shamelessly. We came around to the marbled bell-tower, still laughing, and I veered us toward it. It was secluded and dark and we stopped here for a moment. Amy had her back against the tower, and I pressed gently against her. I put my lips on her neck.

"Hey," she whispered, turning away. "I thought we're going to get some sweets."

"Hey," I echoed, stupid with desire. "Am I not still sweet?" I was already way over the line, by which I mean, I'd have accepted an eternity of hell for a moment inside her. My hand went up her shirt until it met resistance from her hand.

"I'm being serious," she said, pushing my hand down.

"Me, too," I said. "Oh, God, me, too."

"About the pastry shop. You want to go there, or not?"

I kissed her neck and bit her ringed earlobe. "I want you-u-u-u," I began. "I want you so ba-a-ad. It's making me mad. It's make me—"

"Hey, stop it," she said. "You're being ridiculous."

"You don't like this dork singing to you anymore?" I said, pulling back.

She said nothing. Something flashed in her eyes, something like fear mixed with disgust, and I let my head rest on her shoulder in a mock hug. I felt the earth spin and I clung to her as if to keep balance. Desire washed out of me and I felt as filthy as the soot coating the church walls.

It was quiet for a long time.

"I think I know just what you need," Amy whispered after a while.

"Oh, you do, do you?"

"Some pastry puffs with a touch of ecstasy inside. You know you want them?"

I pulled back and looked at her face, its fear now gone. A faint smirk appeared in its place now, a hint of scorn and I pulled away from her then.

As I turned, I collided full-tilt into the flower peddler with his ragged clothes and his shriveled bouquet in one hand, and a single rose in the other. A guttural shriek burst from me from the fright, and Amy snickered. He was real, all right, and the collision had sent him reeling. He regained his footing now, then run over to me with his rose right up my face.

"For your lady," he said in broken English. His eyes, level with my chest, peered up like the eyes of a hungry cat. His maroon shirt was too light for warmth and torn at the sleeves as if he'd been chewing on them while watching us.

"For your lady," he said again. "One rose, one euro. Come, buy. *Dai*"

"Fuck off," I said and pushed him aside with my arm, as if to clear a path.

He didn't flinch. "For your lady, *amico*. Please. One rose."

"*Vattene*," I said, harsher now, and began walking away.

At first I wasn't sure where I was going, then I knew: it was toward Amy's place.

The peddler tugged at my sleeve. "A*mico*. For your lady. Come. *Dai*. Take."

Amy followed, her heels tapping behind me. We turned onto the wide Via del Proconsolo. Her apartment was near

Santa Croce. A group of American male students, smelling of cologne and all dressed alike passed us, but I didn't recognize anyone and no one recognized us.

"So you're *not* going to show me where this place is," Amy said, her voice chilly behind me. "You're just gonna walk me home. How gallant of you."

I swerved now to the side of the street closest to Dante's neighborhood, thinking that at the next intersection I'd turn toward the secret *dolceria*, weaving through narrow streets and alleys that looked like corridors – mere extension of the quaint apartments flanking them. It would be like going into your kitchen for a bite to eat in the middle of the night, after making love. Then I remembered the the pastry shop wouldn't be opened tonight. Tomorrow night, yes, but no tonight. And how absurd it was, the whole idea of it, of a secret pastry shop. What a clever gimmick to entice us stupid foreigners. Oh, sure, they used a secret ingredient. It was the thrill of the illicit, and the unfamiliar. How much more satisfying it made everything.

"There is no secret *dolceria*," I said, halting. "I made that up. God, you're naïve."

Amy stopped walkee, too. She sighed with disappointment, maybe that there was no *dolceria*, or that I was lying, or with everything.

"I made those pastries for you," I went on, with my back to her, while the peddler kept tugging at my sleeve. "From a family recipe," I said. "An old secret recipe. God, you really are naïve."

"I see," she said. "And where did you get the ecstasy for them?"

I stared at a narrow strip of night sky visible between the two parallel eaves above me at this faintly twinkling star, like it might beam on me some saving grace. The peddler quit bugging me now and stood halfway between us. The high of the alcohol had died and the dispiriting process had set in. Still,

I thought to play along, go with something maudlin maybe, end the night on a high note. It was no ecstasy, I thought to say, cliché as that was. But love.

"I made those sweets with love," I whispered, but maybe too softly.

When I turned, I saw Amy just standing there, her arms folded over her chest, her eyes hard on me. The peddler stood between us, his eyes swaying from me to Amy, Amy to me. I wished he were Cupid to shoot us with arrows. But he was just a kid, tired, cold, and probably hungry, and he went on waiting there, his ears red, his shoulders frozen in a shrug.

He glanced at the rose, then extended it to Amy. "Please, take," he said, his breath misty in the cold night air. "*Prego*. Take."

For a moment, Amy just stood there wrapped up in her coat and hugging herself. Then her brow relaxed and her eyes softened and she reached out and took the rose. She sniffed it once, then threw me a dry smirk, and I turned and walked away, conscious of no direction, only of the silence of her heels and the growing space between my feet and hers.

About the Author

Julian Darragjati's fiction has appeared in numerous journals including Adelaide Literary Magazine, Barcelona Review, and Green Mountains Review, and has been nominated for a Pushcart Prize.

Christopher Johnson

The Wall

"So, honey, what are you going to do tomorrow? Are you going to fix the screen door in the back so the flies don't get in? There are so many of them . . . . Anyway, are going to fix it? It's been this way for at least two weeks. For at least two weeks."

Like a movie camera, Herbie, who was eleven years old, shifted his focus from his mother with the crenellated pink skirt and the matching high heels and the incendiary pink lipstick and the buffed up hair and the strange green eyes with flecks of brown in them. Sometimes Herbie caught his mother murmuring to herself as she cooked dinner, carrying on a dialogue with herself. Sometimes he wondered if she heard voices in her head.

Herbie, who tended not to miss a thing although he hardly ever said a word about what he filmed in his head, pivoted to look at his father, who still wore his tie from work even though it was loosened up—his father with the severe-as-steel black crewcut and lips only a few molecules wide and eyes as gray as granite.

"No," his father said. "I can't. Tomorrow's the first Saturday of the month. That's the day—every first Saturday of the month—that's the day every month when I go over to Mother's house and mow her lawn and fix whatever needs fixing. Honey, you know all this. I do it on he first Saturday of every month."

Herbie pivoted his film-camera eyes back to Mother. This was getting interesting. He ignored eight-year-old Buster and six-year-old Maureen, who were slurping down Friday-night fish sticks and French fries and doodling around with their baked beans as if they were tiny animals to be trained and corralled. Herbie ignored his younger brother and sister and secretly anticipated what Mother would say.

"Oh, I forgot," she finally said with a whoosh of a sad sigh. "I forgot all about Mother and her lawn and all the things in her house that need fixing." Grandma was a widow, and her husband and Father's father and Herbie's grandfather had died so very long ago that Herbie had never known him. With his camera eyes, Herbie envisioned Grandpa Hereford having disintegrated completely by now—completely dissipated, bones and all, in the mahogany box buried six feet under at St. Joseph's Cemetery, which they all visited every year on dead Grandpa's birthday, March 15, the Ides of March. Herbie would stare at the gravesite and feel a little creepy and read Grandpa's head stone: Robert John Hereford, Beloved Husband and Father, March 15, 1899 – November 2, 1935. At the gravesite, Herbie would stand beside Grandma Hereford and hold her hand, which felt like leather that had been punished by the desert sun for years upon years. Grandma wept and Father wept but Mother did not weep because she had never known Grandpa Hereford.

Mother's voice brought Herbie back to the dinner table, back to the here and now. "Poor Grandma Hereford," Mother said, while Buster and Maureen, oblivious children that they were, continued to shovel fish sticks and French fries and baked beans into their starving mouths. "Arthur, dear," Mother continued, "why doesn't your mother sell that old house, which would free you up on Saturdays to do the things that need doing around here. Why doesn't she just sell that old house and move into a nice apartment in Elmhurst and that way, you wouldn't have to mow her lawn and fix the things that are always going wrong that need fixing in that house, which must have been built over a century ago."

Herbie cantilevered his head back to Father to see how he would respond. Father continued to eat as if Mother had said nothing. The dining room had fallen quiet—the silence broken only by the sloppy slurping of Buster and Maureen as they shoveled fish sticks and French fries and baked beans into their hungry little childish mouths.

Well, Herbie thought, that's a logical suggestion that Mother just made, but he didn't dare say that out loud because he knew Father would tell him to mind to his own business. Herbie added to the thought—it was a logical suggestion, but he hoped Father wouldn't go along with it. For the simple fact was this: Herbie and Buster and Maureen all loved Grandma Hereford's house. They had never been anywhere else like it. It had the musty odor of the sacrosanct past. The ancient lace curtains and the ornate Victorian furniture and the dark attic still contained the toys from the 1930s that their father had played with when he had been a boy. Grandma's ancient house promised ghosts and was so so perfect for Herbie and Buster and Maureen to play hide-and-go-seek in—so many wondrous places to hide—the cupboard in the cellar that could hide an entire body, the workroom with the enormous coal-burning furnace that dated back practically to the Civil war–the attic, naturally, with its dark mysteries–the dimly lit parlor with the Victorian furniture that camouflaged modern children and made them disappear.

Finally Father spoke. Finally he addressed Mother's logical suggestion. Herbie craned his eyes back to his father. Father spoke slowly and with a voice that was calm and measured, but Herbie saw something more in Father's eyes, as if he were tired or conflicted. "I hear what you're saying, honey," he said. "But I know that she's not ready to sell the house."

He was going to continue talking, but Mother was too quick. "Did you talk to her about it?"

"No."

"Well, then, how do you know how she feels about selling the house?"

"Well, I just know. I can feel it. I know her so well."

There was a pause. To Herbie, the pause felt like a cloud that hung over the dinner table as his little brother and little sister kept scooping food into their mouths as if they were starving to death. The pause reminded him of feelings in the movies he went to in which one character said something and you knew the other character disagreed but for whatever reason didn't say anything, and you knew that the pause was pointing toward something uncomfortable or even bad that was going to happen.

He craned back to Mother, and she was so pretty in her flounced dress, but she stared ahead at the table as if she saw something that was invisible to the rest of them. She didn't look at Father. She sighed and stabbed a fish stick with her fork as if it were a stiletto and raised the fish stick to her mouth and thrust the fish stick into her mouth and chewed it and chewed it and chewed it until it was beaten mercilessly into submission, and only then did she swallow it.

"Well, honey," she finally said, "I just thought that if Grandma Hereford sold that ancient house that she would be happier and you wouldn't have to go mow the lawn every time I turn around, and you would have time to fix the screen so that we wouldn't have scads of flies in the kitchen making everything filthy." Herbie wanted to flinch because Mother's words split the air so that all that was left was a silence that pressed down on the dinner table. Herbie didn't flinch. He just stared at the fish sticks on the plate in front of him and wondered how the heck the fishermen turned a living breathing fish into a fish stick, which didn't look at all like a fish.

For the moment, the only sound in the dining room was of Buster and Maureen clanking the silverware against their plates to scrape up every bit of baked beans, which was smothered in catsup. Buster picked up his plate and started to lick the mucous-like juice of the baked beans—to get every single ounce of it into his yawning eight-year-old mouth.

"Oh, for God's sake, Buster," Mother snapped. "Don't lick your plate. It's just downright rude." She looked at Father. "Arthur," she continued, "will you please tell Buster not to lick his plate."

Father eyed Buster and said, "Buster, please don't lick your plate at the dinner table," which left open the possibility that it would all right to lick the plate when one was away from the dinner table. Herbie could tell that Father wasn't really angry with Buster, but Mother was.

Father picked up his glass that had the gin and tonic in it. "I'm going to have another one. You want one, too, honey?" he said to Mother. Under the glare of the dining room light, Father's skin looked like cheese to Herbie. It was sallow and old, as if he had never been out in the sun. "Well?" he repeated to Mother.

"Oh, I suppose so," Mother said. She handed the gleaming crystal cocktail glass to Father, who took it and stumbled slightly as he made his way out to the kitchen. Herbie thought that his father looked like a dog. His entire face drooped from fatigue. His usually sharp features were melting into one another. Herbie shook his head as if to wake himself from a dream, but the illusion of his father's face remained intact.

The dining room was silent as Father mixed the drinks in the kitchen, clanking the glasses as he mixed the gin and tonic and cut a lime to deposit into each glass. Father finished, and the silence returned. Father returned and handed the drink unsteadily to Mother. She took a deep drink of the gin and tonic. Herbie saw her look at Father. "Thank you very much" she said, her voice wrapped in Arctic ice. Herbie felt the sadness that surrounded her like a wraith. Mother and Father drank deeply from their glasses and stabbed the fish sticks with their forks. No one spoke. The idea of Grandma Hereford selling her house hung like a cloud over the dining room table. In the silence, Herbie stared at the wallpaper of the dining room. The wallpaper had purple and red and green flowers hanging on vines. Hanging on the wall opposite to him were ancient photographs of Mother's mother and father and of her grandparents—ancient photos with a patina of dull brown.

Herbie was used to silence. He would go to his buddy Bob's house, and Bob's mother was listening to Elvis, and his father was telling a corny joke or two and then laughing with a loud, booming laugh that filled the entire house. In his own house—the house of the Herefords—Herbie felt the silences like the cemetery where Grandpa Hereford was buried. Herbie could hear the soft crunch of the wood as the house settled. He could hear the ominous clanking of the radiator in the dining room. He could hear the air conditioning click on. The silence had weight. He didn't like it. He felt alone in it.

Mother took a deep drink of her gin and tonic. Herbie saw her look at Father, and she swayed slightly back and forth like a straw in the wind. She eyed Father for a while and then bit off the silence and said in a voice that was sweet yet darkly insistent, "Arthur, could you please just skip going over to your mother's tomorrow? Could you *please* just skip going over there and stay here instead and fix that screen door and mow *our* lawn, which desperately needs mowing."

Herbie flinched, as if he were Father. He stared straight ahead, trying to find a way to excuse himself and Buster and Maureen from the table. The silence in the dining room felt like the moment before dynamite explodes in the Westerns that Herbie loved to watch. It was that l - o – n – g moment, the moment before everyone knew that everything was about to be blown to kingdom come. Herbie slyly shifted his eyes and only his eyes, without turning to his head, to sneak a look at Father. Father looked down at his plate, which still had several fish sticks on it. He picked up his crystal cocktail glass, which gleamed in the sharp overhead light of the dining room. He swished the glass around so that the ice clinked against the side of his glass. He took a long drink of the gin and tonic. He shook his head back and forth and bit his lower lip with his upper teeth.

Father stopped swishing the drink around in his glass. He lowered his glass to the dining room table and sighed deeply, sighed sadly. Finally he said, "I most certainly *won't* skip going to my mother's house tomorrow. I go on the first Saturday of every month, and it's what I will continue to do. My mother needs me. I don't know why you can't understand that." Father was staring at Mother, and she was staring back. Father took a deep breath and raised his voice and said, "And my mother needs me . . . and I will continue to go on the first Saturday of *every* month and mow her lawn and do whatever else needs to be done at her house." Herbie felt a fear creep like a poisonous snake around his neck and shoulders. It was a fear, never far beneath the surface, of his father and what his father might do.

Suddenly Father and Mother remembered that the children were in the room, still at the table. In a voice that swept through the room like a glacier, Mother said, "You children can be excused." Herbie and Buster and Maureen thrust back their chairs. "Go watch TV," Mother said. "Or do something. Anything." Obediently, the two younger children marched out of the dining room and down the hall to the family room, where the television was located. Herbie hung back of the other two children. He walked slowly down the hall, listening.

The dining room was silent. Then Herbie heard a chair scrape back and bang against the wall of the dining room. He heard the clatter of dishes, and he knew that Mother was collecting them from the dining room table. Herbie stood in the hallway, listening. He heard Father say, "Can I help?" Mother didn't answer. There were no more words after that. He heard Mother's high heels strike against the linoleum as she walked into the kitchen. He heard the clattering of the dishes as she cleaned them off and shoved them into the dishwasher. He heard her slam the faucet on and off. He heard the rattle of the metal sheet on which the fish sticks had been cooked as it plummeted to the floor. He heard her mother say something, but he couldn't tell what it was. Then he heard the metallic sound of the sheet as she cleaned it. As he listened, his heart beat as if a squirrel were racing around in it.

Herbie heard Father's footsteps. He was walking toward the family room. Herbie turned and rushed into the family room and plopped down on the sofa next to Buster and Maureen. They had turned on the TV and were watching *The Brady Bunch*. The children's faces were transfixed by the images on the television. Butch and Maureen both sat with their arms around their knees, nearly retreating into the fetal position. The images of the television flickered in their eyes. When Herbie entered the room, they looked at him—two pairs of eyes squinting with a shadow of fear, of questions. He sat on the sofa near them and started to watch *The Brady Bunch*. He couldn't make heads or tails out of what was going on.

Father came into the family room. He dropped himself into the easy chair—his favorite chair—the one with the slip-cover of beige and orange circles, with the bulge in the back from a broken spring that Father had never bothered to have fixed—the chair that he had inherited from Grandpa Hereford. Father stared at the TV flickering away with *The Brady Bunch*. His fingers were jumpy, and his jaw was clenched. He murmured to himself and kept shaking his head as if it had fleas. He clenched and unclenched his jaw. He shook his head and said unspoken words.

Herbie looked at Father and felt afraid of and sorry for him, all at the same time. Father had his gin and tonic with him, and he twitched the drink around in his crystal glass and took a deep swallow. He stared at the TV, but Herbie could tell that he wasn't really seeing or following the show. Father's eyes were distant, sad. The show ended, and by now Father had drained his glass. He blundered out to the kitchen to refill the glass and returned. In a voice that was thick and indistinct, he said, "Why don't you kids go up and get ready for bed?" Maureen and Buster and then Herbie hugged him. Father returned the hugs. As they left the room, Father stared at the TV without seeing it.

Mother was in the living room. She had finished cleaning the kitchen. She was knitting. She stabbed the yarn with her knitting needles. She looked up, and her eyes were tinged with red. She managed a smile. "Good night, sweethearts," she said. She gave each of them a hug. Herbie felt Mother cling to him, her arms like steel as she enwrapped him. "I love you," she said to each of the children.

Herbie followed Buster and Maureen as they climbed the stairs. On the way, Herbie paused and looked back at Mother. She had a full glass of gin and tonic. She took a drink—a long drink. Then she started to knit, stabbing the yarn with her needles. Her jaw was set like iron, and she muttered under her breath. She stabbed and muttered. Herbie stared at her, feeling the squirrels in his heart in his chest. He went upstairs.

Maureen went to her bedroom, which she had all to herself. Herbie and Buster went to the bedroom that they shared. The room was festooned with pennants for the Bears, the White Sox, the Blackhawks. Herbie had mounted a baseball signed by Ernie Banks. The bedroom was their safe haven. Nothing could harm them here. It was their safe harbor.

They dutifully said their prayers. They had a bunk bed that was like a fantastic pyramid, and brother and brother knelt side by side on the hardwood floor and prayed—prayed as hard as they could that everything would work out between Mother and Father—that God would release their anger—that God would make them friends again—that God would make them love one another again—that God would fix the screen door so that Father could go to Grandma Hereford's home and help her—that God would prevent Father from losing his temper—that God would lead Father to hug Mother just as he had hugged Herbie and Maureen and Buster—that God would lead Father to tell Mother that he loved her. Buster fell asleep, and Herbie kept praying that the angels would watch over Buster and Maureen and him as they slept.

A wall separated Herbie's and Buster's bedroom from Mother's and Father's bedroom—a common wall, four or five inches thick. A loud thud on the other side of the wall woke

Herbie up. He rubbed his eyes and sat up in bed. He heard voices muffled voices, angry voices, penetrating the wall from Mother's and Father's bedroom. Herbie heard and knew right away, and immediately his heart was spinning, churning. He heard another thud against the other side of the wall, and the squirrels in his heart panicked. The voices grew louder, and Herbie felt the anger of the voices. Another thud, then quiet. A muffled sob, violating the wall. Muffled words, angry, thrown against the wall and charging into the boys' bedroom. Words indistinct, but the tone clear—furious.

Buster woke up. "What is it, Herbie?" Buster climbed down to the bottom bunk and sat as close to Herbie as he could get. Herbie saw in the dim light cast by the alarm clock that Buster was rubbing his eyes. The clock read 1:25. The voices grew louder now, angrier. Buster looked at Herbie in the dim light and moved even closer to him. "What is it, Herbie? What's happening?" Herbie felt like his heart would jump into his throat. He put his arm around Buster. "I don't know," he said. But he did know.

The voices grew even louder, even angrier. Through the wall, Herbie could hear his mother sobbing. Herbie heard something—something like a smack or a punch. Another one. Buster leaned against Herbie. "What is it, Herbie?" the boy said. Then, "I'm scared." Herbie could hear Buster start to cry. He heard what sounded like wrestling—the sound of the springs of the bed in his parents' bedroom—the sharp rustling of something—the bed, bodies, then the banging of his parents' headboard against the wall. He heard another thud against the wall and the another. Tears sprouted in the corners of his eyes.

In the dimness, he heard the door open to his and Buster's bedroom, and he knew it was Maureen. She was crying. She climbed into the bunk bed and found Herbie and Buster in the dim light. Herbie's heart raced. He felt like he should do something, but he had no idea what.

He heard his mother sobbing again. The sobs pierced the wall. He heard more rustling and struggling and then the headboard thudding into the wall, the sound traveling through the wall like sharp blow. Herbie thought he heard a punch, and he closed his eyes and fought back his tears. The muffled voices on the other side of the wall were louder now. Herbie had never felt so frightened in his life. The muffled voices were violating the wall, penetrating it. All three children listened, shaking, holding one another. They heard bodies struggling on the other side of the wall, angry struggles of bodies pierced against each other. Muffled, raging struggle. The children clung to one another, their hearts galloping, their tears exploding.

Then, the sound of Mother's and Father's bedroom door opening. Footsteps, running, and Herbie knew it was Mother. She ran past their bedroom, and her angry sobs violated the air in the hallway, pierced the air of the hallway. She slammed the bathroom door shut. Her sobs echoed in the bathroom and reverberated throughout the entire upstairs.

Herbie wiped his tears away in the dim light. He looked at the alarm clock. It read 1:45. He wrapped his arms around Maureen and Buster. They clung to him, their older brother. They slowly stopped crying. None of them said a word. They shivered against one another. Herbie heard the bathroom door open. He heard the soft footsteps of his mother descending the stairs, heard her despairing soft sobs as she climbed down the stairs.

Now the house was silent. Mother's and Father's bedroom, on the other side of the wall, was silent. The tears from Maureen and Buster slowly ceased. They started to breathe regularly. "Everything will be fine," Herbie whispered. But he did not believe it.

Eventually the children fell asleep, huddled together on the bed. Herbie dreamt of sailing alone in a thieving storm, and he was in a tiny rowboat on a disastrous sea, clinging to the rowboat as the cascading waves washed over him. He was washed over the side, was drowning. He woke up and felt himself shivering. He shook his head to make sure he was awake. Maureen and Buster were sleeping next to him. He went to the bathroom, and the light was still on from when Mother had been in there. He looked in the mirror, and he barely recognized himself. His eyes were puffy and sad. He grabbed a washcloth and rubbed his face harshly, cruelly. He returned to bed and lay next to Buster and Maureen and felt his tears creep back. He slept fitfully, uneasily. He knew the worst about his parents.

The next morning, Herbie woke up, and Maureen and Buster were already awake. His heart was murdered when he remembered what had happened the night before. And he knew it has been his fault. It had been his responsibility. There was no rhyme or reason—he just knew it. He was responsible for everything that had happened. His sadness at this realization limned the insides of his eyelids with acid, like some horrible liquid had spilled on him.

Buster and Maureen went downstairs to breakfast, but Herbie lagged behind. He got down on his knees on the hardwood floor. He prayed to God to forgive him for making his mother and father hate each other. He prayed to God to forgive him for not being a good enough son. He prayed to God to make his mother and father love each other again. He prayed to God to prevent his mother and father from getting divorced.

His heart pumping rapidly, he went downstairs to the kitchen. He hoped Father wouldn't be there. He wasn't. He'd already gone to Grandma Hereford's house. Mother was there. She was sitting at the kitchen table, in her pink bathrobe. Her hair was frazzled and destroyed. Herbie looked in her eyes and knew she was lost. There was a welt on her cheek that she had tried to cover up with powder. But it was still visible. Herbie stared at the welt and hated Father. Mascara dripped like poison from Mother's eyes. She stared into the distance. Buster and Maureen slurped cereal into their yawning mouths. Herbie wanted to walk over to his mother and hug her and tell her that he loved her. But he didn't know how. He didn't know how. He poured himself a bow of Cheerios and started to eat. Only the slurping of the children eating their cereal violated the silence.

About the Author

I'm a writer based in the Chicago area. I've done a lot of different stuff in my life. I've been a merchant seaman, a high school English teacher, a corporate communications writer, a textbook editor, an educational consultant, and a free-lance writer. I've published short stories, articles, and essays in The Progressive, Snowy Egret, Earth Island Journal, Chicago Wilderness, American Forests, Chicago Life, Across the Margin, Adelaide Literary Magazine, The Literary Yard, Scarlet Leaf Review, Spillwords Press, Fiction on the Web, Sweet Tree Review, and other journals and magazines. In 2006, the University of New Hampshire Press published my first book, This Grand and Magnificent Place: The Wilderness Heritage of the White Mountains. My second book, which I co-authored with a prominent New Hampshire forester named David Govatski, was Forests for the People: The Story of America's Eastern National Forests, published by Island Press in 2013.